ALL ARE WELCOME

TOWARD A MULTI-EVERYTHING CHURCH

LEON BROWN, GENERAL EDITOR

PRAISE FOR ALL ARE WELCOME

This book needs to be read by everyone who is committed to Christ-centered biblical justice, lived out through the church. The church must be committed to being a multi-everything church where all are welcome, loved, and empowered to minister, for God's glory.

John H. Sather
National Director, Cru Inner City

Racism is a systematic as well as personal sin. Repentance and reconciliation must be both as well. You don't have to agree with everything in this book to profit from its informed arguments and wise exhortations. Usually, racial reconciliation conversations in our churches have been led by largely White leadership. If we're really to grow more and more into one body with Christ alone as our head, it's time to do some listening. I, for one, learned a lot from this book and will recommend it widely.

Michael Horton
J. Gresham Machen Professor of Theology and Apologetics, Westminster Seminary California

There is a long-standing conversation on the church's call to be the multiethnic, multicultural, multigenerational expression of the Kingdom of God. This volume is a substantive contribution to that important discussion. If you are inclined to join the discussion, you would do well to read this book.

Anthony Carter
Pastor, East Point Church

If only I had this book fifteen years ago when I began my journey of leading my congregations into diversity and racial reconciliation! *All Are Welcome* is a timely contribution to the church recently being revived to pursue diversity reflecting the complexion of heaven. From each of these chapters, we get unvarnished historical background, solid biblical foundation, robust theological thinking, and tested practical application. And because each of these authors (my friends) is deeply rooted in the Gospel, these essays bring conviction leading to repentance with hope, rather than mere regret with shame.

George Robertson

Pastor, Second Presbyterian Church, Memphis, Tennessee

All Are Welcome is a remarkable book. It helps us put together a church where people from different cultural backgrounds, races, and economic positions will know they are truly welcome.

D. Clair Davis

Emeritus Professor of Church History, Westminster Theological Seminary

A vital and necessary conversation is currently taking place about the Gospel, the church, and race (or ethnicity). It is long overdue. The issues are complex, and simple solutions are unhelpful. One thing is clear enough: in Christ, the racial wall that divides is broken down (Eph. 2:14). But how to proceed? Reading this book will help enormously. Leon Brown has pulled together a collection of thoughtful and provocative writers, each with distinctive emphases, but collectively addressing the goal of progress and reconciliation. Essential reading that by God's grace will lead to thoughtful and biblical progress. Grateful for this book.

Derek W. H. Thomas
Pastor, First Presbyterian Church, Columbia, South
Carolina, Chancellor's Professor, Reformed Theological
Seminary

This book offers a unique contribution in the genre of
books on diversity and the church. Diversity is not a bad
word, but a good word that the church must engage on a
deeper level. In this book, thought-provoking insights are
offered by a range of voices from various disciplines,
including biblical studies, homiletics, liturgy, history, and
sociology. This text will challenge the reader to engage the
topic of diversity from multiple angles. The driving narrative of the book is the profound hope that the church can
do better in the area of diversity and multiethnic inclusion.
You may not agree with everything in the book, but you
should be challenged by the wide range of issues and questions raised by this book.

Soong-Chan Rah
Milton B. Engebretson Professor of Church Growth and
Evangelism, North Park Theological Seminary, Author of
The Next Evangelicalism and *Many Colors*

How can churches reflect the heavenly reality of God's
people from every nation, tribe, people, and language
worshiping and serving God together? This collection of
essays is unique and thought-provoking reading for all
church planters, leaders, and anyone involved in multiethnic churches creating church bodies that incorporate
various cultures in their worship and service.

Melanie Cogdill
Women's Ministry Trainer, Presbyterian Church in
America

All Are Welcome invites the reader into different cultural facets of the American church, hoping all will gain deeper understanding into their high value and significance in God's house. This chorus of scholarly voices blends to speak of Christian unity in practice, life, thought, and worship, all centered around the transformative person of Jesus Christ. Whether on college campuses, in the marketplace, or in the pews, *All Are Welcome* offers valuable insight to cross-cultural thinking during this unique period in American church history.

K. A. Ellis
President and Co-Founder, Ellis Perspectives, The Makazi Institute

All Are Welcome is both a reminder of what the Scriptures call us to as the new people of God and the unique challenges of what it means to be the church at the beginning of the twenty-first century. *All Are Welcome* needs to be read and studied by all who take the church and its mission seriously. It is both informative, inspiring, heartbreaking, and challenging!

John S. Leonard
Pastor, Cresheim Valley Church, Author of *Get Real*

CONTENTS

Portions of Chapter 3 overlap with Jarvis J. Williams, *One New Man: The Cross and Racial Reconciliation in Pauline Theology* (Nashville: B&H, 2010) and with articles he wrote for the Reformed African American Network (RAAN) website, (now called "The Witness") Williams uses overlapping material with permission. He delivered portions of the material in his essay in a lecture about multiethnic church planting at the Arise City Summit in Tampa, Florida. The original lecture was called "Kingdom Multi-Ethnicity as the Ground for Urgent Multi-Ethnic Church Planting and Reform."

Cover design by Orlando Arias

Typesetting edited by Claire Berger

ABOUT WHITE BLACKBIRD BOOKS

White blackbirds are extremely rare, but they are real. They are blackbirds that have turned white over the years as their feathers have come in and out over and over again. They are a redemptive picture of something you would never expect to see but that has slowly come into existence over time.

There is plenty of hurt and brokenness in the world. There is the hopelessness that comes in the midst of lost jobs, lost health, lost homes, lost marriages, lost children, lost parents, lost dreams, loss.

But there also are many white blackbirds. There are healed marriages, children who come home, friends who are reconciled. There are hurts healed, children fostered and adopted, communities restored. Some would call these events entirely natural, but really they are unexpected miracles.

May this collection help you in your quest to know Christ as he is found in the Gospel through the Scriptures. May you look for and even expect the rare white blackbirds of God's redemption through Christ in your midst. May you be thankful when you look down and see your feathers have turned. May you also rejoice when you see that others have been unexpectedly transformed by Jesus.

ALSO BY WHITE BLACKBIRD BOOKS

Heal Us Emmanuel: A Call for Racial Reconciliation, Representation, and Unity in the Church

The Organized Pastor: Systems to Care for People Well

Everything Is Meaningless? Ecclesiastes

Urban Hinterlands: Planting the Gospel in Uncool Places

Birth of Joy: Philippians

Choosing a Church: A Biblical and Practical Guide

A Sometimes Stumbling Life: Making Sense of Our Struggles and God's Grace in the Journey of Faith

Follow whiteblackbirdbooks.pub for upcoming titles and releases.

AUTHORS

Eric M. Washington
Eric M. Washington is an Associate Professor of History
and Director of the African and African Diaspora Studies
at Calvin College. He received a BA in Sociology from
Loyola University-New Orleans, an MA in History of
Africa from Miami University, and a PhD in African and
African American history from Michigan State University. In 2012, the *Puritan Reformed Journal* published his
article, "I Agree to Election: The Influence of Calvinism
Among African American Baptists in Slavery and Freedom." Washington also contributed a chapter to *Black
Scholars in White Space: New Vistas in African American
Studies from the Christian Academy* titled "An Open
Door and a Welcome Hand: Lewis Garnet Jordan's
Ethiopian Vision." He is the co-author of *African Americans: We've Come This Far by Faith* and "From Cary to
Colley: The Ethiopian Factor in the Formation of the
Baptist Foreign Mission Convention" in *Between Fetters
and Freedom: African American Baptists Since Emancipation.*

Irwyn Ince
Irwyn Ince is a graduate of Reformed Theological Seminary (MAR) and Covenant Theological Seminary (DMin).
He serves as Pastor and Director of the GraceDC Network
Institute for Cross-Cultural Mission. He is the author of
the chapter "Reconciliation or Bust" in *Heal Us,
Emmanuel: A Call for Racial Reconciliation, Representation, and Unity in the Church.* His ministry passion is to see

the Gospel message of reconciliation with God and people lived out in the context of the local church.

Jarvis Williams

Jarvis Williams has served as an Associate Professor of New Testament Interpretation at Southern Seminary since 2013. He's published numerous academic works including: *Maccabean Martyr Traditions in Paul's Theology of Atonement: Did Martyr Theology Shape Paul's Conception of Jesus' Death?; For Whom Did Christ Die? The Extent of the Atonement in Paul's Theology*; and *Christ Died For Our Sins: Representation and Substitution in Romans and Their Jewish Martyrological Background.* He's published essays on soteriology in Romans and in Second Temple Judaism in Brill Academic and in the Society of Biblical Literature Press. He also has published books and articles on racism and racial reconciliation.

Alexander Jun

Alexander Jun, PhD, is a TEDx speaker and Professor of Higher Education at Azusa Pacific University's School of Behavior and Applied Sciences. He has published on issues of postsecondary access for historically underrepresented students in underserved areas and conducts research on equity, justice, and diversity issues in higher education. He is author of *From Here to University: Access, Mobility, and Resilience Among Urban Latino Youth* and *White Out: Understanding White Privilege and Dominance in the Modern Age.* He serves as associate editor for the *Journal of Behavior and Social Sciences.* A ruling elder at New Life Fullerton in southern California, Jun also serves on the Study Committee on Racial Reconciliation for the Presbyterian Church in America (PCA), the PCA Unity Fund, and the Committee for Mission to the World. Jun was elected Moderator of the 45th General Assembly of the PCA in 2017.

Leon M. Brown

Leon Brown is a husband, father, pastor, and professor. He received his BA in Communication Studies from the University of San Diego, an MDiv from Westminster Seminary California, and an MA in Historical Theology from Westminster Seminary California. In his MA thesis, he proposed that Joseph Smith Jr., the founder of The Church of Jesus Christ of Latter Day Saints, constructed a uniquely blended Christology and soteriology that included aspects of Arianism, pre-existentialism, and Hermeticism. Brown is an adjunct professor of Old Testament at Erskine Theological Seminary (Columbia, SC), a visiting professor of Old Testament at Covenant Theological Seminary, and is presently pursuing a PhD in Hebrew from the University of the Free State in Bloemfontein, South Africa. Prior to pastoral ministry, he served in the US Navy for ten years.

Russ Whitfield

Russ Whitfield serves as Pastor of Grace Mosaic, a cross-cultural church he helped plant in Northeast Washington, DC. He is also a visiting lecturer in Practical Theology at Reformed Theological Seminary's Washington, DC, campus. Whitfield received his BM from New York University and his MDiv from Westminster Theological Seminary. Whitfield is the author of the chapter "Moving Forward" in *Heal Us, Emmanuel: A Call for Racial Reconciliation, Representation, and Unity in the Church.*

Sherrene DeLong

Sherrene DeLong received her BA in the Study of Religion

from the University of California, San Diego, and her MA in Theological Studies from Westminster Seminary California. She previously worked with Mission to the World developing curriculum based on the Apostles' Creed for women in South Asian villages, and has taught at a classical school in Alabama for three years. Sherrene and her husband, Matthew, have served with Reformed University Fellowship International at Auburn University for four years before transferring to George Mason University in 2018. The DeLongs have one son, Isaac, who was adopted from India.

Howard Brown
Howard Brown is a native of Charleston, South Carolina, and Senior Pastor of Christ Central PCA in Charlotte, North Carolina. He planted the church, a multiethnic work in the arts district, in 2003. Howard has a BA from Clemson University and an MDiv from Covenant Theological Seminary. He and his wife, Kellie, have two boys.

Alexander Shipman
Alexander Shipman is the Senior Pastor at The Village Church, a cross-cultural and multiethnic church located in NE Huntsville, Alabama. He received his BFA from Valdosta State University and MDiv from Reformed Theological Seminary. He has spearheaded the African American Presbyterian Fellowship (AAPF), a denomination-wide ministry that focuses on recruitment of African Americans into the Presbyterian Church in America, as well as serving as a resource to increase cultural awareness.

Jahaziel Cantu
Jahaziel Cantu is pastor with Providence Presbyterian Church in Dallas, Texas. He previously served as Associate

Pastor at Christ Presbyterian Church in Flower Mound, Texas, where he planted Iglesia Gracia, a multicultural, bilingual church. After giving up a successful career as an engineer in his native Mexico, Cantu moved to Texas in 2005 and soon began helping a Hispanic church plant, Cristo Rey PCA, where he served as a pastoral intern for seven years. During that time, he assisted with and led multiple English as a Second Language programs for Dallas churches. He holds a BS from the Universidad Autónoma de Nuevo León in Mexico and anMDiv from Westminster Theological Seminary in Dallas.

C. Stanley Morton

Stan Morton is Assistant Pastor for Diaconal Ministries and Outreach at Second City Church PCA in Harrisburg, Pennsylvania. He is the founding pastor of New City Fellowship in Lancaster, Pennsylvania, where he served for nine years. He received his BS in Psychology and Economics from the University of Pittsburgh and MDiv from Westminster Theological Seminary in Philadelphia. He also is a certified facilitator for the Faith and Finances classes of the Chalmers Center.

Lance Lewis

Lance Lewis serves as Pastor of Soaring Oaks Presbyterian Church (PCA) in Elk Grove, California. He previously served as pastor for twelve years at Christ Liberation Fellowship in Philadelphia. Over the past two decades, he has served in various capacities within his denomination, the Presbyterian Church in America. Currently he serves as a trustee on the board of Covenant College, as the chairman of one of the denomination's regional committees for starting new churches, and on the board of the African American Presbyterian Fellowship. As part of his general pastoral ministry, Lewis has contributed chapters in the following books: *Glory Road: The Journeys of Ten African-Americans Into Reformed Christianity*; *Aliens in the Promised Land: Why Minority Leadership is Overlooked in White Christian Churches and Institutions*; and *Heal Us, Emmanuel: A Call For Racial Reconciliation, Representation, and Unity In the Church*.

Darryl Williamson

Darryl Williamson is Lead Pastor at Living Faith Bible Fellowship in Tampa, Florida, where he has helped transition the church from a primarily middle-aged African American membership to a multicultural, multiethnic, multigenerational congregation. Williamson leads Arise City a ministry focused on seeing the Gospel advance in marginal urban communities in the US and abroad, especially in the areas of leadership and theological development. He also has served on the management team of a global software company, where he has engaged with business executive teams in North America, Europe, South Africa, and Australia. He earned his BS in Mathematics and Philosophy from Boston University and is working toward his MDiv at Reformed Theological Seminary Orlando.

Jemar Tisby

Jemar (BA Notre Dame; MDiv RTS Jackson) is the president of The Witness: A Black Christian Collective where he writes about race, religion, and culture. He is also the co-host of "Pass The Mic," a podcast that amplifies dynamic voices for a diverse church. His writing has been featured in the Washington Post, CNN, The Atlantic, and the New York Times. He has spoken nation-wide at conferences on racial reconciliation, US history, and Christianity, and is the author of *The Color of Compromise: The Truth about the American Church's Complicity in Racism.* Jemar studies race, religion and social movements in the twentieth century as a PhD student in History at the University of Mississippi. Follow him on Twitter @JemarTisby.

Christina Edmondson

Christina Edmondson is committed to bringing diverse people together to promote personal and team flourishing. She serves as the Dean for Intercultural Student Development at Calvin College, which is committed to inspiring, challenging, and equipping domestic and international students to engage in meaningful and intentional intercultural interactions within a global society. As a Certified Cultural Intelligence facilitator, public speaker, and mental health therapist, she is often contacted by churches to consult about both diversity and mental health issues. She received a BA in Sociology with an emphasis in race, class, and gender from Hampton University, an MS in Marriage and Family Therapy from the University of Rochester, and a PhD in Counseling Psychology from Tennessee State University.

INTRODUCTION

DO WE NEED ANOTHER BOOK ON THE CHURCH?

Demographics are changing. California, Hawaii, New Mexico, and Texas are all majority-minority states. According to the US Census Bureau, there were more than twenty million children under the age of five living in the United States in 2014, and 50.2 percent were minorities. Additionally by 2044, the United States as a whole is expected to be a majority-minority country.

How will the church respond to the new normal? While these ethnic demographics will be represented in the church universal in the US, will individual congregations reflect the various forms of diversity within their cities? Asked differently, will the makeup of our churches remain the same—segregated?[1] If we are going to reach the nations at our doorstep, something has to change.

As the subtitle of this book indicates, we want to move toward *a multi-everything church*. While the term "multi-everything" is meant to be hyperbole, it expresses the heart of the authors who contributed to this book. Our congregations should be welcoming to everyone, affirming the good of the various cultures expressed in one's community, and seeking to implement those cultural distinctions in our church services. Is that biblical? Is that possible?

One thing is certain: what the American church has done thus far has not worked. Keep in mind that the means to achieve a multi-everything church is not pragmatism. However, we must state the obvious—we are divided, and it is often for reasons other than doctrinal distinctives.

If separation is not the goal, what must we learn, and what can we do to see the chasm closed to bring various forms of diversity into our congregations? One answer is to hear from the people we desire to see in our churches.

Within these pages you will hear from men and women, African Americans, an Indian American, a Hispanic, and those of mixed-ethnic heritage. Their insights are valuable. Their perspectives—like yours—have been shaped by their cultures, ethnic heritages, histories, and financial standings.

While every contributor is united as an ethnic minority, we also are all unified by confessing that the Scriptures of the Old and New Testaments are infallible and inerrant. We believe there is only one God, who exists in three persons—Father, Son, and Holy Spirit—and there is no salvation outside of the person and work of the Lord Jesus Christ. We value the local church, and we love all our brothers and sisters in the faith.

For some, this book may be a corrective. For others, it may affirm what you already believe. Wherever you are on the continuum of learning, embracing, and implementing the perspectives of different cultures, I hope you are encouraged by what you read. I pray we would truly become a multi-everything church where all are welcome.

1

THE MOST SEGREGATED HOUR: ROOTS AND REMEDIES OF AN AMERICAN EVANGELICAL PROBLEM

ERIC M. WASHINGTON

After giving a speech at Western Michigan University in Kalamazoo in 1963, Dr. Martin Luther King Jr. fielded questions from Dr. James Miller, President of Western Michigan. During this session, Dr. Miller raised this provocative question to Dr. King: "Don't you feel that integration can only be started and realized in the Christian church, not in schools or by other means? This would be a means of seeing just who are true Christians." In response, Dr. King uttered these words:

> As a preacher, I would certainly have to agree with this. I must admit that I have gone through those moments when I was greatly disappointed with the church and what it has done in this period of social change. We must face the fact that in America, the church is still the most segregated major institution in America. At 11:00 on Sunday morning when we stand and sing and Christ

has no east or west, we stand at the most segregated hour in this nation. This is tragic. Nobody of honesty can overlook this. Now, I'm sure that if the church had taken a stronger stand all along, we wouldn't have many of the problems that we have. The first way that the church can repent, the first way that it can move out into the arena of social reform, is to remove the yoke of segregation from its own body. Now, I'm not saying that society must sit down and wait on a spiritual and moribund church as we've so often seen. I think it should have started in the church, but since it didn't start in the church, our society needed to move on. The church, itself, will stand under the judgement [sic] of God. Now that the mistake of the past has been made, I think that the opportunity of the future is to really go out and to transform American society, and where else is there a better place than in the institution that should serve as the moral guardian of the community. The institution that should preach brotherhood and make it a reality within its own body.[1]

Sadly, these words still hold true. For the most part, American Christians worship within their own racial group. According to a 2008 ABC News report, only 7 percent of the nation's churches are multiracial.[2] In January 2015, *Christianity Today* published an article on church segregation based on a LifeWay Research survey. The research found eight out of ten American churches consist of one main racial or ethnic group, and that church-goers accepted that their particular churches are just fine as is.[3] Out of all church communities, Evangelical and Protestant churches especially must address reasons why this still persists long after the legal destruction of Jim Crow segregation.

Writing in the late 1990s, psychologist Beverly Daniel Tatum in her book *Why Are All the Black Kids Sitting Together in the Cafeteria?* revealed that as she traveled the country and spoke about racism, there were members of the audience who believed that racism was something of the past, an ugly relic of yesterday's America. Evangelicals may have expressed the same sentiments during that period as movements like Promise Keepers attempted to break down racial barriers between men of color and White men.

Now in light of the killings of Trayvon Martin, Michael Brown, and the whole Black Lives Matter movement, white Evangelicals have tended to assert that people of color actually exacerbate racism by calling attention to unfortunate incidents that may or may not be attributed to racism. In the aftermath of the Michael Brown killing, it became clear how racially divided America is. This includes the church. When Emerson and Smith published their now landmark study on racial attitudes within Evangelicalism, *Divided by Faith,* it shocked many white Evangelicals. Yet it affirmed what most African American Evangelicals felt.

In this new day, the attitudes have changed little, if at all. This chapter provides historical perspective regarding why a Black Church came into existence, and even continues, in light of calls for multiracial and cross-cultural churches.[4] This chapter's argument is that the Black Church is a product of White racism beginning in slavery and extending even now. African American churches function as a safe haven from the ravages of a racist society where African Americans can worship unashamed of their culture and lead in distinct cultural fashion.

That there is a distinct Black Church is an occurrence with a deep, complex history. During the colonial period of American history through the Revolutionary War, people of African descent, who were Christians, worshiped with

European-descended Christians. There is no evidence that Protestant churches consigned enslaved Africans or free Blacks to a seating gallery segregated from the rest of the congregation. Though churches may not have been segregated during those times, enslaved Africans and free Blacks had defined roles in the churches. For example, the leadership of these churches consisted exclusively of White men.

There were rare exceptions such as the ministry of Lemuel Haynes, who was the minister of all-White congregations in Connecticut and Vermont from the end of the Revolutionary Era into the 1810s. The rule was African members of biracial churches suffered under racial prejudice that relegated them as second-class citizens of the Kingdom of Christ. Once the nation emerged from the Revolution, and free Africans in the North began to challenge slavery more and more, and as free Africans migrated from the South to the North, churches began to react negatively against their presence in sacred spaces.

This is when churches began to segregate African American congregants. African Americans in the North responded to this segregation in these biracial congregations by organizing their own churches under their own leadership. These actions by Free Black Baptists and Methodists led to visible Black Christian communities in the North at the turn of the nineteenth century.

This segregation of churches situation was different in the South. Independent African Baptist churches started appearing. Those were encouraged and promoted by the Whites. These churches emerged from plantation missions with African leadership from the outset. Independent churches in the South remained few, mostly because Whites in power refused to sanction independent African churches in light of the sporadic slave rebellions during the first half of the nineteenth century. Once Whites rejected the idea of endorsing the legitimate establishment of independent African churches, very few churches started. Thus, since the vast majority of the African American population were enslaved, most black Christians worshiped in the same church with their masters. Whites were able to control both free and enslaved African Americans.

Biracial Churches Under Colonial Slavery

Christianization was sporadic and slow during the majority of the colonial period. There are two key reasons for this.

First, slave owners were uninterested in catechizing their slaves. Second, slave owners refused to catechize slaves because they believed that Christian baptism was a means of manumission. By the 1660s, the latter issue received clarification when both Maryland and Virginia passed legislation that stated baptism had no bearing on the status of a slave.

During this period, few Africans came to faith in Christ. There were some who came to learn the faith in their master's households, and even made professions of faith, making them members of Christ's church. In the Dutch colony of New Amsterdam, the Dutch West India Company began to import enslaved Africans as early as 1626 to work on various building projects. From this point, individual Dutch-speaking burghers (citizens of the colony) began to purchase Africans. Enslaved Africans worked on farms and in Dutch-owned households. The Dutch Reformed Church emphasized that slave owners should seek the salvation of their slaves. As a result of catechism, conversion, and confession of faith, enslaved Africans became communicant members of Dutch Reformed churches. African enslaved persons had clear rights and privileges, including the privilege of marriage in the church and the baptism of their children. However, despite being given membership, there is no evidence that any enslaved members could serve as deacons or on the consistory.[5]

Further to the north in Massachusetts, slavery became legal in 1641 (this was before legalization in Virginia, Maryland, and South Carolina). Congregationalist pastors, like their Dutch Reformed ministerial counterparts, strongly urged Puritan slave-owners to catechize their slaves in their households and encourage their conversion.[6] As a result, Congregationalist slaveholders believed slaves were part of their covenant households owing to their application of Genesis 18:19, which states Abraham would teach his children and his household to *keep the way of the Lord.*" Those enslaved Africans who converted to Christianity were members with their masters in Congregational churches. Phillis Wheatley, the slave poet and writer of the 1770s, was a Christian convert through catechesis in the household of the Wheatleys of Boston.

The number of Africans in Christians churches grew in the eighteenth century. The Church of England founded the Society for the Propagation of the Gospel (SPG) in 1701. This group undertook work throughout the English-speaking Atlantic World, but in the British American colonies its goal was the evangelization of American Indians and Africans. SPG engaged in mission work in Virginia, New York, and Maryland, along with urban areas such as Boston and Philadelphia.

Samuel Thomas' work in South Carolina should be deemed successful. In 1705 there were twenty African communicant members in his mission. He also reported that one thousand enslaved persons were under instruction and could read the Scriptures. According to historian Carter G. Woodson, some resisted this work because they objected to Africans coming to the Lord's Table.[7] As work in that part of South Carolina continued, Africans would come to compose half of the congregations.[8]

A few catechism schools began to teach Africans the faith, in addition to reading and writing. In 1704 a French Protestant, Elias Neau, founded one such school, and the work done at this school caused a ripple effect as other catechism schools extended to other parts of the colony.

SPG had modest success, but the main point here is that Africans who became communicant members of the Church of England worshiped in biracial congregations. However, there is no record of African communicant members holding office in these Anglican churches.

Presbyterians in colonial Virginia began catechism schools among enslaved Africans during the 1750s. Late historian Luther Jackson noted that New Light Presbyterians (Presbyterians who emphasized revival) put forward the first effort among Evangelicals to reach enslaved persons in that colony as early as 1755. The Rev. Samuel Davies reported that as many as three hundred enslaved persons attended his ministry and about one hundred had received baptism. A colleague of Davies, John Todd, reported two hundred enslaved persons in each of his churches in Hanover County, Virginia. A similar situation occurred in Cumberland County under a Rev. Wright. The enslaved people who attended these churches learned to read and write "true to the traditions of their [Presbyterian] church." According to Jackson, "This revival represents the first time in Virginia that any considerable number of Negroes embraced the Christian religion."[9]

In New England there is evidence that African converts became members of Baptist churches during the eighteenth century. For example, in 1762 First Baptist Church of Providence baptized eighteen Africans. In 1771

First Baptist in Boston received Africans as members. Again, here is evidence of biracial churches.[10]

The First Great Awakening (1734–1770s) brought more Africans into churches, especially in the South. Raboteau notes, "The Great Awakening represented 'the dawning of the new day' in the history of the conversion of slaves to Christianity."[11] White revivalist preachers came from New England and the Mid-Atlantic to the South during the middle of the eighteenth century and preached to multiethnic audiences, including Africans.

Formation of Independent African Churches and African Congregations

During the 1770s, the first independent African American Baptist churches appear in the South. These were Baptist churches that had their foundation as plantation missions in South Carolina and Georgia. The majority of African American church historians state that the Silver Bluff Church in Aiken County, South Carolina, is the first African American Baptist church. A white "New Light" Baptist preacher, Wait Palmer, helped to organize this church with one George Liele, who was the first ordained African American Baptist minister in American history. Liele was a slave, but manumitted to preach on plantations along the Savannah River in South Carolina and Georgia. Silver Bluff Church started sometime between 1773 and 1775. One of the members, a slave, David George, became the pastor of the church until 1778 (when the British occupied Savannah). The other church founded during this time was First African in Savannah (now known as First Bryan). This church began in 1778, and it had a close tie with Silver Bluff across the river in South Carolina. Like Silver Bluff, this church began as a plantation mission, and its first pastor was George Liele until he had to flee the colonies to settle in Jamaica. The church disbanded and had to be reorganized.

In Virginia, it was largely through the initiative of free African Americans that independent African American Baptist churches started. Gilfield Baptist, founded in 1788 by African Americans, was biracial, but by 1809 the African American segment separated and formed the Sandy Beach Baptist Church.[12] In the South, independent Baptist churches organized because of slave preachers preaching to other slaves on plantations. The Baptist polity of sovereign and independent local congregations proved advantageous for the formation of these churches by an oppressed and marginalized population.[13]

The beginning of independent churches among African American Methodists is a different story from the Baptist churches which formed among slave populations. For the purposes of this chapter, the story of Richard Allen and the founding of the African Methodist Episcopal Church (AME) will be highlighted.

Richard Allen was born a slave in Philadelphia in 1760. His master moved to Delaware, where Allen remained enslaved until 1786. Upon his emancipation, he returned to Philadelphia the same year. As a teenager, Allen and his brother were converted through the preaching of a Methodist circuit-riding preacher. Allen eventually became a Methodist preacher himself. Upon his return to Philadelphia, Allen joined St. George's Methodist Church, which was a biracial church. He was a pastor there, preaching to fellow African Americans.

Allen's ministry at St. George's proved to be remarkable. Upon joining the church in 1786, there were only five African American members. Owing to his tireless ministry to African Americans, there were forty-two members at the beginning of 1787. Because of this, Allen began to plan to organize an independent black church. The first steps toward such was the founding of the Free African Society in 1787, which was a mutual aid society. From 1786 to 1792, the overall membership of St. George's grew, as well as the Black membership. With more and more African Americans joining St. George's (as a result of the preaching of Allen), the White church leaders decided to cast African American congregants to the balcony sometime in 1792.

This proved to be the perfect opportunity for Allen, Absalom Jones, William White, and other respected African American members to stage their exodus. One Sunday in 1792, Allen, Jones, and White led the entirety of the African American membership out of St. George's by refusing to sit in the segregated balcony. Black members had sat among their fellow White members during prayers that morning, but White officers insisted that they remove themselves to the balcony.

Incensed, the Black members walked out of the church. This action resulted in the founding of two black churches: the African Church of St. Thomas and Bethel African Methodist Episcopal Church.[14] In 1796 another group of African American Methodists in New York City left their church. This group would found the African Methodist Church in Zion under the leadership of James Varick.[15]

Formation of independent churches among Baptists in the North took on much of the same pattern as the African American Methodist beginnings. Racial prejudice and the need to have churches under their own leadership prompted free Blacks in the urban North to start churches in the early nineteenth century.

In 1805 African Americans in Boston founded First African, the (aptly named) first African American church in the city, with Thomas Paul as its first pastor. What gave rise to this church was both racial discrimination and the need for African Americans to be free to express themselves in the worship. In integrated churches, African Americans had to sit in segregated seating in the galleries, and the leadership prohibited them from singing or speaking in worship. This was the case in both First Baptist and Second Baptist churches. These African American Bostonians retreated to meet in private homes rather than undergo this type of indignity. They did this for a decade. Thomas Paul would be this church's first pastor.

In 1808 African American Baptists in New York City founded Abyssinian Baptist Church. This church came into existence because of White prejudice and an African American desire to have their own congregation like their Methodist and Episcopalian counterparts. The same Thomas Paul of First African became the founding pastor. He served as what we might call an interim pastor, taking a leave of absence from First African in Boston to do so. He had traveled to New York City to give a series of lectures. In 1809 thirteen African Americans formerly of First Baptist in Philadelphia founded First African. First Baptist Philadelphia had been a church pushing for anti-slavery, yet the church resorted to treating its African American members prejudicially. The historian Carter G. Woodson explains that this prejudice came from the succession of Southern pastors at First Baptist Philadelphia. The prejudicial treatment also followed in the wake of many fugitive slaves joining the church at the same time.[16]

Biracial Churches During the Antebellum Period

In the South, the majority of African American Christians worshiped in biracial churches either with Whites, although they were segregated in the actual worship space, or as a separate church under White leadership (the "colored branch"). The First Baptist Church of Columbia, South Carolina, had been a majority African American church since 1796. These congregants were slaves. The pastor of the church was White, Richard Furman. First Baptist in Richmond was majority African American until the 1840s when the church decided to have a separate church, First Colored. Rev. Robert Ryland, a White pastor, led it.

Because of the fear of slave insurrection both after the uncovering of the plot by Denmark Vesey (an African Methodist) in 1822 and Nat Turner (a Baptist) in 1831, Southern states and localities placed harsh restrictions on African Americans meeting independently of Whites, and this included both enslaved and free African American Christians. According to historian Ira Berlin in his classic study of free African Americans in the South during the antebellum period, *Slaves Without Masters*, during the 1820s Whites ceased to sanction independent churches. States passed laws that eroded the independence and the ability of free African Americans from forming their own churches under their own control. Because of the Nat Turner rebellion, African American men were no longer permitted to preach legally without White supervision.[17]

Though technically the Presbyterian Church in the USA was biracial, the church in both the South and the North planted all-African American congregations. During the nineteenth century, one African American Presbyterian home missionary stands out amidst the relative meager effort of the church to evangelize the enslaved population of the South. He was a free-born African American man named John Chavis. In 1801 Chavis was the first ordained African American minister in the Presbyterian Church in the USA and the first missionary commissioned by the General Assembly to work specifically among African Americans, both enslaved and free.[18] After receiving his ministerial education and serving in Hanover County, Virginia, Chavis returned to North Carolina in 1805, where he preached to audiences of African Americans and Whites.[19] From that year until 1831, he served as a missionary-teacher among free African American and White children. In the aftermath of the Nat Turner rebellion in 1831 in Southampton, Virginia, the state of North Carolina stripped Chavis of his privilege to teach and preach.[20] Though unable to teach and preach publicly, Chavis used his pen to educate others during the 1830s.

As relatively few African Americans joined the Presbyterian Church in the South, a smaller yet more influential number joined the church in the North. Throughout the late eighteenth century and into the early nineteenth century, Presbyterians welcomed African Americans, and they could participate fully in the government of the church, even serving as moderators of presbyteries potentially (though none did). What is evident is African American Presbyterians worshiped in their own congregations in the North like in African Presbyterian Church in Philadelphia and Liberty Street Presbyterian Church in Troy, New York.[21]

Civil War and Reconstruction

After the Civil War, newly freed, formerly enslaved African Americans began to join African Methodist churches in large numbers. The AME denomination flooded the South with missionaries who planted churches. At the end of Reconstruction, there were AME churches from Florida to Texas. One reason for such growth was the obvious newfound sense of independence among African

Americans. The AME also successfully implored freedmen to join the church to be under African American leadership.

Baptists organized independent churches during the 1860s and 1870s. Author William Montgomery states that this phenomenon occurred because slaves were displaying their newly acquired independence.[22] Forming their own churches was one of the easiest ways to display their freedom. They broke away from the white-controlled churches. New Baptist churches organized district associations and state conventions. Eventually, Baptists organized regional conventions and then the National Baptist Convention in 1895.

In Presbyterian circles during this period, something interesting transpired, the creation of all-Black governing bodies in the South. During Reconstruction, two northern Presbyterian churches, the Presbyterian Church in the USA (PCUSA) and the United Presbyterian Church of North America (UPCNA) established presbyteries which consisted of all African American congregations. This phenomenon occurred in North Carolina and Tennessee primarily, where there were large concentrations of the small number of African American Presbyterians in the South. Even in a national church like the PCUSA, it had to adopt a "Southern strategy" that excluded African Americans within their ranks from the governance of the entire church.[23]

After years of social, political, and economic oppression, African American Baptists and Methodists wanted to control their own ecclesiastical affairs. In the aftermath of the Civil War, African American Christians in the South seized their opportunity to build local churches, regional associations of churches, and denominations under their own control. African American Presbyterians found themselves in a similar position as their Baptist and Methodist counterparts as their churches decided to form governing bodies in the South that would allow African American pastors and elders to run their own affairs. In all of these cases, church segregation was more a force perpetuated by white racism and gerrymandering than attitudes by African American Christians despising fellowship with their White brothers and sisters.

In Christ There Is No East or West

Christians confess the oneness and catholicity of the church. In more liturgical churches, both African American and White churches recite the Apostles' Creed, in which they confess together (albeit in separate worship spaces), "I believe in the holy catholic church." The question for us now is how can a local church, or larger church denomination, live out the holiness and catholicity of the church? Does this mean that majority African American churches willingly become cross-cultural, intent on including different people groups? Does this mean that predominantly White churches become only cross-cultural, or also multiracial? Who should bear the burden to break down congregational segregation?

Taking another look at Dr. King's lament over the church being the most segregated American institution in 1963, and still largely segregated now, it can be argued—though some would argue against—that White churches carry the burden to work to eradicate ecclesiastical segregation.

The history is clear. White Methodists and Baptists in the North segregated their African American brothers and sisters in their shared houses of worship. African Americans refused to be disrespected in this manner and started their own congregations. In the South, Christians who were slaves had limited roles in their biracial church contexts, and even when allowed to "have church" on their own, those meetings had to be supervised by Whites. During Reconstruction, African Americans struck out on their own to liberate themselves from second-class existence in the church. Even Presbyterians decided that African Americans should worship in their own congregations and even organized all-African American governing boards in the South. According to the history, White Americans erected the racist structures that prompted independent African American churches.

A large portion of the burden lies on White churches. In recent years, predominantly White churches have apologized publicly for slavery and racism. In 1995 the Southern Baptist Convention (SBC), a convention of churches born amidst controversy regarding slavery in 1845, issued an apology for slavery.[24] Currently, Russell Moore, a SBC leader, has stood for further efforts at racial reconciliation with his own convention and within Evangelicalism.

In 2002 the Presbyterian Church in America (PCA) published a paper on racial reconciliation in which it confessed its involvement and complicity in racism as well as a complacent attitude in terms of witnessing against racism.[25] In 2016 the PCA made even more strides to confess and repent of their sins of not loving their neighbor during the Civil Rights era.[26] These are important, necessary steps. However, African American churches must help White churches bear that burden, as called upon by the Apostle Paul in Galatians. History demands White churches repent from their past and present racism and that African American churches walk with them down the road of repentance from racism.

In his statement, Dr. King cited the hymn "In Christ

There Is No East or West." The hymn writer Michael Perry published his version of this hymn as a testimony of the glory of Christ who died for people from all nations and brought them into one in the Church.

There is one special line in the hymn: "For God in Christ has made us one from every land and race; he reconciled us through his Son and met us with his grace." This teaches Gospel truth. If all Christians live this out, then our churches could begin to look differently. The church's place in society would be more counter-cultural as she stands for the Gospel and its social and communal implications rather than standing against mere cultural norms and values.

In the United States, the predominant culture has tended to devalue African American life, culture, and experiences. Christians must recognize how deep racism runs throughout the history of American society and be purposeful and committed to do the hard work of rooting it out both in the household of faith and in the broader society. This work must be done by Whites and African Americans hand in hand.

REGAINING WHAT WE'VE LOST: THE FIRST-CENTURY CHURCH

IRWYN INCE

Here there is not Greek and Jew, circumcised and uncircumcised, barbarian, Scythian, slave, free; but Christ is all, and in all.
—Colossians 3:11

There is neither Jew nor Greek, there is neither slave nor free, there is no male and female, for you are all one in Christ Jesus.
—Galatians 3:28

He said to me, "And you're... you're Black."

I couldn't help but laugh. I tried not to let him see me laughing at that. And I wondered why is it so awkward for him to say something to me that is so obvious? There are various reasons why this happens. And it happens all the time. I think on one hand, he was unsure of whether that was an insulting thing to say. And on the other hand, maybe he was unsure as to whether that was how I see myself.[1]

Journalist Afua Hirsch describes identity as a crucial aspect of humanity with which people grapple. In her TEDx Tottenham talk, she relays the (above quoted) personal encounter with a former colleague. The gentleman, although attempting to flatter her with compliments on her qualifications, felt the need to nervously point out in a whispering tone, "You're Black."

Questions arise from encounters like this. How should we relate to those who are different from us? What is and what isn't acceptable in those relationships? Whether people ask those direct questions or not, they demand attention because people's differences are implicitly or explicitly evident.

These differences are no accident. Even if people may prefer sameness, "God apparently loves difference; he created so much of it," writes Duane Elmer.[2] He continues, "Comfort in another culture only occurs when you understand difference."[3] What's more, "People become aware of their culture when they stand at its boundaries."[4] These abundant human differences become a source of difficulty because people must navigate their differences in the context of relationships with others.

Yet in Galatians 3:28 and Colossians 3:11, the Apostle Paul directly and clearly addresses the explicit differences that so often serve as a source of our division and difficulty. He is not declaring that in Jesus Christ those distinctions are now obliterated. Rather they should no longer separate people. In the body of Christ, our ethnic identities are maintained, and they contribute to the beauty of the body. At the same time, texts like these indicate for today's world that the conundrum of people coming together across lines of difference is not a new phenomenon. It is as old as humanity. Since the fall of humanity into sin, the long-awaited solution is in the plan of the Triune God, who purposed to rescue a people for himself.

The plan of the Triune God to rescue a people for himself includes the fulfillment of humanity's need for connection to others. This need, while unavoidable for every person, only finds ultimate completion in the work of God. Dutch theologian Herman Bavinck argues the strongest bonds of human connection are found in religion. He wrote:

> The family, society, the state, associations of various kinds, and for various purposes, bind people together and cause us to live and act in concert with one another. Even stronger than all these institutions and corporations, however, is the bond that unites people in religion. There exists in religion a powerful social element. The reason for this is not hard to find: religion is more deeply rooted in the human heart than anything else.[5]

For Bavinck, people's central and foundational relationship with God flows out into relationships with other human beings. Bavinck speaks of religion in general, not Christianity in particular. However, in Christianity, Jesus claims that allegiance to him is central and foundational. Jesus says, for example, *"Whoever loves father or mother more than me is not worthy of me, and whoever loves son or daughter more than me is not worthy of me"* (Matt. 10:37). Then using the language of family, Jesus promises that allegiance to him brings about human connection that leads to life. He says:

Truly, I say to you, there is no one who has left house or brothers or sisters or mother or father or children or lands, for my sake and for the Gospel, who will not receive a hundredfold now in this time, houses and brothers and sisters and mothers and children and lands, with persecutions, and in the age to come eternal life. (Mark 10:29–30)

Jesus promised to form those who gave allegiance to him into a connected community, the church. Indeed, theology professor and author John Frame notes that an important image for the church is the family of God. This image reflects the intimacy of life in the church.[6] It is significant that Jesus authorizes his followers to call on God as their Father.[7] If his followers all have the right to call on God as their Father, it means that they are all brothers and sisters. To be a Christian is to belong to an eternal family created by God himself.

This family, as implied by Jesus' words quoted above, is not theoretical or only future oriented. It exists "now in this time." Reflecting on the words of the Apostle Paul in Ephesians 2:14–16,[8] Steven Guthrie marvels: "In the church Paul sees nothing less than the completion of God's purpose in creating humanity."[9] God breaks down barriers so we can have intimacy of life in church family. Social barriers aren't supposed to be legitimate dividers for brothers and sisters in Christ. Jesus puts those hostile barriers to death.

Thus in Jesus Christ the restoration of humanity includes the restoration of community. More specifically, Jesus Christ's salvific redemption created a new normal of redemptive ethnic unity for his people.

This redemptive ethnic unity may seem like an elusive dream for the church today,[10] but the early church began to embrace its pursuit as normative for Christianity. Thus the purpose of this chapter is to show how the announcement of the good news in Jesus Christ contradicted the acceptance of ethnic, gender, and socioeconomic division. The reality of union with Jesus Christ manifested itself in his people striving for union and unity with one another across dividing lines. Thankfully many American churches are taking more seriously the biblical call to build and participate in multiethnic churches and communities.[11] However, this chapter is not an examination of the church's current dilemma with regard to race and class. It is rather an articulation of how Jesus brought the church to pursue its new normal of redemptive ethnic unity, and a call for the church to regain what we have lost.

The New Normal

The Prophet Isaiah wrote:

> *In that day there will be a highway from Egypt to Assyria, and Assyria will come into Egypt, and Egypt into Assyria, and the Egyptians will worship with the Assyrians. In that day Israel will be the third with Egypt and Assyria, a blessing in the midst of the earth, whom the Lord of hosts has blessed, saying, "Blessed be Egypt my people, and Assyria the work of my hands, and Israel my inheritance." (Isa. 19:23–35)*

How did Isaiah's words start to become realized in the New Testament? We will turn our attention to the storyline in the first half of Acts to see how the new normal of multiethnic worshiping communities developed for the people of God.

What may be described as the first multinational

worship service in the New Testament took place on the Day of Pentecost. The set up for this never-before-seen scene was the 120 disciples of Jesus (Acts 1:15) gathered at a house in Jerusalem. The Day of Pentecost was upon them. This is the day that Jesus told them to wait for, the day that they would be clothed with power from on high (Luke 24:49, Acts 1:8). As they are gathered, still devoted to prayer (Acts 1:14), the Holy Spirit comes in dramatic fashion. A sound like the mighty driving of the wind fills the entire house. Individual tongues like fire appeared to them, and a tongue sat over each one of them. Luke says they were all filled with the Holy Spirit. Because of the Holy Spirit, they spoke in other languages.

The coming of the Holy Spirit was not a private matter; it was a public declaration to the nations that the Kingdom of God had come. How large was the crowd in Jerusalem? Luke doesn't say, but the delegation of international representatives is unmatched—Parthians and Medes, Elamites, residents of Mesopotamia, Judea, and Cappadocia, Pontus, Asia, Phrygia, Pamphylia, Egypt, and the parts of Libya belonging to Cyrene, and visitors from Rome, both Jews and proselytes, Cretans, and Arabs (Acts 2:9–10).

What did they hear? They all heard the disciples declaring the mighty works of God. What they experienced left them confused, astonished, amazed, and perplexed. It left them with two conclusions, neither of which included understanding. They asked, *"What does this mean?"* And they surmised, *"These people must be drunk"* (Acts 2:12–13). Peter then preached a sermon to bring clarity, conviction, and resolve (Acts 2:14–36).

The message everyone needed to understand was that the end had come, the end that marked a new beginning. The new beginning was the lavish pouring out of the Spirit of God. Peter says, "What you see might be new, but it's not unexpected." What he explains to his multinational audience is that what's happening is all rooted in God's promise through the prophet Joel (Acts 2:17–21). The coming of the Holy Spirit was a public declaration that the Kingdom of God had come. God would fill his people with his Spirit for the purpose of Kingdom mission. And God's Kingdom expansion program would reverse the tragic effects of Babel (Gen. 11:1–9). The expression of unity in humanity would be for the praise and glory of God, not for the establishment of people's own kingdoms in rebellion against his rule.

Luke's description of this multinational audience is not a passing remark. It is key to the narrative. This multinational audience came to Jerusalem because they were religiously bound by a commitment to Judaism. But they didn't stay that way! About three thousand souls were added to the church that great Gospel day (Acts 2:41). This multinational audience is transformed into the multinational body of Christ. Their commitment as such went beyond the day of Pentecost. They became devoted to the apostles' teaching and corporate worship (Acts 2:42). Further, that devotion extended to a commitment to one another (Acts 2:42, 44–45).

Theologian Daniel Hays makes the important point that biblical scholarship has tended to overlook much of the ethnic diversity in the New Testament world. We have the same tendency. In our connected world we clearly hear, see, and often experience the diversity of our multinational world. We may live in an age of radical multinational connection due to development of social media and new technology, but there is a drought of multinational communion. How often do we look at, study, or preach on a passage in the Bible like Acts 2 and miss the multinational communion? How often do we read Peter's sermon and the people's response, yet do not find our hearts pierced and convicted by the dearth of multinational communion in the contemporary American church?

The multinational communion we hear about in Acts 2:42–47 sets the trajectory for the church's new normal. We may miss its significance because the New Testament regularly categorizes humanity in terms of Jew and Gentile. Hays asserts that biblical scholarship assumes subconsciously that the New Testament world consisted only of two ethnic groups: Jews and Greco-Roman Gentiles. But people in the Greco-Roman world of the New Testament were neither mononational nor monoethnic. While there definitely was a Greco-Roman culture, "there was not really any Greco-Roman ethnic group."[12] It may be simple, and sometimes even useful, to categorize people of the Greco-Roman world into either Jew or Gentile. However, that does not go far enough when examining God's work in the New Testament.[13] In other words, God is not simply interested in reconciling two categories of humanity. His delight and desire is to reconcile all nations.

Multiethnic communities in the United States are similar to what was the reality of the Greco-Roman world of the New Testament. Hays describes the types of events that took place, influencing the ethnic makeup of the region:

Migrations and invasions occurred, such as that by the Celts into Macedonia and Asia Minor. Merchant-driven colonization occurred. Jews were scattered throughout the region. Roman soldiers and foreign auxiliary soldiers retired and settled in areas away from their homes; and slaves were captured from a variety of areas of the Roman frontier and transferred throughout the Empire to be incorporated into the diverse mix of peoples that inhabited the cities of the first century AD.[14]

This large diverse mix of peoples in Jerusalem heard the disciples proclaiming the mighty works of God. They heard Peter proclaim the message of the Gospel of Jesus Christ for the nations—for them. Peter clearly articulates and reiterates God's message through the prophet Joel, which stated: *"it shall come to pass that everyone who calls upon the name of the Lord shall be saved"* (Joel 2:32; Acts 2:21). After hearing Peter's message, those in the crowd were cut to the heart. They asked Peter and the apostles, "What shall we do?" Peter says:

> *Repent and be baptized every one of you in the name of Jesus Christ for the forgiveness of your sins, and you will receive the gift of the Holy Spirit. For the promise is for you and for your children and for all who are far off, everyone whom the Lord our God calls to himself.* (Acts 2:38–39)

They had come to Jerusalem from "every nation under heaven." Unbeknownst to them, God planned to call people in those "nations under heaven" to himself in Jesus Christ. Now in Christ, the multi-everything people would have one Lord, one faith, one baptism, one God and Father of all.[15] Peter's "congregation" was exposed to what would become the new normal. Luke's audience needed to hear that their new normal was the fulfillment of God's promise. And we need to ask ourselves whether or not we've embraced the new normal, or have we forsaken it for something else?

The reason the message was important for them and is still important for us is that while the new normal is wrought by the Spirit of God, it is extremely difficult to break out of our cultural comforts to pursue it wholeheartedly. Acts 6 and Acts 10 remove the covers to reveal this struggle in the church. The multinational audience in Acts 2 came together as people who were religiously committed to Judaism. They were either ethnically Jewish or converts to Judaism. In spite of this commonality, discrimination reared its head in the early church quickly.

In Acts 6, as the disciples were multiplying, a complaint arose from the Hellenists against the Hebrews (Acts 6:1). The complaint was that the Hellenists' widows were being neglected in the daily distribution of resources for those in need. Some of the new disciples were native to Jerusalem, and they spoke Aramaic as their primary language. These were the Hebrews, and they were probably the majority. The others weren't native to Jerusalem but came from other parts of the Roman Empire. These people were the Hellenists, and they spoke Greek. Given Luke's description of the church's unity up to this point, the lack of negative comment about the neglect leads us to believe it was unintentional. However, the language barrier did not excuse the magnitude of neglect the Hellenist widows were experiencing. The struggle for a new normal of unity in diversity was evident.

We can almost hear the Hebrews saying to the apostles, "We didn't mean to do it! That wasn't our intent!" But we see that intent doesn't much matter when the impact is marginalization, neglect, and lack. We still wrestle with this in the church today. We are implicitly biased towards those in our group (language, culture, etc.). It is easy to ignore the needs of those outside of our group. When our group is the majority, this natural bias can have a negative impact on the lives of those in the minority. Dr. Alexander Jun puts it well when he says, "How much does intent really matter if the impact continues to perpetuate feelings of marginalization or oppression for minority brothers and sisters in our churches?"[16]

The struggle did not end in Acts 6 but continues in earnest in Acts 10:1–23. The Holy Spirit has to make it clear that the promise of Jesus' Kingdom is not limited to any ethnic, socio-economic, political, or any other group. Peter, who preached the powerful Pentecost sermon, is confronted with his own ethnic bias when the Lord calls him to preach the Gospel to a Roman centurion named Cornelius. Cornelius stands in need of the Gospel's comfort, and Peter stands in need of some radical theological correction. Peter has to hear Jesus' non-discrimination clause, *"What God has made clean, do not call common"* (Acts 10:15).

The unfolding of this new normal begins to reach a pinnacle in Acts 11 in Antioch. Jesus chose Jerusalem to be the birthplace and launchpad for Christianity. Jesus chose Antioch to be the nurturing place where the Gospel would begin to go deep. The Spirit is at work breaking down the inherent discrimination between Jew and Gentile. Overt exclusion has been replaced through faith in Jesus Christ by radical inclusion. And this radical inclusion was not going to be accomplished without conflict and previously held assumptions about people from other "tribes" being turned on their heads. In Acts 11:19, Luke takes his audience back to Acts 8 when persecution of the believers occurred. He says in verses 19–20:

> *Now those who were scattered because of the persecution that arose over Stephen traveled as far as Phoenicia and Cyprus and Antioch, speaking the word to no one except Jews. But there were some of them, men of Cyprus and Cyrene, who on coming to Antioch spoke to the Hellenists also, preaching the Lord Jesus.* (Acts 11:19–20)

There were some men who were natives of Cyprus and Cyrene, who came to Antioch and decided to break out of their cultural container and tell the good news about the Lord Jesus to non-Jews. The word "Hellenist" simply means a Greek speaker and is used in Acts 6 to refer to Greek-speaking, Jewish believers in the church and in Acts 9 to refer to Greek-speaking Jews. In Acts 11 it refers to Gentiles. God is bringing new people, unexpected and diverse people, into the church.

This beautiful painting of international evangelism and discipleship leads to God's people receiving a new name. In Antioch, Luke says the disciples were first called "Christians." It's a new identity for a new people who will express the new normal. It's no accident that we don't find the word "Christian" ascribed to the followers of Jesus until the church has a massive influx of Gentiles. Jesus, has created —and is creating—a new normal. Pastor theologian Derek Thomas observes:

> Up until this moment, *everyone* belonged to one or the other grouping. What was so distinctive in Antioch is that a *third way* emerged—someone who was neither a Jew or a Gentile, but a Christian! Just as Antioch was regarded as the third city (after Rome and Alexandria), so these followers of Jesus Christ were regarded as a "third race of men.[17]

Their identity was now: people who follow Jesus Christ. When the nations began to turn to the Lord, not only did they receive a new identity, but the church received a new identity, a new normal.

Why the New Normal?

Why was this new normal necessary? Why a "third race of men"?

Yes, it was God's plan. Yes, it was and is for God's glory. Yes, it was God's original intent that humanity would multiply, fill the earth, and cultivate it in their life of worship together. But sin and the Fall resulted in a worship problem. So, the answer is that the new normal became necessary because of our idolatry. In particular, our ethnic identity became a form of our idolatry. We describe the events of Acts 2 as the reversal of Babel. The result of God's judgment of humanity at Babel was confusion and separation. As humanity spread out over the earth with separate languages, separate cultures and ethnic identities developed, which in time created barriers (e.g., John 4:9).

Our ethnic identities within our people groups came to feel so instinctive.[18] That is, ethnic identity came to feel absolute, as if it were inherent to one's identity.

The new normal from Acts was necessary to move people to locate their primary identity in Jesus Christ. This was to guard against making ethnic identity absolute. Put another way: the new normal of the multiethnic church in the New Testament moves the focus to Jesus Christ, and finding our identity in him helps avoid cultural idolatry. Jewishness was not to be at the center of anyone's identity. Egyptian-ness, Libyan-ness, and Arabian-ness were not to be at the center of anyone's identity. The Spirit of God worked to press the people of God into the new normal with Jesus Christ at the center of identity. Again, this did not mean that ethnic identities were no longer apparent or significant. The work of God was not a call to strike a balance between identity in Christ and ethnic identity, as if too much of one washes out the other. Instead, those who belonged to Christ were to understand ethnic identity as subservient to identity in Christ.

We still stand in need of looking to the new normal of the New Testament church for our way forward in the church today. Sociologists Brad Christenson, Korie Edwards, and Michael Emerson demonstrate this in their research. They examined racial integration in religious organizations. They describe the effect of religiously empowered ethnocentrism when it comes to understanding cultural differences. In religious organizations, because "members interpret most of life through a religiously informed grid, differences in culture are often talked about in absolute terms."[19] In our ethnocentric churches, differences in preference get framed in absolute terms. As Miroslav Volf says, both parishioners and clergy are often "trapped within the claims of their own ethnic or cultural community."[20] In other words, our Blackness, our Whiteness, our Asian-ness, and our Latino-ness still tend to be at the center of our identities even after faith in Jesus Christ!

Only Jesus is able to bear the weight of the center. Your Blackness cannot. Your Whiteness cannot. Your American-ness cannot. Your "Whatever-ness" cannot. What's further, "God alone has the wisdom, power, and grace to weave the tangled threads of different people, with different cultures, customs, and languages into a single tapestry of glorious beauty."[21] This is precisely the new normal. May we regain what we've lost.

THE GOSPEL: A UNIQUELY PLANNED STRATEGY FOR RECONCILIATION

JARVIS J. WILLIAMS

In today's Christian culture, discussions about reconciliation are becoming more and more common.[1] Some Christians disagree about the usefulness of the phrase "racial reconciliation" since this phrase (some say) wrongly assumes the need to restore a previously existing relationship in this country between Blacks and Whites. Regardless of what some may think about the terminology, Bible-believing Christians should gladly embrace the Gospel's power to unify all things and all people in Christ and to unite those alienated from God and from one another into reconciled friends (Eph. 1:9–3:8). In this essay, I briefly discuss the Gospel as a uniquely planned strategy for reconciliation.

Approaching Reconciliation from the Bible

The Bible should be the starting point in our conversations about reconciliation for Bible-believing Christians. God's original creation was in perfect harmony. God called his creation good (Gen. 1–2). Humans were in right relation with God and each other, and they enjoyed the fruit of the ground without thorns and thistles. But when sin entered creation, it destroyed the unity of God's creation and shattered everyone's relationship with God and with each other (Gen. 3). Sin introduced both physical and spiritual death and individual and cosmological sin into the world (Gen. 3, Rom. 5:12).[2]

An example of spiritual death in the real world is human depravity. All human beings are dead in trespasses and sins (Eph. 2:1). The sin of Adam and Eve and God's universal curse of them, and of the entire cosmos because of their disobedience, resulted in the shattering of both vertical and horizontal relationships (e.g., Gen. 1–4). Human transgression also resulted in a universal curse that fragmented and devastated the entire creation (Gen. 3:14–19). As a result, all of us sin and fall short of God's glory (Rom. 3:23). One way we sin and fall short of God's glory is by the way we treat others. Our sin often results in broken relationships.

In the Old Testament, we see this relational brokenness illustrated in Cain's murder of his brother Abel (Gen. 4:8). We also see relational brokenness in the various factions in the churches in certain New Testament letters (e.g., 1 Cor. 12–14; Phil. 4:2). We ultimately see human brokenness in personal relationships through the efforts of humans to execute God's Son (Matt. 26:47–56). As a result of broken individual relationships with God, broken relationships with one another, and the brokenness in the actual cosmos itself, God must act to restore or reconcile this brokenness to himself and to unify all things and all people to himself. He has acted to crush the seed of the serpent through the seed of the woman (Gen. 3:15) by the

unification of all things and all people through Christ
(Eph. 1:9–3:8).

Thus, Christians need to understand that the entire
world needs to be reconciled in at least three ways.

First, humans need to be reconciled to God. Second,
humans need to be reconciled to each other.[3] Third, the
entire cosmos needs to be redeemed from the curse of sin
and reconciled to God. Bible-believing Christians must
begin the conversation about reconciliation (both vertical
and horizontal reconciliation) by surrendering to the
authority of the Bible, listening to the Gospel, and listening
to what both say about the Gospel's plan for reconciliation.

Approaching Reconciliation and Race as Bible-Believing Christians

Christians must start the conversation about reconciliation
with the Bible.[4] Yet we must also critically work to understand the complicated reasons humans in general and
Christians in particular are not reconciled to one another.[5]

One reason Christians are disunited is because of race.[6]
As a result, Christians must diligently work for and carefully consider the meaning of race and the way in which
race has historically functioned in the American experience. Race in the American narrative has prioritized
majority White culture and dehumanized and marginalized minority (and especially Black) cultures.

Scholars debate whether race or racism existed in the
ancient world.[7] The Bible's concept of categorizing people
into diverse groups and the reasons for that categorization
differ greatly from how race has historically functioned in
the American experience.[8] Race in the American experience is a negative word with a racist beginning.[9] Race, as it
has been socially constructed in the American experience,

and the negative ideas attached to this concept, does not occur in the Bible.[10]

The origins of race and modern racial reasoning are complex.[11] Basically, race in the American experience is a social construct that took on a life of its own around the 1600s and later in the American experience. The construct of race in the American experience enabled the majority White culture to establish and maintain a racial hierarchy over Blacks.[12] The construct of race has functioned in the American experience as a racialized (i.e., the act of giving racial characteristics to) way to dehumanize and marginalize black and brown people and to subjugate them to the White majority.[13]

Racism is very real in the American experience, because race is a "social fact."[14] But race in the American experience is a biological fiction, not rooted in any established or fixed biological reality.[15] Race and racial hierarchy in the American experience have historically dehumanized people of color, especially Blacks. Though certain White Christians courageously worked for the equal rights of Blacks in both abolition movements and during the Civil Rights Movement, other White Christians wrongly used the Bible to justify racial hierarchy and racist practices against Blacks, like slavery and Jim Crow laws.[16]

To support their views of racial hierarchy, others within majority White culture used pseudo-scientific arguments to justify racial hierarchy and White superiority.[17] The construct of race in the American experience has historically operated as a category of privilege for the majority White culture over black bodies and as a category granting to majority White culture social, economic, and political power and privileges over black and brown bodies both inside and outside the church, and even in many other Christian spaces.[18] If Bible-believing Christians desire

36

reconciliation in our churches, we need to grow on a regular basis in our understanding of the complexity of race, race relations, and the ways in which race still socially privileges and marginalizes different races in the church, in Christian institutions, and in society.[19]

The Reconciling Power of the Gospel and Reconciliation

The Gospel creates both vertical and horizontal reconciliation (Rom. 5:6–10; Eph. 2:11–3:8). The Gospel also demands Christians to pursue horizontal reconciliation.[20] The Gospel is the power of God unto salvation for everyone who believes, for the Jew first and also for the Greek (Rom. 1:16).

Paul summarizes Jesus' cross and resurrection as the first important matters of the Gospel (1 Cor. 15:3–8). Jesus' death justifies (declares not guilty) sinners by faith in Christ. Jesus died for us to make us right with God (Rom. 3:21–4:25). We call this justification by faith. God declares sinners to be not guilty because of Christ's death for their sins and their union with Jesus' death and resurrection by faith (Rom. 3:21–4:25). God reckons to the account of sinners the righteousness of Jesus Christ by faith (Rom. 4:6–8).[22]

Jesus' death and resurrection are foundational to the sinner's right standing with God (Rom. 3:21–5:10). Because all of us are sinners (Rom. 3:23), everyone needs to be justified by faith in Christ through the blood and resurrection of Jesus Christ (Rom. 3:21–4:25). We all likewise need to be reconciled to God (Rom. 5:8–10). Justification by faith in Christ happens through God's redemption provided through Christ's blood (Rom. 3:24) and resurrection (Rom. 5:6–10). This redemption delivers us from the future wrath of God (Rom. 5:8–9), emancipates us from our current bondage to sin (Eph. 1:7, 2:1–10), reconciles us to God (Rom. 5:9–10), and delivers us from the present evil age (Gal. 1:4).

Jesus' blood and resurrection emancipate all different kinds of sinners from the penalty of their sin (Rom. 3:24–25). His redemption (and reconciliation) is for "all" without distinction, all who have sinned and fallen short of the glory of God (Rom. 3:23; 2 Cor. 5:20). God, through the work of Jesus on the cross for sinners, is now the God of both Jews and Gentiles by faith through the death and resurrection of Jesus apart from the works of the law (Rom. 3:29–30). God's redemption of the justified is for "all" who have been justified freely by faith through Christ's redemption (Rom. 3:21–22, 24–25; 5:1).

Through Jesus' death on the cross, God was pleased to reconcile to himself all things in heaven and on earth by making peace through his cross (Col. 1:20). Jesus reconciles, in his body, by his death on the cross, those who were once alienated from and hostile toward God to present us blameless if we continue in the faith (Col. 1:21–22). His work of reconciliation with God enables us to live in hot pursuit of reconciliation and Christian unity in community with each other (Rom. 14–15; Eph. 2:11–5:33).[22]

Jesus' death also delivers us from the present evil age (Gal. 1:4) and from the curse of the law (Gal. 3:13). Jesus' death gives to various groups the Spirit by faith (Gal. 3:14). Factions, quarrels, divisions, and other social vices are manifestations of the present evil age (Gal. 5:19–21). These vices (and vices like these) are lusts of the flesh (Gal. 5:16–21, 25–26), works of the flesh (Gal. 5:19), and contrary to the Spirit (Gal. 5:16–26). Love and the pursuit of unity are the work of the Spirit (Gal. 5:16, 22; cf. 1 Cor. 13). Jesus' death and resurrection then deliver sinners united to him by faith from the present evil age, which is marked by disunity, division, factions, and a curse.

Christians redeemed by Christ's blood and walking in the Spirit will therefore inherit God's future kingdom (Gal. 5:21). The Kingdom of God in Galatians is a reference to the new heavens and new earth, which Paul calls "new creation" (Gal. 6:15), and which John identifies as the New Jerusalem coming down from heaven (Rev. 21–22; cf. Isa. 65:17–25). God's future kingdom invaded the world and was inaugurated in the ministry of Jesus (Mark 1:16).[23]

The Kingdom of God is already here, but not yet fully realized. This is one reason why the New Testament speaks of the kingdom as both a present reality (Mark 1:15) and also as a future hope (Gal. 5:21). The future kingdom is currently experienced in the here and now in real space and time by Christians from different tongues, tribes, and nations as we inherit by faith the indwelling presence and power of the Spirit (and live in community with each other Acts 2; Gal. 3:14; Eph. 4:1-6:9), and as we live in step with the Spirit by a consistent pattern of Christian obedience (Gal. 5:16–26; Eph. 4:17–5:21).

Christians are recreated by faith as children of Abraham filled with the indwelling presence and power of the Spirit (Gal. 3:1–14). We are bound for the Kingdom of God and experience a foretaste of the kingdom as we live as a unified people from diverse backgrounds (Gal. 3:28), because Jesus died and resurrected to unify us into a reconciled community redeemed by the cross (Gal. 1:1, 4; 3:1, 13). We, the different tongues, tribes, and people for whom Jesus died and who live in faithful obedience to him, represent the beautiful diversity gathered around the throne who will worship the lamb forever and ever (Rev. 7:9). Jesus' death for all kinds of people purchased salvation for some of those people for the purpose of recreating them from different races and ethnicities and backgrounds into a new, chosen race and reconciled community (1 Pet. 1:1–2; 2:9). This redemption neither guarantees every church will be multiethnic, nor that Christian unity will happen without hard work and intentional efforts. Monoethnic locations make it difficult for churches to become multiethnic, and multiethnic locations bring many multiethnic challenges to multiethnic churches.

Still, Jesus makes the many different tribes, tongues, peoples, and nations into a kingdom of priests, a holy nation, and a royal priesthood by his blood in both monoethnic and multiethnic contexts (1 Pet. 2:9). Consequently, the universal church will live in a perfectly reconciled community when the kingdom consummates at the end of history (Rev. 21–22). And, when location allows and the Spirit enables, Christians should live now in imperfect reconciled communities in our local churches on earth as we reflect in part the inaugurated presence of the kingdom on earth with redeemed brothers and sisters from different tongues, tribes, peoples, and nations in Christian spaces (Eph. 2:11–3:8).

As Revelation 5:9–10 says:

And they sang a new song by saying: worthy are you to take the scroll and to open its seals, for you were slain, and by your blood you ransomed people for God from every tribe and language and people and nation, and you have made them a kingdom and priests for our God.

John says God builds his kingdom by the blood of Jesus Christ shed for Jews and Gentiles, and he makes those for whom Jesus died into a kingdom of priests. The redeemed throughout all of the ages are the people of God who live in the presence of God and who have access to God together as a unified people in the Kingdom of God. We should live out the certainty of this future hope now in this present evil age as we walk in the Spirit and gather corporately together in local Christian churches and live in community with each other.

Concluding Practical Applications

The Gospel is a unique strategy for reconciliation. The Gospel drips with the red blood of Jesus, the Jewish and brown-skinned Messiah, for all people without ethnic or racial distinction (Rom. 3:24–25; Eph. 1:7). The Gospel victoriously announces that the crucified Messiah triumphantly reigns in the heavenly places over all things at the right hand of God (Eph. 1:20–22). The Gospel creates all Christians to live in Christian unity (Gal. 2:11-14). Jesus demands Christians from every tongue, tribe, people, and nation to deny self, take up the cross, and follow him (Luke 9:23). The Gospel demands all Christians to pursue Christian unity with each other whether one's context is monoethnic, multiethnic, poor, middle-class, upper-class, poorly educated, educated, urban, or rural.

Below I list a few practical ways Christians can live out the Gospel's strategy for reconciliation in churches located in communities where multiethnic expressions of reconciliation are possible.

1. Pursue Multiethnic Friendships!

One strategy the Gospel outlines for reconciliation is the need for Christians to pursue multiethnic friendships. Living multiethnic lives can help us begin to understand and pursue multiethnic friendships, which would help us see our blind spots. This understanding could help us begin to ask the question of how to esteem others to be more important than ourselves by putting the needs of others in the Christian community ahead of personal preferences when our personal preferences have nothing to do with the Gospel. This requires a flexibility for Christians, especially Christians from the majority culture, a willingness to sacrifice some preferences when possible to achieve reconciliation in an increasingly ethnically and racially diverse world (1 Pet. 2:9; Rev. 5:9). Negotiating preferences is hard for many of us, especially when those preferences are also attached to a particular ethnic or racial culture. With that racial or ethnic culture comes a certain theological culture with which we identify.

Reconciliation requires sacrifices from both majority and minority cultures. Those of us who are minorities serving in majority cultural Christian contexts ethnically negotiate on a regular basis by default because of our minority status in majority cultural spaces. This reality requires majority cultural Christians to be aware and intentional about their need to negotiate, to share, and to leverage some of the privileges and preferences they have due to their majority cultural status for the sake of reconciliation.

2. *Ask God to Help Us Embrace the Racial and Ethnic Diversity in Our Communities*

Cultures and ethnic groups that differ from ours may make us uncomfortable or even afraid. We may think our individual culture or ethnic group is normal for everyone. We may perceive of people ethnically different from us as the "other." Christians should remember we are the other, and each one of us in the Christian community shares the status of other to someone from another racial, cultural, or ethnic community within the Christian community. God created different tongues, tribes, peoples, and nations.

Depending on where we live, we may see the beautiful ethnic diversity of God's creation in our very own communities. We should be intentional Christians, committing to understand, embrace, and learn from the beautiful ethnic diversity in our neighborhoods. If we lack ethnic or racial diversity in our communities, we can still read books written by and about women and men from different racial and ethnic groups and cultures. We can listen to music, lectures, and observe art from cultures that represent the beautiful racial and ethnic diversity of our world. We can attend Christian conferences led and hosted by ethnic and racial groups different from our own. These things will not be easy for many of us, for we all have preferences and fears of the so-called racial and ethnic other. Yet seeking to understand, appreciate, and embrace the beautiful ethnic and racial diversity that God created should be an intentional pursuit of the Christian community.

3. Rely upon the Spirit

Reconciliation is impossible without the supernatural power of the Spirit. The Spirit gives life (John 6:63). The Spirit is also our helper (John 15:26), who guides us into all truth (John 16:13). The Spirit produces unity in the bond of peace (Eph. 4:3). As God's people rely upon the power of the Spirit both individually and corporately in our churches, he enables us to achieve the very unity that he commands us to pursue (Eph. 2:1–22). May we embrace the Gospel's unique strategy for reconciliation as we pursue and walk in the power of the Spirit.

MULTIVOCALITY IN THE CHURCH: STRIVING FOR MORE HARMONIOUS AND DIVERSE FAITH COMMUNITIES

ALEXANDER JUN

Once upon a time there lived a giraffe. He recently built the perfect house that met his family's needs and met all his unique specifications—narrow hallways maximized space and high windows allowing for privacy and plenty of light. This masterfully designed house was the pride of the neighborhood, and it also won awards by *Giraffe Home Magazine* for its design.

One day while the giraffe was working from home, he looked out the window. Down the street he saw his neighbor, the elephant. Wanting to befriend him and extend hospitality to the elephant, the giraffe invited him in. Delighted, the elephant made his way over to the giraffe's house, but immediately encountered the first of many problems—the elephant could not get through the narrow doorway. The giraffe noted the problem but was able to accommodate the elephant by expanding the door so that the elephant could get inside. The complications continued once inside. Being asked to make himself at home, the elephant's every move led to broken fixtures, cracked walls, a damaged staircase, and the like. The mildly irritated giraffe soon recognized the problem and made his suggestions to the elephant. The giraffe suggested weight loss, ballet lessons, and some aerobic classes for the elephant. If the elephant could slim down, become more nimble, and essentially change who he is, then the elephant would be happier in giraffe's house.

The fable concludes with the elephant being unconvinced of the giraffe's assessment, because the elephant knew that a house built for a giraffe was never intended to be one for an elephant.

I begin this chapter by embellishing upon this fable. This was originally written as part of an introduction to a book on diversity by Thomas and Richards in 1999, and I retold the story at a seminar on race at the 43rd General Assembly of the Presbyterian Church in America (PCA) in 2015. The fable is still relevant today and continues to offer many lessons for members in a dominant group to see their inability to recognize blindness, privilege, power, and mindset of a subordinate group.[1] This fable offers much when applied to what I refer to as Predominantly White Churches (PWCs).

Multivocality in the church simply means many voices are needed in the faith community. It also means that multiple perspectives, cultures, and ethnic backgrounds ought to be represented and have equitable say in conversations of any given church and denomination. Due to pervasive racial homogeneity in American church leadership today, faith communities continue to be one of the most segregated aspects of US life. More than 40 percent of Americans attend some religious service each week.[2] What exactly makes a church diverse, and how might one measure the effectiveness of multicultural ministry? A common standard for diversity is a statistic put forth by scholars Pettigrew and Martin, who state that a culturally or ethnically diverse church can be defined as one that has no racial or ethnic group comprising more than 80 percent of attendees.[3] With this working definition, some scholars have determined that less than 10 percent of US churches are racially/culturally diverse.[4] In their seminal work *Divided by Faith*, Emerson and Smith state that 90 percent of church congregations are composed of 90 percent one race.[5]

Often when one considers the racial gaps and disparities in churches, one's natural impulse might be to examine the patterns, behaviors, and idiosyncrasies of The Other in order to identify the problem. Perhaps like the giraffe in the fable, we might shift our gaze upon the elephant. Perhaps we problematize elephant culture as the root cause of the elephant's failure to succeed or thrive. Often we unintentionally focus on The Other as the cause of division. However, we must also shift the gaze to ourselves, thus turning our windows into mirrors. In addition we ought to interrogate the larger systemic issues in which we all find ourselves. Systemic and structural barriers continue to be significant challenges toward building robust multiethnic faith communities and denominations.

One goal of this chapter then is to highlight how systemic as well as individual change is at the heart of both the problem and the solution. To that end, I offer a few points to consider. First, I will examine systemic issues that plague us, and then by extension look at how internalized issues such as homophily and the Homogenous Unit Principle (HUP) have reinforced our leaning toward homogeneity. This discussion will be followed by a broader examination of the idea of White normativity. I then focus on the benefits and costs associated with diversity. I conclude with a call for intentionality as a way forward.

Systemic and Internalized Barriers

In the United States there are systemic forces along racialized lines that contribute to the ongoing divisions seen across the country. These systems also have significantly impacted the church in America. In this chapter I discuss both systemic and individualized internal factors that perpetuate homogeneity.

Structural racism has been defined by some scholars as the

> normalization and legitimization of an array of dynamics—historical, cultural, institutional, and interpersonal—which routinely advantage Whites while producing cumulative and chronic adverse outcomes for people of color. It is a system of hierarchy and inequity, primarily characterized by White supremacy—the preferential treatment, privilege and power for White people at the expense of Black, Latino, Asian, Pacific Islander, Native American, Arab, and other racially oppressed people.[6]

Some race scholars contend that all forms of racism, such as interpersonal, internalized, and institutional racism ultimately stem from systemic racism. Structural racism can be found within multiple aspects of American society and culture, including:

> 1) history, which lies underneath the surface, providing the foundation for white supremacy in this country, 2) culture, which exists all around our everyday lives,

providing the normalization and replication of racism and, 3) interconnected institutions and policies, the key relationships and rules across society providing the legitimacy and reinforcements to maintain and perpetuate racism. Examples include racialized laws and institutional policies, dominant cultural representations, popular myths, and compounded and chronic inequities, etc.[7]

Several remnants of a racialized system, which are still at work today, continue to prevent ethnic diversity and cultural unity in churches and denominations in the United States. The PCA for example, is a denomination made up of many Predominantly White Churches across the country, with a heavy concentration in the South. It has been struggling to acknowledge its racist past, particularly toward African Americans, and the remnants of these historical experiences continue to manifest through low representation of black PCA pastors. The PCA is also largely middle-class. We have likewise struggled to reach and embrace people of lower socioeconomic standings.

Homophily and HUP

Scholars such as psychologist Kathryn Ecklund[8] and others[9] who are concerned with diversity in the church, write about microsystems and macrosystems that impact daily living. A microsystem refers to the immediate surroundings, such as the family, school, or peer group, while a macrosystem refers to the overarching institutional patterns of the culture or the subculture, such as the economic, social, or religious systems.

Adjunct to micro and macro systems is the internalization of our desire for homogeneity. More specifically

Ecklund addresses the notion of homophily, which may best be described as the tendency of individuals to gravitate toward those who have similar background or demographic attributes. Because attendance at a particular church or religious institution is not assigned and is based on a desire to be there, people will go where they feel drawn, which can be affected by homophily. When one visits a new church, one often has an initial reaction regarding the community. One has either a good feeling about the place and the people or not.

Soong-Chan Rah, like other evangelical scholars, expands upon the notion of homophily further as he describes the concept of the Homogenous Unit Principle (HUP) as a primary method of numerical church growth in the twentieth century.[10] In his book *The Next Evangelicalism*, Rah contends homogenous churches grow faster because people are more inclined to be around those from similar ethnic, cultural, and socioeconomic backgrounds. The more "successful" churches (as defined perhaps simply by numerical growth) simply removed any barriers such as racial and cultural differences to draw more people into the church. Rah goes on to state that one of the biggest obstacles in the establishment of multiethnic churches is the system of White privilege in the American church. He argues that when the majority group continues to define and shape the parameters of discussion on what the church ought to look like, the multiethnic voices of the non-dominant group are silenced. Building upon Rah's ideas, I focus on the notion of what members of a dominant majority often consider perfectly logical and normal rationale for thoughts and actions. While both systemic and internalized factors account for the lack of ethnically diverse churches and denominations in the US, nothing dominates the consciousness for majority culture more than the notion of White normativity.

White Normativity

An often invisible system that contributes to a reduced sense of belonging for minorities in PWCs and diminished cultural unity is the prevalence of White normativity. White normativity is defined as "the normalization of Whites' cultural practices, ideologies, and location within the racial hierarchy such that how whites do things, their understandings about life, society, and the world, and their dominant social location over other racial groups are accepted as just how things are."[11] As a result, anything that deviates from a dominant white cultural norm is seen as abnormal.[12] Emerson describes the process by which White normativity is perpetuated, stating:

> Whites uphold practices and beliefs that sustain their dominant position in the racial hierarchy. Thus the practices and understandings of Whites are normalized, and their interests affirmed.[13]

Harken back to the story of the elephant and the giraffe. Any house that is built *by* a member of a majority group and *for* a member of a majority group would naturally be viewed by members of that group as being architectural pleasing, simply because it was designed logically, intuitively, and naturally. It makes sense to the dominant majority group. Extending this concept into the church, a ministry that has been built by members of a dominant majority group might also conclude all their decisions that have been prayed for and carefully considered, can only be perceived as not only normal but also orthodox and biblical.

Too often, dominant majority culture churches—and by extension, evangelical denominations across the United States—are dominated by culture that has been influenced and reinforced by a dominant worldview. To be clear, this in no way means to suggest that folks in a dominant group are bad people, or that individuals are themselves racist. However, local churches and denominations ought to recognize that sometimes ministry philosophy, approach to church planting, and styles of worship (from songs that are selected, to instrument selection, and delivery method of the sermon) may be implicitly biased toward a dominant ideology, culture, and worldview. Often, that worldview means a Eurocentric, Western, White lens that is normalized and perpetuated. Failing to acknowledge that one's own views may be rooted in normativity can lead to cultural myopia for a majority of members and their leaders.

Moreover, churches seeking to be multicultural may also have neglected to recognize a fundamental dominant culture in the design of their churches, which is to simply say some multicultural churches are still White. In other words, even though the membership in the congregation is compositionally mixed and well-balanced, and perhaps even though the leadership is non-White, the overwhelming culture and climate (how a place inexplicably feels) that is embedded into the very fabric of a church, is often influenced by a dominant White paradigm. Although a church may be compositionally diverse, the underlying concern for minority church members is often one of assimilation, perhaps being left to regularly question whether or not they "fit in" with the prevailing culture of a particular church or denomination. Is their ethnicity too visible? A recent study by Jenkins found that due to the lack of structural diversity in one church, ethnically diverse members had to deny their desires and preferences associated with their race in order to achieve a sense of unity and community within the church community.[14]

Individual churches often have distinct styles of worship and preaching tied to cultural and historical traditions. If these traditions are not changed to reflect the diversity of the surrounding church community, it seems unlikely that unity and diversity will grow there. White normativity in churches is often revealed within the music style, preaching style, and perhaps even the time management of a church.

A study of one institution found that even though the church's band had diverse members, this diversity was not shown in the band's primary characteristics like tempo, rhythm, song selection, and instruments selected. Author and researcher Lydia Veliko discusses the negative effects of ~~White normativ~~ity in churches, stating: "for those accustomed to the patterns of our early years, there is a tendency to explain to new members how to do it 'the correct way'... when we do that, however, new communities coming into the church hear that they are welcome, but only when their patterns fit an ecclesial and cultural norm that is determined by the majority culture."[15] Edwards asserts that interracial churches still perpetuate racial inequality, even though the aim was to abolish it, and that mixed-race churches still strongly adhere to White culture and White norms.[16] As a result, African Americans in these churches often have to adapt their behavior to fit the White norms and to make White attendees feel comfortable.

What about leaders and their impact on the direction of churches and denominations? The overarching normative assumption among a majority of leaders from a dominant group is perhaps that members of color will join existing Predominantly White Churches and embrace or

[handwritten margin note: rightway' / white way.]

assimilate to the existing culture, checking their identities at the door.

But as discussed in other chapters in this book, what about the music, liturgical style, preaching, and outreach focus? What are the denominational priorities in terms of time, people, and money, and how might the colored perspectives among leaders be normalized by a dominant lens that causes well-intentioned leaders to fail to see? Would multiple voices and perspectives not aid greatly to enhance perspective? In the next section, I elaborate on the benefits of and challenges with having a diverse and multi-cultural community.

Costs and Benefits of Diversity

I grew up playing the clarinet. Throughout elementary, junior high, high school, and even through college, I was part of organized music clubs—symphonic orchestra, jazz ensemble, marching band, and the like. Every group required what are called sectional rehearsals or simply sectionals. Sectionals were essentially a time for individual instruments to be isolated for group instruction and practice.

For me that meant joining with all my fellow clarinet players. We would gather together and squeak our way through our portion of the music. Other instruments also rehearsed separately within their own instrument groups. I hated sectionals. The music and the sound of all clarinets playing the same clarinet parts the same way quickly became repetitive, predictable, and boring. Only when the entire band convened (the brass, strings, and percussion joined the flutes, oboes, saxophones, and clarinets) did the music begin to sound melodious, harmonious, full, and complete. I got chills every time we all came together. I still do. The multivocality of the various complementary instruments orchestrated with perfection is what turns an individual sound into a beautiful symphony.

As I have outlined above, the systemic problems of diversity are manifold. Not only are the overall numbers of ethnically diverse participants low at any given Predominantly White Church, but the focus has primarily been placed on compositional diversity of membership, and not on more important aspects such as leadership, education, and funding. One particularly provocative thought by scholar Steven Monsma in highlighting one of the benefits of diversity, stresses the need for both diversity and unity, stating: "unity without diversity is at best boring and at worse totalitarian; diversity without unity constantly threatens to degenerate at best into tensions and failures at cooperation and at worst into genocide."[17] While Monsma uses strong language in describing the worst cases of a lack of diversity, I concur there is a figurative death in terms of the fellowship of the saints, which should make any given faith community vibrant and mutually enriching.

Benefits of Diversity

Renowned psychologist Gordon Allport argued for structural diversity as early as the mid-twentieth century, encouraging equal status among church members, which might then result in positive interracial contact and community.[18] More recently, educational researcher Mitchell Chang has found that racial diversity in higher education institutions has a direct positive impact on White students and the more diverse the institution the more likely a White student will interact with someone of a different ethnicity.[19] His study also determined that having a diverse student body results in "stronger commitment to multiculturalism, a greater faculty emphasis on racial and gender issues in their research and in the classroom, and more frequent student involvement in cultural awareness workshops and ethnic studies courses."[20] These attributes also have been shown to have positive effects on college satisfaction, student retention, the GPA of students, and the intellectual and social self-confidence of students.[21] In another study of college students, Gurin, Dey, Hurtado, and Gurin reported that students in the dominant White majority had the largest gains of any racial group in several learning outcomes as a result of engaging with diverse groups of students, in both formal classroom settings as well as informal social gatherings.[22] Alger reports that having a diverse student body in higher education allows all students to "have the transformational experience of inter-acting with their peers who have varied perspectives and come from different backgrounds. These experiences, which are highly valued by employers because of their importance in the workplace, also prepare students with the skills they need to live in an interconnected world and to be more engaged citizens.[23]

Research by Espinoza-Gonzalez et al. has found that multicultural institutions promote greater work of social justice, reduce prejudice, and change negative effects of stereotypes, while also promoting empowerment, combatting deculturalization, and enhancing other-group orientation.[24] Ghosh and Galczynski asserted that multicultural institutions also help their members affirm their cultural identities.[25] Several evangelical scholars found similar benefits, confirming that members of multicultural churches have more progressive racial attitudes and beliefs than members of primarily White churches.[26, 27] Other scholars have stated that "a more racially/ethnically diverse student body increased cross-racial interaction in the classroom for all students. Greater engagement with diverse peers in the classroom in turn was related to greater intellectual ability, social ability, and civic interest; this relationship was especially salient for students of color."[28]

Multicultural churches help congregation members become more aware of diverse perspectives, beliefs, and expressions of worship. This awareness then helps people from both dominant and subordinate groups to reflect on the experiences of The Other, which are often vastly different from their own experiences, thus helping people from all groups seek to understand God from a different vantage point.

Some scholars have examined how to create more multicultural faith-based institutions. For example, Joel Perez submits that leaders from "both clergy and lay, must come together with a common vision and must be equipped with the skills and resources to address the needs of congregations constantly living with change, especially when the favorite stance of most churches is 'this is how it has always been done.'"[29] Perez underscores the importance of perspective by stating that when diversity is viewed as a gift from God and not something that should be feared, real change and diversification become part of church stewardship. However, in order to incorporate these changes, the entire congregation needs to be mindful of how diversity both defines and surrounds them.

Finally, a study conducted by Jenkins finds that the most significant factors in creating and maintaining congregational diversity are the development of inclusive worship styles, creating small and racially/ethnically mixed groups within the church, and having a formal organizational commitment.[30] These studies from various disciplines and traditions capture the essence of the benefits of having multiple experiences and perspectives that enhance our overall understanding and appreciation of God and his people.

I recently had an opportunity to spend time with a seasoned and successful long-term missionary who served the Lord overseas for more than a decade. She is a living example of the impact cross-cultural ministry had in reconceptualizing some of her long-held assumptions of what she considered normal about people, culture, and the worship of God. Scholars also, through various academic disciplines, have stated the numerous benefits associated with multicultural institutions. Diversity has been proved to benefit both ethnic majority and ethnic minority groups.

Just as some music lovers might argue that an entire eighty-eight-piece orchestra of only clarinets would sound monotone, so too does a Christian community, church, and denomination become monotonous when only one dominant voice is represented. The final product of a well-rehearsed orchestra always sounds like heaven on earth to me.

The Costs of Multivocality

Sometimes orchestra rehearsals did not go well. This was often true whenever young musicians tried performing a new composition for the first time. No one was familiar with how all the sounds were supposed to come together, even as everyone was trying to be intentional about creating a unified sound. The problem was we failed to listen to one another. Sometimes one section, usually the lower brass section, thought their horns should be the ones that should be heard the longest, loudest, and most frequently. On those days, rehearsals do not go well, and rather than creating a harmony, we created cacophony.

The same could be said of diversity within a variety of

Christian settings and institutions. Whenever a church or denomination tries to diversify work in our faith communities, our much-anticipated initiatives and programs may not go smoothly at first, and that cacophony can last a while. When church leaders intentionally make efforts to gather a diverse group of people, they may just get what they wanted—a diverse group of people, but with a diverse set of opinions, experiences, and expectations.

So once compositional diversity is achieved, then what? One can be sure that when diversity is brought into the church, there are bound to be challenges. In fact, there may be more rather than fewer problems.

This has been my experience in multicultural spaces. Diverse people with diverse worldviews rarely work issues out by themselves naturally in some process of social osmosis. The reality is more conflicts arise. We are conscious of and talk about race more, not less, with increased instances of misunderstandings, hurt feelings, and hard conversations. White normativity is revealed for those in dominant groups, and deep-seated pain and bitterness is revealed among people in subordinated groups. Without intentionality, and without a critical consciousness about race, many multicultural efforts can lead to the opposite of the intended goal of unity. If left unattended, faith communities can be left with fractured and broken relationships, full of misunderstood and defensive people who never want to engage in this type of social experiment again.

Professor Roxanne Lalonde takes a slightly different approach in discussing unity through diversity, stating that rather than just tolerating diversity, individuals must work toward a more complex sense of unity that is based on knowledge of how differences enrich our collective human experiences.[31] Lalonde's statement strikes a chord with me on a very personal level. As an Asian American I would hate to think that my White brothers and sisters in a majority culture merely tolerate my existence. I would hope they would affirm that my humanity and presence has made their lives more meaningful.

Anyone who has had a negative experience in multicultural settings might be the first to acknowledge the challenges of diversity in real life. These individuals might also be the most resistant to engage in another attempt at diversification. This kind of silent or vocal resistance might ultimately keep churches and denominations from becoming ethnically and culturally diverse. Many might balk at the notion that racial divisions still exist and say that only cruel individuals with malicious racist intent refuse to diversify. I, perhaps naively, doubt that most of the time people's resistance is ever truly malicious. Rather, I would submit that we are often driven more out of fear than by faith. We draw largely upon our own past failed efforts to engage with and understand The Other. We might also be misinformed by the rhetoric from conservative media and in the pulpits across the country that diversity is driven by a secular, leftist, liberal, ungodly, socialist and Marxist agenda and that by pursuing diversity one is watering down the Gospel.

The early church certainly experienced tension along racial lines when the Hellenist Christian widows were being neglected in the daily distribution of food by the Hebraic Christians in the book of Acts. In our churches today, who is in charge and whose concerns take precedence? Having Whites in leadership positions within churches, professor Emerson explains, could often perpetuate White normativity. Researchers Meeussen, Otten, and Phalet with their recent research, highlight how so-called color blindness of leaders within a multicultural group affected how minority and majority members of their group felt accepted and connected.[32] They said leaders' consciousness toward multiculturalism was linked to minority members' feelings of acceptance, while leaders with color-blind ideologies were linked to relationship conflict for the minority members as they distanced themselves from the majority group.

Thus far I have discussed the notion of White normativity and its prevalence in the culture of Predominantly White Churches across the United States. I outlined both systemic and internalized barriers to diversity that continue to plague our Christian communities. I also discussed the costs and benefits of diversity. But what is still needed to combat normativity is greater awareness and a critical consciousness that is intentional. In what follows, I offer thoughts on how to make consciousness more intentional.

Intentionality

It takes great intentionality and effort to regularly surround oneself with people who look, act, and think differently from you. It certainly takes us out of our comfort zones and our natural inclinations might be to seek spaces where we feel comfortable. I argue here that an unforeseen barrier that prevents greater efforts toward diversity is the lack of intentionality to counteract the structures of homogeneity within churches and denominations.

Justice scholars argue that intentional efforts toward diversification have yielded some positive results toward ethnic representation in a variety of spheres in society such as business, education, and civil services. While some leaders in the corporate arena employ intentional diversity practices that may be driven more by financial rather than altruistic motives, they have nevertheless improved the ethnic representation among their employees. Though their efforts have led primarily to compositional diversity among staff and not significant changes in leadership, their business practices can offer much for nonprofit groups and churches, which operate not out of an obligation to the bottom line, but are driven by the sacred.

Some scholars and practitioners have offered practical solutions that may prove helpful. Professor Ammerman for example suggests churches can become more diverse by creating an inclusive organizational identity that replaces group boundaries rooted in cultural differences.[33] These boundaries are often changed due to an increase in "the proximity and diverse racial-ethnic groups and recognized similarities across the groups." In order to help congregations discover these similarities, Dougherty recommends the use of small groups. These small groups have been proven to create a culturally diverse religious community. In a study of 625 churches, Dougherty found that churches with small groups that met regularly were more diverse than churches that did not have them.[34] This makes one wonder whether the lack of small groups is contributing to a lack of diversity and unity within American churches.

Lack of intentionality prevents diversity within churches. One cannot merely hope and pray, in the midst of our inaction, that something will dramatically change in our denominations. I am not suggesting prayer has no power; however, I think prayer should be joined with intentional action. We need both.

A Way Forward

Moving forward, there are numerous ways in which intentionality regarding creating diversity within small groups, church leadership, and churches in general can be pursued. To create diversity within a local church community, I submit the following ten introductory recommendations for consideration.

1. Be intentional about putting yourself in social and ministerial situations where you are not the majority. Be especially intentional about listening to those with different experiences, beliefs, and backgrounds from your own.

2. Identify individuals who would be able to provide you or your small group with diverse perspectives so that all can grow, learn, and mutually benefit from a cross-fertilized fellowship.

3. Connect groups of people with other groups (neighboring churches, schools, community organizations) on a regular basis to foster community, growth, and shared learning opportunities.

4. Hold yourself accountable for being intentional about learning from other cultures. Identify someone who can serve as a mentor to you on issues of diversity.

5. Read and study more about diversity and the church. Yes, reading this book is a good start. There also are many good lectures and seminars available online, as well as books or other materials you can use for discussion groups at church.

6. Talk with the leaders in your church about a vision of intentionally building relationships, both within the church and in the surrounding community.

7. Hold those in leadership accountable for being proactive or responsive to racial reconciliation. Some churches may want to have church leadership provide regular updates on how they sought to create a diverse leadership team.

8. Seek feedback from your congregation if you are a ministry leader. Conduct regular roundtable discussions and individual interviews that facilitate the exchange of ideas and recommendations from members of a non-dominant group. Be prepared to listen and work through the painful stories without rationalizing or justifying your own internal biases or the impact of unintentional practices in the church.

9. Consider how to diversify those in visible positions of leadership. Inviting guest speakers of color to preach occasionally, and not just on topics of diversity, may help normalize different interpretations, ministry styles, and backgrounds.

10. Think differently about the delivery of the elements of worship. From music and song selection, speaking styles, delivery of God's Word, and communion, all of these elements may be helpful in meeting the many different needs of a diverse community while still maintaining a focus on the primacy of the Lord during worship.

Finally, intentionality needs to be nurtured. By that I mean intentionality toward diversity ought to be discussed regularly, and race ought to be addressed critically and carefully rather than be avoided. This allows momentum to be built and racial harmony to remain a priority as a biblical mandate.

How might an enthusiastic "Amen," "Alleluia," or "Praise the Lord" rupture normalcy in our churches? What systemic, though unseen and unspoken, principles have we built our churches on that require examination? Often leaders believe their churches are purely founded upon Christ. However, our respective cultures, mindsets, and practices are much more influential than we might realize.

A majority of what has been presented in this chapter has focused on an unintentional and unconscious yet dangerous assumption of normativity among those in a dominant majority. This normativity has been built over generations and is reinforced by racialized structures and systems that continue to benefit some at the expense of others. This problem permeates society as a whole, including in the church. I also have focused on the merits of a diverse community, while also acknowledging the challenges that can come with it.

I conclude with this reminder from the abolitionist William Wilberforce, who famously said, "You may choose to look the other way, but you can never say again that you did not know." My hope is that we all recognize the systems we are unwittingly part of, and with this knowledge we would be intentional and critically conscious of structural and internal factors that hinder greater diversity. We need multiple voices, styles, perspectives, and forms of expression to be valued. We need these perspectives to be seen as necessary and beneficial to our faith communities.

In the end, God's house was built for all of us. We can choose to look the other way, but we can no longer say we did not know.

5

LITURGY: A RHYTHMIC
EXPRESSION OF WORSHIP
AND TOOL FOR LIVING

LEON BROWN

Matthew Anderson wrote, "One thing is certain—that unless the Presbyterian Church takes greater interest in the colored people, she will lose her opportunity."[1] Anderson pastored Berean Presbyterian Church in Philadelphia beginning in 1880. To assist others in better understanding the Presbyterian Church's need to evangelize and engage African Americans, he wrote a brief sketch of his church's history. There, he boldly declared:

> We have always thought, and we believe rightly, that the Presbyterian Church has an important mission to perform among the colored people of the United States. The doctrines held by the church are the best calculated to correct the peculiar faults of the Negro, his legacy from slavery, and thus give him that independence and decision of character necessary to enable him to act nobly and well his part as a man.[2]

His calculated approach to mission among African Americans also included his involvement in the Berean Building and Loan Association and the Berean Manual and Industrial School. The latter "provided a number of business and vocational courses for Blacks when the doors of other institutions were closed to them."[3]

Despite such efforts, more than a century later we are still wrestling with how to take interest in "colored people." We ask: "What will assist us"—those in predominantly White denominations, networks, and federations, as Anderson was—"in attracting and retaining more ethnic minorities?" If our primary interaction with African Americans is through ministries of mercy, food pantries, education, financial assistance, or medical assistance, will our churches garner interest among them? Should we found churches in communities that are primarily populated by African Americans? Is adoption of Black children a satisfactory means of increasing our ethnic count? Is it as simple as hiring a Black minister, thereby increasing the ethnic diversity within the church's leadership, or catering to African American musical preferences? What must we do to see the demographics within our communities enter our congregations, thereby knitting together a beautiful tapestry we call the church?

Many of these discussions, as indicated by conferences, articles, and books, highlight a standard approach to increasing ethnic diversity. However, within these conversations, a very important element is lacking.

While ascribing to a culturally diverse musical arrangement on Sunday is important, what houses the music is also important. Preaching and the sacraments are the means God utilizes to strengthen his people and draw all men and women to himself, but what escorts us to these elements? Ministries of mercy are necessary. Nevertheless, into what will you bring those whom you are serving? What is often missing in our communication about diversifying our churches is *liturgy*; that is, the order and flow of our church services.

In this chapter, I will explore liturgy as a rhythmic expression of worship. I also will discuss freedom of expression within liturgy and consider the movement of liturgy. Finally, I will examine how liturgy is a pedagogical tool for living. I hope these thoughts will add one more piece to the puzzle that will enable you to more effectively minister to African Americans and other ethnic minorities in your communities.

Liturgy: A Dialogue or a Dance?

During my first year at seminary, my wife and I moved, which meant we had to settle into another church. Like many Christians looking for a new congregation, we became church shoppers. For a short period, we visited churches that other seminarians frequented. These churches were affiliated with different denominations, networks, and federations, and each of these churches maintained a different ethos. Some were more formal, others utilized more or less instrumentation during the singing, and some had more responsive readings. Of all the churches we visited, only one church elicited this remark from me to my wife: "We're not going back."

Perhaps at the time, I said more than I should have. Maybe it was my immaturity that kept me from seeing the beauty in the Lord's Day service at that church. Whatever it was, I have since visited that church again. While I have come to more fully appreciate all that is occurring in that congregation, I have retained one of the reasons that caused me to say we weren't going back. It wasn't the preaching that gave me pause, though I wasn't familiar at the time with three-point sermons. It wasn't the singing, though I preferred a different music style. It wasn't the cries and squeaks of the children, though I wasn't used to children staying during the entire service. It was the liturgy.

Like a military formation, it was rigid: step one, two, and three until the company commander, or in this case the pastor, said, "Company! Halt!" or declared the benediction. I stood when the pastor said stand. I confessed sin when we arrived at that part of the service. I sang when I was told. I sat when commanded. I even left when I was dismissed. In the words of one church tradition, "It was done decently and in order." After spending ten years in the United States Navy, I did not mind the structure, but something in this church service did not quite resonate with me. I later discovered what it was.

Some have suggested corporate worship functions as a dialogue. Like any good conversation, one person speaks and another responds. Upon entering the corporate worship of God, the Lord speaks to his people, calling them to worship him. A pastor or ministry leader uses a portion of Scripture—often from the Psalms—to announce to the people, "*Let us come into his presence with thanksgiving; let us make a joyful noise to him with songs of praise!*" (Ps. 95:2). The congregation then responds in song or in some other fashion. This dialogical principle affords the saints the privilege of replying to God's work and words in praise, prayer, tithes, and listening intently.[4]

The inerrant Word of God is filled with this pattern. After the Lord gives Moses the ceremonial and civil laws—a rubric for life—that promote justice, service, and worship, Moses descends the mountain and speaks on behalf of God. The people respond, "*All this we will do*" (Ex. 24:3).

On the day of Pentecost, Peter lifts his voice to multitudes and exclaims that King David died and was buried (Acts 2:29), but Jesus, though he died, was not abandoned to Hades, nor did his body see corruption, as God raised him up and we are all witnesses (Acts 2:31–32). The people responded, *"Brothers, what shall we do?"* Peter said, *"Repent and be baptized"* (Acts 2:37–38).

God's Word demands a response. Hence, our Lord's Day services are dialogical in nature. He speaks and we reply. The problem was not with the principle the church practiced. The problem was what we in attendance did with it. And as I mentioned previously, the principle is only one part of the Lord's Day worship narrative.

When I was younger, I grew accustomed to hearing my mother repeat certain phrases. Statements like, "I brought you into this world and I'll take you out" were routine idioms. Other cultural utterances included, "While you're living under my roof, you'll abide by my rules," "Don't talk to me that way. I'm not one of your nappy-headed friends," and "Don't bring the outside inside. Wash your hands."

Perhaps one statement that transcends ethnic and cultural boundaries is, "You'll speak when spoken to." Some elder in your family likely has borrowed that line to ensure children "zip their lips." However, when applied to the dialogical principle, it creates an atmosphere suggesting one can only speak during the routine responsive sections of the worship service. Demonstrative outpourings during the sermon, for instance, are off limits. Since you are being spoken to for an extended period, your responsibility is solely to listen.

While the dialogical principle, as it is called, has its place, and although others have described corporate worship as the reliving of the unfolding grand narrative of God, the dialogical principle only provides part of the story, which indicates that it does not describe the Sunday worship experience completely.[5] What is lacking?

The missing piece can be found in many African American and Hispanic congregations. Have you been? If so, you will recall the liturgical ethos being much different. Amid the responsive readings, prayers, Scripture, and sermon, people are much more verbally expressive. Why? It is because African Americans and other minorities speak to each other differently. While at times we embrace the motto, "Speak when spoken to," we also consider our conversations more like a dance.

A dance requires rhythm, give and take, ebb and flow, a keen awareness of when to proceed and when to delay, as well as the wherewithal to understand when to improvise. There are five elements to dance. Each element is represented in the acronym BASTE, which stands for Body, Action, Space, Time, and Energy.

The body demonstrates the holistic approach to dance. Dance requires the involvement of the head, eyes, torso, shoulders, breath, senses, perceptions, thoughts, and emotions. Dance inevitably includes one's actions, which demands bending, stretching, rising, and falling. One's entire body is involved in dance. Likewise, we must bring both body and soul into the dance we now call liturgy. In theory, we confess that we bring ourselves into the liturgy. In practice, we may appear gnostic, only engaging the ebb and flow of the worship service cognitively. However, when we approach this event as a dance, bringing our body and actions, we navigate the liturgy within the space and time allotted, expending our energy for the glory of God.

Let's Dance

What do you notice about the liturgist during Sunday worship? Is he—are you—holistically involved, or is the presentation more subdued? Is he gripping the pulpit with his hands throughout the liturgy? Is he moving his arms and head? Or is he more akin to a mannequin placed in a storefront window? These are not theatrics. This bodily movement communicates to many of us as minorities that you actually believe in what you are doing, and you are firmly convinced of what you are saying.

No person exclaims, "I am excited!" while having her hands in her pockets. No lottery winner tells his family he has selected the correct numbers with a solemn look on his face. No family member remains in his seat while his son or nephew walks across the stage to receive his college degree. Those events bring something out of us that require our synapses to fire and our muscle to act, which ultimately produces movement. When we are gathering corporately before the God of all creation, should there not be some resemblance of these actions (Ps. 47:1, Ps. 95:6, Ps. 149:3)?

While I am not suggesting that you, as the liturgist, should be something you are not, having our personality and character stretched and conformed to the image of the creator is consistent with the Word of God. Unlike the Ten Commandments, our personality is not carved in stone. Therefore, it seems we can make adjustments for the sake of the other. That may require you to release your hands from the side of the pulpit in order to produce hand gestures consistent with what you are saying. It may force you to make more eye contact with the congregation so you get a sense of how they are responding to you. In this dance, you may need to start moving from side-to-side instead of standing stationary. Your knees may be more engaged than

73

you are accustomed, as they bend back and forth. Even in an elevated pulpit, you feel as if you cannot be contained. These movements—this dance—occur throughout the liturgy, which means you may sweat or actually be tired after service, as your body is acting within the given pulpit space and worship auditorium provided.

Such enthusiasm, as the Holy Spirit leads, may evoke responses from the congregation. Inevitably, this will prolong the time of the worship experience. Furthermore, the liturgist must be willing to improvise during this time. That is, he cannot transition from one segment of the service to another without giving credence to what the Holy Spirit may be doing in his midst.

Unlike my children, I was not raised in the church. It was not until I joined the Navy and was invited into the household of saints that I was introduced to the Christ through his Gospel. I was made spiritually alive as the Holy Spirit breathed life into me. My guilt and shame were omitted, and I was newly clothed in the righteousness of Jesus.

The message that gave me hope was proclaimed at a Pentecostal church. Sometimes well-meaning Christians ungraciously classify the entire movement as consisting of verbal acrobatics containing no substance. This was not true of any Pentecostal church I have visited, but they definitely did spend a large amount of time in worship. I came to faith in the Lord in a church that spent a ton of time in vigorous worship.

But regardless of the affiliation of a church, each congregation has a liturgy. Some are compacted into an hour while others take place over three or four hours. If the liturgy is choreographed like a dance, on some occasions the same dance may take longer than others because of improvisation. When necessary, liturgists must be willing to improvise. The Holy Spirit can neither be constrained by the contours of earth nor the time allotted to worship services. If a church member brings two guests to church and amid the sermon, the guests begin crying out for mercy, will the preacher stop his message to tend to those who are being saved? Improvisation requires one be sensitive to what requires attention or more time throughout the liturgy.

Being keenly aware of your body and actions, space and time requires energy (i.e., BASTE). Each Lord's Day, the liturgist will be exhausted because along with his physical muscles being exercised, his spiritual faculties are also taxed. Indeed, the one leading the service should be holistically occupied.

In predominantly African American churches, the preacher often will take a cloth into the pulpit along with his Bible. There is a reason for this! When he is engaged in the preaching event, his eyes are tuned to the sensibilities of the church. If his point was received with great enthusiasm, he may repeat it once or twice more. That extends the length of the service. If God is mending broken hearts, restoring relationships, and pouring out more grace on the hearers, brothers and sisters may exclaim, "Amen!" or "Say it again, Rev!" The second recitation of the point may come with more enthusiasm, which causes the preacher, or liturgist, to be even more involved bodily, requiring action and energy, as he covers more space on the platform, all of which takes more time, energy, and sweat.

The entire service is a dialogue. The entire service is a dance, which is a rhythmic expression of a movement between the liturgist and God's people.

Movement

As my wife and I attended different churches during that first semester at seminary, I noticed many of the same trends. When we walked into the church building, we were greeted, given a bulletin, and soon thereafter took a seat. Once the service started, there was a call to worship and confession of sin followed by singing, more Scripture reading and preaching. The service typically ended with a benediction. While the elements of a dance could have been improved upon in those services, something else was missing—movement.

While one could argue transitioning between each section of the service necessitated movement, it was more static than directional. Our liturgies should have forward anticipatory movement. We must take people, like a dance, from one part to another that ultimately terminates in a climax. There are two aspects to movement that are directional: simply put, it's *here* and *there*. They are both eschatological categories.

Although the phrase is sometimes used pejoratively, there is something to liberation theology. Carl Ellis observes:

> In the early foundations of Southern Black theology, the *second exodus* became a major theme. The River Jordan represented death. On this side of the Jordan we lived in the Egypt of slavery, where we were the least among the American cultures. On the other side of the Jordan we would be free to be with our Lord in the Promised Land, and we'd be the first among the American culture.[6]

Liberation theology, at its core, is a message that

bespeaks freedom. Any marginalized people wants a taste of independence, a taste of being able to freely dance without the shackles. Its genesis is in the Bible, and while the message has been surgically altered, its theme is still valid—you will be taken from this place of pain and sorrow and delivered to a new world. Instead of being treated like a slave, you will be recognized as a king.

As we craft our liturgies to be directional, the terminus must first be *here*.

Think about redemptive history. There is a beautiful, though shortened, display in the prologue of John's Gospel. He writes: *"In the beginning was the Word, and the Word was with God, and the Word was God. He was in the beginning with God. All things were made through him, and without him was not any thing made that was made"* (John 1:1–3).

As John continues the narrative, he tells us the word is life, light, and truth. There is a messenger who will announce his arrival. His name is John the Baptist, but ultimately do not fix your eyes on him. He is a witness standing in the courtroom of Jerusalem testifying to the coming one, who now has taken on flesh and tabernacled among us, and *"we have seen his glory, glory as of the only Son from the Father, full of grace and truth"* (John 1:14). Along with anticipation being embedded within the prologue, there is a terminus. John, the author, took us from the way the world was and took us to Jesus. The terminus must always be Jesus. *"Come to me, all who labor and are heavy laden, and I will give you rest"* (Matt. 11:28).

African Americans, as well as other minorities, need rest. The yoke of this life is too heavy. We have to deal with the perils of being in a fallen world like you, but the color of our skin adds an additional burden. Our hearts skip a beat for different reasons than others when we look in our rearview mirror and notice law enforcement behind us. According to one source: "African Americans serve virtually as much time in prison for a drug offense (58.7 months) as Whites do for a violent offense."[7] In general, "sentences imposed on Black males in the federal system are nearly 20 percent longer than those imposed on White males convicted of similar crimes."[8] Alexis de Tocqueville (1805–1859), a French historian, wrote: "I do not imagine that the white and black race will ever live in any country upon an equal footing. But I believe the difficulty to be still greater in the United States than elsewhere."[9]

Although African Americans are fearfully and wonderfully made, God's providence has brought us certain circumstances that cause burdens simply because of the amount of melanin that is produced within melanocyte cells in our skin. Therefore, we need to be taken to a place of rest *here and now*. We want to feel the momentum rushing over our bodies much like driving on a freeway in a convertible. That momentum is felt and observed throughout the liturgy as with every turn of the worship event, we experience being brought one step closer to Jesus. We know he is present among us, but after a wearisome week, we need the liturgist to guide us to him.

Our liturgies must also take us *there*. We must be taken to a place that is other-worldly. While the benefits of salvation are offered to us now, they are fully realized later. We need to be taken to a place that says, "There is more to come." We need to be taken to a place that says, "There won't always be tension between image-bearers because of the color of our skin, political affiliation, or class." We need to be taken to a place that says, "All the tears you have cried because you could not change your circumstances will one day be wiped away." Take us to heaven with the universal church where Jesus is seated upon the throne as judge and merciful savior (Heb. 12:18–24)!

Is that not what the sacraments do? They are directional. They take us *here* and *there*. In Matthew 26:26–28 we are told:

> *Now as they were eating, Jesus took bread, and after blessing it broke it and gave it to the disciples, and said, "Take, eat; this is my body." And he took a cup, and when he had given thanks he gave it to them, saying, "Drink of it, all of you, for this is my blood of the covenant, which is poured out for many for the forgiveness of sins."*

That is the *here* of the sacrament. You have transitioned from having a meal to feasting upon Christ *in this world*. There is an otherness to the sacrament as well. "*I tell you*," Jesus said, "*I will not drink again of this fruit of the vine until that day when I drink it new with you in my Father's kingdom*" (Matt. 26:29).

There! Anticipation is embedded within the sacrament and words of institution that assures us something greater is coming.

The liturgy should maintain that same appeal. Anticipation for the next stage of worship should be placed at every stage. What about your verbal interludes promotes movement? How do the songs build upon each other? How does the flow of the service lead to the preaching of the Scriptures and the administration of the sacraments? Does the liturgy prepare us for prayer? Much like a scavenger hunt that provides exciting clues leading to the next portion of the adventure, each part of the liturgy should propel the hearers forward to the next stage with a sense of expectation, awe, wonder, and excitement. Take us *here!* Take us *there!*

You may have heard the phrase, "Less is more." It is sometimes ascribed to minimalists, who believe it is better to devote oneself deeply and to fewer tasks than to many things and spread too thin. In any event, the same idiom is also applied to liturgy. Some would say that in order to attract minorities to your congregation, develop a worship experience that is less structured.

Again, less is more. The backdrop of that type of suggestion appears often to be birthed out of the Pentecostal experience. In that tradition, many churches do not corporately confess sin as it often occurs in Reformed or Presbyterian churches. The Nicene Creed or Lord's Prayer also are not consistently recited in many Pentecostal congregations.

Hence, some suggest that in order to make allowance for those from that background, who are newly entering churches with more formal liturgies, it is best to remove those portions of the service (e.g., the Lord's Prayer, Nicene Creed, corporate confession of sin). If however, liturgy is a pedagogical tool for living, and life is multifaceted, then our liturgies should be multifaceted. Simplistic services will struggle to teach us how to live complicated lives. In fact, as I observe the landscape of African American churches, many of them have standard liturgies with responsive readings, multiple Scripture passages, prayer, preaching, and even a confession of sin.

When people from our congregation are on vacation and visit other churches, I encourage them to ask two sets of questions pertaining to the liturgy. First: What is the structure of the service? In other words, why does a church sing two or three songs in a row? Do they publicly confess their faith in the service? Why or why not? While the New

Testament does not provide an exact outline for our church services, God is still serious about how we worship him (Heb. 12:28–29). It seems, then, that we should think thoughtfully, incorporating paradigms from both the Old and New Testaments, when we construct our liturgies.

Second, I encourage them to ask: How does this help us live? James K. A. Smith, in his book *Desiring the Kingdom: Worship, Worldview, and Cultural Formation*, offers key insights in this area. If the liturgist provides little time to pray, how does this help us to live? If the service is focused almost exclusively on the sermon, does that suggest that singing and prayer are unimportant? What about the service's order will enable my family to live throughout both good and bad days?

As a general outline, our congregation's Lord's Day service begins with a call to worship. A responsive section using Scripture and prayer follows the call to worship. We then sing and soon thereafter confess our sins corporately while kneeling. We hear an assurance of pardon, declaring that those who have embraced Christ by faith are forgiven, after which we rise to our feet to sing in response. There is and Old and New Testament Scripture reading, a sermon, prayer, more singing, the Lord's Supper, and a benediction. All of this takes place within an hour and twenty minutes to an hour and forty-five minutes (remember we must be mindful of improvisation).

Who would attend such a service? Our congregation is 60 percent minority. They believe this is an acceptable way to worship the living God and receive good gifts from his hand. Our service is bathed in Scripture, filled with shouts of joy, and it seeks to collapse the binary nature of this present age. Who among us does not look forward to bowing before the Lamb of God in humble submission and joyful worship (Phil. 2:9–11, Rev. 7:9–12)? On that day, our bodies and souls will finally operate as one. The war that presently ensues between the flesh and the spirit will cease (Gal. 5:16–26, Col. 3:5–17). We therefore seek to enact that now. For example, in kneeling to corporately confess our sin, we unite the posture of our bodies with the disposition of our hearts. Does it not appear a bit strange to humbly confess one's sins while standing? In that posture, we might suggest that our hearts are contrite, but what about bodies? Kneeling to confess sin teaches us that before both God and man, we are to maintain a humble disposition when we confess sin.

Why does our church have both an Old and New Testament Scripture reading? Simply put, it is to help our people learn how to study and understand the Word of God, as well as demonstrate how the whole Bible elevates the Triune God and more particularly the salvation that Christ offers. Jesus used the Old Testament Scriptures to demonstrate how they pointed to him (Luke 24:13–27, John 5:46). Paul preached from the Hebrew Bible (i.e., the Old Testament) to proclaim the Kingdom of God and his Christ (Acts 28:30–31). The Bible is sixty-six books of interwoven tapestry that declares the message of hope for all people. We ought not conclude that the Old Testament is filled with rules and wars that have no relevance for us. Having complementary testament passages read within our liturgy displays the unifying message of the Bible and assists the people in comprehending the saving power of God from both passages.

More broadly, the overarching composition of the liturgy teaches us how to navigate the beginning, middle, and end of our days. Just as our service begins with God (i.e., the call to worship), our days begin with God. We do not wake up merely because our hearts are beating, our brains are functioning, and we are breathing. Our life is held in Christ's hands (Col. 1:17). He is the catalyst for our breathing and moving. Hence, just as we are called to worship on Sunday and reply with a responsive reading of Scripture, prayer, and singing, so too, we respond to the Lord with Scripture, prayer, and singing when we arise in the morning or evening after he calls us to awake. This paradigm might cause us to rearrange the liturgies of our lives. Instead of immediately wondering what someone posted on social media or having the urge to check your favorite news broadcast upon getting out of bed, might you first acknowledge that it is God who called you to rise? Upon recognizing his care for you, might you also reply in prayer and song?

Our call to worship is followed by a confession of sin. In light of God's goodness and our lack thereof, an appropriate response is necessary. We confess who he is and what we are not (Isa. 6:1–7, Rev. 1:17). This, as indicated, takes place on our knees. This, followed by a declaration that we are forgiven in Christ, produces an excitement and joy that may well cause us to shout for joy (Ps. 100:1–2)! After all, James wrote that if you are cheerful, sing (James 5:12). Is there anything that should make you happier than what God has done for you in Christ?

From there, we read the Bible and preach the Bible. The Lord's Supper and benediction follow the sermon.

Superimpose this liturgy upon your daily activities.

Once you acknowledge God's goodness in waking you, you respond with Scripture reading, prayer, and singing, and after you have taken care of your other normal morning duties, you eat a meal. Once your meal is complete, provided you have not already started work and do not work at home, you leave your domicile to begin the workday. In a similar manner, just as God meets you at the Lord's Table and sends you on your way with his name and blessing upon your life (i.e., the benediction), you leave the church building to serve and love your neighbors. Likewise, the Lord meets you at your meal table in the home, grants you blessings of nourishment, and sends you into the world for love and good deeds.

The liturgy is a pedagogical tool for living as it teaches us how to respond when we sin, causes us to better understand the Bible, enables us to more fully embrace the God of the Scriptures, prompts us to give God glory when we wake, and provides a fuller vision of how God is with us every moment of our days. If the liturgy of Sunday service replaces the liturgy of your life, you will be more likely to confess sin immediately upon its recognition, you will sing more throughout your day as you are frequently reminded of God's goodness, you will navigate the Scriptures more responsibly, you will bless God at every meal as you recognize he has provided your daily bread (Matt. 6:11), and you begin your work day more fully confident that his blessings are upon you.

Closing Remarks

If you have already utilized many of these suggestions or you are considering implementing them, how do you know if you are satisfactorily orchestrating the liturgy as a dance, incorporating forward movement, and providing a pedagogical tool for living? Since the focus of this chapter is ministering to minorities, consider reaching out to those presently in your congregation or others in the community. Ask them to be critical of your liturgy by providing feedback on how changes to the liturgy might make them feel more comfortable.

Often they will not respond that you should reduce formal liturgy. Rather, you will hear them articulate that they want to feel freer to express themselves demonstratively. African Americans and other minorities desire a fluidity that is more than, "Stand up, sit down, say this, and say that." We want to be taken *here* and *there*, and we want to know that you believe in what you are doing and what you are saying while you are navigating the worship service.

Will you dance with us? Will you converse with us?

PREACHING: TO THE PREACHER, TO THE CHOIR, AND TO THE EMPTY SEAT

RUSS WHITFIELD

When I sit on my front porch in Washington, DC, and look at my neighborhood, I see African Americans, Anglos, African immigrants, Asian Americans, and Latinos. On a casual walk around my block, I encounter mixed-race families with young children and elderly folks who remember when Dr. Martin Luther King Jr. came to town to deliver his famous "I Have a Dream" speech. On that same neighborhood walk, I cross paths with single professionals who work on Capitol Hill, blue-collar city workers, and people who are not sure if they will receive the help they need for their next meal. The cultural, ethnic, socioeconomic, generational, and vocational variations are seemingly endless.

Now, I realize that I'm describing my own neighborhood in Northeast Washington, DC, and it's possible that your neighborhood does not look like mine. However, if demographers and social trend experts are correct in their projections, it will not be long before your neighborhood does indeed look like mine. We live in a time where the global is becoming local. Our neighborhoods, schools, and places of work are undergoing rapid social change. Yet our call to neighbor-love has never changed. We must wrestle with the reality that the church will fail to communicate the heart of God *to* her surrounding neighbors if she does not have the heart of God *for* her surrounding neighbors. If we do not love our diverse neighbors in word and deed, then why would we ever expect to find our diverse neighbors in our churches? It is a sad fact that the one place where this cross-cultural love should be found in full measure is the very place where it often seems to be most absent: the church.

It should be said that this cross-cultural love has nothing to do with being politically correct. Rather, this cross-cultural love has everything to do with the good news of God's grace in Jesus Christ. Theologically our goal is not to seek diversity as an end in itself because this would be too small an endeavor relative to God's Kingdom calling. Rather the great end of this pursuit is doxology through diversity. Our goal should be to glorify our cross-cultural Savior by cultivating a cross-cultural community that maintains a cross-cultural witness to the grace and glory of God. When rightly considered, the Christian life and the Christian community should be a symphonic expression of the *"breadth and length and height and depth, and to know the love of Christ"* (Eph. 3:18b—19a). This love requires humble listening, an ability to be taught, understanding, and the proactive pursuit of individual and institutional change. This love requires faith, repentance, renewal, creativity, and perseverance.

It's a tall order, but this is precisely the community for which Jesus Christ prayed in the Upper Room (John 17) and for which Jesus Christ died at . If this oneness is on the heart of Christ, it should be on the heart of the Christian.

To put a finer point on it, I would argue this should be a particular concern and conviction of the local pastor when it comes to the ministry of preaching. These demographic changes signal the need for homiletical changes if we are going to spiritually form the people of God according to the beauty of the Lord's vision. If we hope to have a resonant corporate witness amidst our diverse cultural contexts, then our preaching must meaningfully minister to the diverse peoples of our local contexts. We need a growing cultural dexterity and theological facility if we are to meaningfully engage the entirety of our diversifying mission fields. In this chapter, I will suggest three considerations for growth in cross-cultural preaching: preaching to the preacher, preaching to the choir, and preaching to the empty seat.

However, we should start with a word about preaching itself.

Preaching the Word

Most Christian pastors would acknowledge their calling is primarily directed toward the ministry of the Word of God. We shepherd, counsel, disciple, equip, and nourish our people by the authoritative Word because we know our congregations and our neighbors need more than good advice on how to have a nice life. They need the good news of resurrection life in Christ. Our calling is to announce again and again the Lord Jesus has risen from the dead with all power over sin, death, and the powers of evil!

Jesus is mighty to save, ready to restore, and worthy of our highest thoughts, our greatest affections, and our deepest devotion. For this reason, preaching has rightly held a place of primacy in the life of God's community. We have been called into an altogether different kind of life that is sustained by an altogether different kind of power.

The new age has dawned, and the old is passing away. We must turn from BC living in order to thrive in this new AD context. The announcement of the King's victory is simultaneously a summons to live as a participant in this new Kingdom administration. The preaching of the Word is one of the central means by which God graciously forms his people for their mission to the world. We need a complete reordering and restructuring of our individual lives and our corporate life so that both align with the life of God, the grace of God, and the Word of God.

But what exactly is the nature of this Word we preach? The Word of God is a cross-cultural document of cross-cultural origin, with a cross-cultural message about a cross-cultural Savior, and it was written to produce a cross-cultural community that glorifies the Lord. We have more than just a few isolated proof texts to support this outlook. In fact, every chapter of redemptive history leads us in this cross-cultural direction.

The narrative arc of God's story, with all of its thematic trajectories, is leading us to see that God's plan for the fullness of time is to unite all things in Christ, restoring harmony and unity to the world God created, through Christ (Eph. 1:10). In Colossians 1:25–27, the Apostle Paul says God called him to his apostolic ministry in order to make the Word of God fully known. He then goes on to clarify that full knowledge of the Word of God entails understanding that, through Christ, God has brought peace to the sociocultural polarities of the world through the indwelling Christ. Paul acknowledges the inclusion of the Gentiles, the "outsiders," was indeed a mystery to the Jewish "insiders." However, the apostle says it is a "glorious" mystery. Mark that word "glorious." It's more than a great thing or a nice thing. It is a *glorious* reality. Should not this mention of glory send us back to the purpose of creation and forward to the fullness of the consummation in which Christ will receive all the glory from all his people from all over the world throughout all time?

We need to rehearse this script if we aspire to be compelling players in God's redemptive drama. If we are committed to faithful proclamation of God's Word, then we must begin with our own heart-level submission to the Lord's transforming Word.

Preaching to the Preacher

Theologian John Owen once said, "No man preaches that sermon well to others that doth not first preach it to his own heart."[1] What Owen implies here is we pastors need the same grace, the same healing, and the same nourishment we offer to others on Sunday morning. The cross-cultural Gospel[2] we deliver should enliven our own hearts if we are to have the confident expectation that it will enliven the hearts of our people. But it's at this very point that many experience a tension. Many pastors struggle, and they end up with monocultural preaching, because they do not recognize the cross-cultural dynamic in the biblical text. When first exposed to the idea of cross-cultural preaching, many suppose this is the result of some type of liberal or pluralistic ideology that has crept into the church from culture. Others believe this way of thinking is theologically sound, even important, but they have difficulty connecting the dots. But why is this so hard to see?

In many cases, pastors have attended seminary and have learned to interpret the Bible but have not acquired a cultural self-awareness regarding the baggage they bring to the interpretation of Scripture. They have learned how to do theology in a particular cultural context that governs the way in which they theologize through cultural issues. They operate under the false impression they are approaching the Bible and doing theology in a purely objective, culturally neutral fashion.

But there is no such thing as an acultural interpretation of Scripture. We do not, and indeed cannot, theologize in a cultural vacuum. However, one of the things we can do is bring different questions to the text, questions that result from authentic cross-cultural relationships in which we can learn and grow. We must humbly approach the Scriptures with a growing self-awareness regarding our cultural baggage, asking the right kinds of questions, fully acknowledging we need the Spirit to minister the Word to our own hearts before we can graciously minister to the diverse people of our community.

The pastor must be the chief repenter as it pertains to racial pride, socioeconomic idolatry, and ethnocentrism if he is going to lead his people into the beauty of cross-cultural love. Self-righteous, pride-filled preachers will only proliferate social, emotional, and cultural dysfunction within the congregation. However, pastors with increasing degrees of cultural self-awareness and humility cropping up in their personal lives will see the Lord graciously working through their weakness and expanding their understanding of the cross-cultural dynamics of the sacred text.

But how do we begin to ask the right kinds of questions? How can we gain fresh angles on the Word that bring these cross-cultural considerations into view?

We must be good pastors. If you want to be a faithful cross-cultural preacher, then you must be a faithful cross-cultural pastor. Your congregation may not be diverse yet, but you can have a pastoral presence among the representative people in your neighborhood. As you care for different people with different stories, different values, and different assumptions, you will start to come to Scripture with different questions that bring new interpretive vistas before you.

We must remember that our primary calling is to shepherd our people. A faithful cross-cultural pastor will be a faithful cross-cultural preacher because he will carry his beloved people in his heart and into the study. The pains, struggles, and needs of his people will become his burden as he prayerfully pores over the text in sermon preparation. In time, he will develop a cross-cultural intuition, sensing when homiletical choices might alienate certain members of his flock. He will translate extensive, theologically dense material for members lacking formal education or exposure to a particular theological heritage. He will avoid making exclusive sermon applications to the world of the upper-middle class, nuclear family that owns a home, has 2.5 kids, and a dog. He will illustrate points with material drawn from the music, movies, and references of various cultural worlds. He will humbly confess his own ethnocentrism to illustrate points and will celebrate his own personal growth in cross-cultural understanding from the front.

Furthermore, his conscience will not allow him to remain silent on issues of injustice when Scripture speaks so forcefully on behalf of the oppressed. He will not minimize or trivialize the sufferings of his beloved, even if he does not quite understand the depth of their pain. He will not canonize his cultural particulars in the worship context, but will invite both the godly expression of emotion and the godly silence of contrite reflection. In other words, the pastoral ministry of the cross-cultural pastor will lead him to preach sermons in which the cross-cultural diversity of the community is both affirmed and challenged by the message of the Gospel. Our homiletic is greatly enriched and broadened through this pastoral reflection on the diversity of our congregation and neighborhoods.

The cross-cultural shepherd will work to understand the precious and peculiar souls with whom he shares little commonality and cultural experience. Cross-cultural shepherds understand this nuance: Jesus doesn't deal with a vague, generalized notion of sin. He deals with particular sins of particular, culturally located people, with a particular ministry of Gospel transformation. Furthermore, he deals with the particular wounds of particular people who have been sinned against. This involves a particular call to particular repentance of particular sins. It involves a nuanced understanding of social power dynamics and how these realities affect those who have it and those who lack it. But the cross-cultural shepherd begins with his own need for Christ, as revealed through his honest reflections on his own broken soul. Then he moves toward his people in the preaching moment with our common hope.

Practically speaking, the pastor must create the necessary space to listen well to his people. Your schedule will reveal your shepherding values. At this point you must be honest about the story that your schedule tells and ask yourself the hard questions. Do you spend time with the poor in order to love them well and solicit their valuable feedback on how your preaching can be more helpful to them? Do you build friendships with local Black, Latino, or Asian residents that could helpfully inform your sermonic emphases and applications?

Do you spend any time learning from other pastors and leaders of color who are peers? Or do you really think the learning can only go in one direction? Do you spend time cultivating and encouraging cross-cultural leadership, or have you exported the weight of this burden to the seminaries? We're not talking about ecclesiastical parlor tricks or manipulating Sunday morning optics. We're talking about the faithful ministry of a local pastor who is committed to seeing people of different ethnicities, socioeconomic distinctions, and cultures living in everyday, loving community together. We must allow our own souls to steep in the Gospel, and we must take up the habits of Christian spirituality, working out the implications of our shared faith for our shared life and our corporate witness to our neighbors.

I can say I have learned as much from the personal repentance and faith of cross-cultural leaders in my life as I have from their sermons and lectures. Their personal witness added weight to their proclamation. We must not shrink back from proclaiming to our people what is profitable for their souls. We must teach them the whole counsel of God (Acts 20). But we must begin with ourselves. If we do, we will become living witnesses who are able to confirm the transforming power of the Gospel we preach with a peculiar gravitas. The weight of our own testimony and the evidence of grace in our own lives and relationships will be felt by our people and impressed upon their souls with a singular urgency. This personal change is essential if we are to care for our people with grace and patience, connecting the dots, asking the tough questions, and issuing the costly call of discipleship for these divisive times.

Preaching to the Choir

We are all too familiar with the idea of preaching to the choir. It's a simple way of identifying when a person is trying to make a believer out of someone who already believes. But when we see cultural mistrust, ethnocentrism, and racial pride plaguing the community that has been called to oneness, unity, and mutual love, we can't help but ask: Do they really believe?

Do *we* really believe? Do we really believe all people are equally desperate for the grace of the Lord? Do we really believe the work of Christ has made us one family? Do we really believe discipleship involves a death to the sin that separates us and a rising up into the virtues that functionally restore our communion? At the very least, we must pray like the desperate father of Mark 9, "*I believe; help my unbelief!*" (9:24). The choir will never graduate from the school of grace, so we must continue to preach Christ to the choir. We must give them the Christ, the whole Christ, and nothing but the Christ of Scripture.

Admittedly, there is much to learn about humanity through sociology, anthropology, and psychology. However, the most important lens on diagnosing and restoring humanity is Christology. The pastor's work is not editing or adding, but expressing and proclaiming Jesus Christ as the representative and rescuer for every cultural, ethnic, and socioeconomic group in the world.

Pastors and elders, are your people hearing about the Jesus of Scripture who meets the needs of the diverse people groups that surround them? Does the Jesus you proclaim love, befriend, and empower the poor and disenfranchised? Does the Jesus you proclaim warrant the kind of faith that leads people into the cultural fray as gentle peacemakers and courageous mediators? Does your Christ unequivocally compel and demand brother-from-another-mother love? Does your Jesus call people to repurpose their privilege for the benefit of the outsider? Does your Christ lead people out of their false, life-stealing narratives and into God's story of redemption?

These questions are important because we all have a tendency to fashion Jesus into our own cultural image. You must appreciate the fact that when you endeavor to proclaim the cross-cultural Christ, the only Christ there really is, you will be pushed into under-explored Christology. It's both humbling and exciting because knowing this Jesus will enable you to traverse the cultural frontiers of your particular mission field, helping you to encourage, challenge, and care for your people. But knowing this Jesus will, at times, prove to be excruciating because the love he warrants from you will mean the death of you. Of course, this is the entire point. The old you must die so that the new you can rise up clothed in the moral and ethical beauty of Jesus. The road to glory goes through the cross. As it was for Jesus, so it is for us. We preach free grace, not cheap grace.

Many of us have heard throughout our entire lives that God is out to conform us to the likeness of Jesus Christ. This is absolutely stunning! But it has become increasingly apparent we have barely scratched the surface of what this christo-formity entails. We must dig more deeply into the identity and activity of Jesus Christ if we are to be faithful preachers and practitioners of pastoral ministry.

We must preach the Jesus of Scripture who was, in himself, a breathtaking union of two radically different worlds—God and man—without confusion, unchangeably, indivisibly, and inseparably, as the Chalcedonian Creed puts it. The very person of Christ screams "unity in diversity!" Do we spread this particular vision of what it means to be called the body of Christ? Do we water down "community" to fit our existing cultural framework and biases toward homogeneity? Union is central to the identity of Christ and is to be central to the corporate identity of the church.

This Jesus becomes what he was not, out of love for the Father, so that the "other" might share in that most profound love. Do we call our people to this cross-culturally transformative love?

This Jesus fully inhabits a particular culture (Jewish) without falling into racial pride, ethnocentrism, or idolatry. Jesus Christ embodied his Jewish culture in a way that did not demean other ethnicities, but rather, dignified them. Are we equipping our people with a vision broad enough to burst the doors of their cultural prisons? Are we calling our people to embody their ethnic identity in a way that dignifies rather than demeans all the others?

The Son of God allows his existence to be permanently altered by the needs and afflictions of the "other." He remains a true man to this day, a true man with the scars to mark the depths to which he was willing to go for love's sake! Does our preaching allow people to think they can safely elude such life alteration in the fulfillment of God's mission? Do they come away from our preaching, week after week, with the impression that cross-cultural engagement is optional? The million-dollar question is: Do we really want to be conformed to the likeness of Christ?

If we answer this question in the affirmative, then we must understand that this cross-cultural dynamism is precisely what Christlikeness entails. We must connect the dots for our people. They must understand that this was so important to God that he would give the treasure of heaven to secure our harmony and unity. Jesus empathizes with the "other" and is fully engaged with the "other" in mind, will, and emotions. Do we call our people to such cross-cultural empathy and engagement?

The person and work of Christ are an absolute ethical gold mine for the church. It's no wonder that the Apostle Paul said, "We proclaim him!" We've only scratched the surface of the vast treasury held in the person and work of

Christ! Keep searching his many excellencies and you will realize the countless implications.

We must consider how the Son of God enters into a foreign context and willingly relocates in order to be present with the "other." We must allow this reality to confront us when we are inclined to remain geographically distant from the undesirable neighborhoods, allowing fear, selfishness, or apathy to rule us. We must marvel at the way Jesus mediates between the holy culture that he owns and the broken culture that he embraces in order to make that which was his by nature become ours by grace. This type of christological reflection will help us craft sermons that equip our people to become a community of mediators, bringing healing in fractured neighborhoods through repentance, faith, and courageous action.

Paul tells us in the book of Ephesians that Jesus brings the outsider, those historically estranged from himself, near. Do we suggest, through sermonic omission, that our people can safely refuse to do the same?

Paul tells the Philippians that Jesus humbly and willingly repurposes his privilege for the advantage of the "other" (Phil. 2). Do we call our people to repurpose their privilege for the benefit and blessing of those who are socially disempowered and culturally foreign to them? There would be no Gospel if Christ refused to use his power for the benefit of the weak! There would be no Gospel if Christ did not care for, and empathize with, the poor! As the old French carol puts it: "Thou who wast rich beyond all splendour / All for love's sake becamest poor / Thrones for a manger didst surrender / Sapphire-paved courts for stable floor."[3]

This truth is central to the Gospel message, and we must not allow these realities to remain peripheral to our proclamation and framing of discipleship. The heart of

Christ was so large, so enflamed with love, that he wept over the brokenness of his place. Are we touching the hearts of our people with such longing for renewal and concern for the welfare of their city, town, or neighborhood? Do our people understand the Father's plan is to clone the heart of this same Jesus in each one of us? This is the Jesus who is held out to us in Scripture. Therefore, this is the Jesus whom we must hold out to our people.

Here is the big picture: God's plan is to conform us to the image and likeness of Christ because Jesus is the archetype of divine image bearing. He shows us what human beings were always meant to be. In as much as we resist preaching this cross-cultural Gospel, we unwittingly oppose the spiritual and anthropological development of our people. We are hindering, through sermonic passivity, their trajectory toward their true human telos embodied in the true man, Jesus Christ. The choir needs to be reintroduced to Jesus. By all means, preach to the choir! But give them the cross-cultural Christ of Scripture.

Preaching to the Empty Seat

A few years ago, there was a story in *The Atlantic* about a Canadian epidemiologist who was researching anemia in rural Cambodia.[4] As you may well know, anemia is typically caused by an iron deficiency, and it results in serious health problems. The researchers knew that iron-rich foods and supplements were too expensive for most rural Cambodians. Even cast-iron pots, which transmit iron to food as it cooks, were financially out of reach for the people. So the researchers distributed small blocks of iron to local women, telling them to place the iron blocks in their cooking pots before making soup or boiling drinking water. However, because this epidemiologist failed to culturally connect with the women, they promptly put these iron blocks to use as doorstops. The people really needed this iron, but they just wouldn't use these iron blocks.

So, after talking with village elders, the researchers learned of a fish that the locals frequently ate and considered to be a symbol of good luck. Then they handed out smiling iron replicas of this fish and the women actually started cooking with them, and within twelve months, anemia in villages where the fish were distributed virtually disappeared. They were working with the same substance, but they were able to fashion that substance in such a way that the people could receive it and be made well.

At the end of the article, the researchers note that the genius of the iron fish is that it does not have to be shaped like a fish at all. If you were to go to another culture you could very easily change that same block of iron into a meaningful symbol for that culture in order to cure their iron deficiency.

Our neighborhoods, our cities, and our world have a Christ deficiency. This deficiency results in spiritual problems, relational problems, and all sorts of other issues that threaten human flourishing within and among all people groups. God has called his church, but especially his ministers, to know Christ, to know our people, and to know our neighbors in such a way that we can give them Christ in a culturally accessible fashion. But what additional, practical changes can we make in our preaching to improve our cross-cultural communication?

We can preach to the empty seat. This is to say that we should craft our sermons with the expectation that our diverse neighbors will actually be present on Sunday mornings.

We often fail to realize that as we preach, we are revealing our expectations about who will show up on

Sunday mornings. After all, *"From the overflow of the heart, the mouth speaks"* (Matt. 12:34, NIV). Sadly, our words often reveal little love and interest in our hearts for the people of our place. When we use language, illustrations, and stories that are only intelligible and resonant with cultural and spiritual insiders, we are subtly conveying the message that only cultural and spiritual insiders are welcome in our places of worship. If by chance, a cultural or spiritual outsider does show up, they hear loudly and clearly: "I'm not welcome or wanted in this place." When we only address the saints from our pulpits, we inadvertently alienate people in the very place where they should encounter the most profound welcome: in the community made by grace.

We see this theological commitment at work when the Apostle Paul addresses the church in Corinth. They were a people who thought themselves wise and spiritual, but they enjoyed using their gifts and flaunting their knowledge for the sake of self-advertisement. A modern example of this weakness occurs in how some use Christian worship in self-aggrandizing ways, aiming to display their vocal abilities, theological prowess, or knowledge of doctrinal and confessional categories with little regard for blessing the "other" in their midst. Paul challenges the Corinthians to grow into a maturity that is expressed in concern for the "other" and a desire to make their worship accessible to the spiritual outsider. The apostle says:

> *If, therefore, the whole church comes together and all speak in tongues, and outsiders or unbelievers enter, will they not say that you are out of your minds? But if all prophesy, and an unbeliever or outsider enters, he is convicted by all, he is called to account by all, the secrets of his heart are disclosed, and so, falling on his face, he*

will worship God and declare that God is really among you. (1 Cor. 14:23–25)

We see here the apostle not only *expects* non-Christians to be present in the worship service, but he also expects Christians to conduct their worship in a way that will be intelligible, resonant, convicting, and transformative for non-Christian people. It seems the Apostle Paul envisions Christian worship as a time of transformative encounter with the living God for both Christian and non-Christian alike. Paul seems to suggest Christian worship is neither exclusively for Christians, nor exclusively for non-Christians, but rather, for both. We do not need to embrace false dichotomies.

An important point to keep in mind is that our people will take their cues from us. They will either learn to translate the riches of our faith in ways that are accessible to non-Christians, or they will adopt the insider exclusive language that blunts our corporate witness to our non-Christian neighbors.

If you preach about evangelism and mission, your people will eventually sense the need to engage their neighbors. However, they may also begin to ask questions like, "Would my neighbors feel welcomed in our Sunday morning worship? Would they resonate with what my pastor is saying in his sermons? Would my neighbors feel respected and fairly represented by the way my pastor speaks about non-Christians? Would my pastor's preaching alienate my neighbor and tear down the relational credibility for which I've worked so hard?"

I'm suggesting your preaching will either build cross-cultural and missional trust with your people, or it will create mistrust through homiletical and sermonic myopia. If you preach to the narrow confines of your existing congregation, your community will remain culturally static. This kind of preaching will dash any hopes your people might have for including their neighbors in your community. However, if you preach to the diversity of your neighborhood as if the diversity of your neighborhood is already present, if you explore their cultural references, using their heroes in your illustrations, if you address their particular fears, insecurities, and needs with the grace of Christ, then your community will eventually have a compelling cultural dynamism, and you will foster the hope and reality of cross-cultural community growth.

An additional effect of preaching to the empty seat is you will simultaneously be shaping and equipping your people to follow your lead in their Monday through Saturday encounters with neighbors and coworkers. Your preaching will serve as a model for cultural teachability and interpretation that is nuanced, empathetic, and winsome in a time where there is so much noise and confusion on these issues. We certainly cannot forsake the exclusive truth claims of our faith. However, the humble, honest, empathetic, and gracious way in which we interact with the alternatives from the pulpit is critical to advancing a cross-cultural mission.

Finally, it is important to acknowledge that cross-cultural preaching can be incredibly frustrating because we are constantly confronted with our own inadequacies, cultural blind spots, and smallness of heart. But when we find ourselves in this place of weakness and insufficiency, we are prepared to prayerfully invite the power of God into the study. It is in these times of felt weakness that we find assurance and comfort in the fact that Christ is the true preacher who is able to convey his Word to the people with transforming authority, even through our limitations. The good news for inadequate preachers like us is that Christ is more committed to cross-cultural preaching than we could ever be, and he delights to involve his beloved to participate in building a church against which the gates of hell cannot prevail.

Our calling, as God's heralds, is to proclaim that Jesus Christ is Lord of all. He is the Lord of men and women, rich and poor, young and old, married and single. The Gospel is good news for PhDs and GEDs, those in the boardroom and those in the courtroom, insiders and outsiders, the oppressed and the oppressor. Jesus Christ deserves worship from those who clap on the 1 & 3 and those who clap on the 2 & 4. *"Everyone who calls on the name of the Lord shall be saved"* (Rom. 10:13).

But how will these diverse segments of humanity call on him in whom they have not believed? And how will these distinct people groups believe in him of whom they have never heard? And how are these multifaceted cultural groups supposed to hear without someone preaching the good news that Jesus Christ cares for people like them, and addresses their central concerns, and meets their particular needs? Our God is no mere tribal deity of parochial concern. Nor is he a regional governor, hindered by the constraints of a limited jurisdiction. He is Lord of all. We believe that one day every knee shall bow and every tongue confess this truth. But Christian preachers must begin bowing the knee and confessing this universal authority right now through our message and our methods. As we prayerfully take up this labor of love for the diverse people of our place, may it be said of us, *"How beautiful are the feet of those who preach the good news!"* (Rom. 10:15).

THE SACRAMENTS: A CATHOLIC, CROSS-CULTURAL, AND MULTIETHNIC EVENT

SHERRENE DELONG

The terms "multiethnic" and "cross-cultural" are arguably the most popular buzzwords in the church today. Multi-ethnic usually refers to the demographics of the congregation. How many different ethnic groups are present? Do we have a diversity of members? Would anyone, from any background, with any skin color be comfortable and welcomed here?

For churchgoers, cross-cultural may indicate some sort of ministry (e.g., a short-term mission trip to a non-domi-nant culture or a college campus ministry to international students). The phrase could also encompass the variety of music a church sings on any given Lord's Day.

Unfortunately, we've unnecessarily limited the use of the aforementioned buzzwords.

Being multiethnic and cross-cultural expand beyond the music we sing at church, the demographics of the congregation, the amount of mission trips we take to other parts of the city or country, and even the personal relationships we maintain. A necessary but sometimes overlooked element of Sunday service also bears the brand of being multiethnic and cross-cultural: the sacraments of baptism and the Lord's Supper. They present multifaceted layers of immersion and digestion of other cultures. And far from creating consternation within the broader church, as many conversations about race, justice, and reconciliation do, the sacraments bespeak unity within diversity. That is, they proclaim, among many things, the catholicity of the church. The way these layers work together may seem mysterious to us, but it is a mystery worth pursuing. In this chapter, we will consider how baptism and the Lord's Supper teach us to live joyfully in the tension of being cross-cultural Christians in multiethnic communities while embracing the catholicity of the church.

Living Cross-Culturally

You should know I live in three very different cultures. While I currently reside in Alabama, I was born and raised in California, and both of my parents were born and raised in India. (Take a moment to let that sink in.) For our purposes, let's consider being both Indian and American. Growing up, I went to a private, Christian, very American school. I spent time with my dominant-culture friends throughout the day, and I came home to the scents of Indian cooking, Indian accents, and, to my chagrin, Indian culture and rules.

Every day, I grew up balancing living as an American in an Indian family and as an Indian in an American school. As many second-generation children will tell you, straddling these two worlds isn't easy. At some point in my youth, I realized that I didn't want two cultures. More specifically, *I didn't want to be Indian anymore.*

This, of course, was impossible. My parents and sprawling extended family met together regularly, and when we did, we were very Indian. There was always a reason to celebrate: birthdays, anniversaries, Indian Independence Day, American Independence Day, and everything in between. No matter what the occasion, the gatherings always included traditional Indian food, clothing, languages, and customs. What drove me crazy was how they always talked about India like it was so much better than anywhere else. "In India, the mangos are so much sweeter." "In India, everyone in the neighborhood was friendly and trustworthy." "You would understand if you grew up in India."

As an American-born, I didn't understand it. We're in a new country now, I would think. Why is there still such a tie to India? How can they live in the United States and still feel such a close connection to their home? Why did they have to be so... Indian?

It's been several years since I went through that phase, and since then I have gained much more respect for India and Indian culture. I also have learned that my large, boisterous Indian family has inadvertently taught me much about being a Christian.

I frequently hear these words from the lips of Christians around me: "This world is not my home." We try to cope with the struggles of a fallen world by reminding ourselves now is not forever, and our true home is in heaven with the Lord.

But what does it mean to live in this world while recognizing it is not our home?

My immigrant family knows plenty about this. While they are grateful for the opportunity to live in the West, they try hard to maintain Indian culture. India, to some degree, will always be home. Because of this, my family lives everyday in the cross-cultural tension between our home culture and our present and surrounding culture.

The Cross-Cultural Christian

No matter what your ethnic background is, as Christians, we also are called to live cross-cultural lives. We too should experience the challenge of having a true home and a current home. The third chapter of Colossians provides an excellent overview of the cross-cultural nature of the Christian life. After spending much time earlier in his letter to the Colossians demonstrating the preeminence of Christ and how we are reconciled to him, Paul delves into the contrast between our previous culture and our true culture. He begins in verses 1–4:

> *If then you have been raised with Christ, seek the things that are above, where Christ is seated at the right hand of God. Set your minds on things that are above, not on things that are on earth. For you have died, and your life is hidden with Christ in God. When Christ who is your life appears, then you also will appear with him in glory.*

Paul immediately sets up a distinction between the things of the heavenly kingdom and the things of the earthly kingdom, just as Jesus did when he said, *"My kingdom is not of this world"* (John 18:36). We are united to Christ and his kingdom, and this union should result in our lives being focused around the things of his kingdom, despite our present reality in the world. The Kingdom of God has come here and now, inaugurated by Christ (Luke 17:20–21), yet we still pray *"Thy kingdom come"* as we look forward to being in the final consummated kingdom, the new heavens and earth (Luke 11:2).

Until that glorious day, God has us here. We long to be in our true home, our true kingdom, with our true Father who is also the true King. Yet even though we remain away from home, we are still called to live as citizens of heaven, practicing the culture and ethic[1] of the Kingdom of God and resisting the culture and ethic of our natural selves. Paul goes on to describe what that looks like, noting that we are to avoid *"sexual immorality, impurity, passion, evil desire, and covetousness, which is idolatry"* (Col. 3:5). Though we are apart from our King, we still abide by his rules for his kingdom. We bow the knee to the One True King alone, and not to the many false gods littering the streets of the earthly kingdom, as we once did. Our allegiance is to the King of Kings, the King with no rivals, the King victorious.

Paul summarizes by saying we *"put off the old self with its practices and have put on the new self, which is being renewed in knowledge after the image of its creator"* (Col. 3:10). Like a child told to put away her dirty clothes, we are to "put away" (verse 8) all facets of our culture that are sinful and instead "put on" the clothing of the new culture. There is a new way of life for the people of God, a new culture and a new ethic that we must embrace as our own, modeled after our King. Since we have gained citizenship into the Kingdom of God, we must now dispose of all crude manners of the world and rise to the standard of the kingdom. Paul shows us what kingdom citizens look like in Colossians 3:12–14:

> *Put on then, as God's chosen ones, holy and beloved, compassionate hearts, kindness, humility, meekness, and patience, bearing with one another and, if one has a complaint against another, forgiving each other; as the Lord has forgiven you, so you also must forgive. And*

above all these put on love, which binds everything together in perfect harmony.

In contrast to the laundry list of culturally offensive faux pas, Paul describes how true citizens reflect the King. By including recommendations for dealing with complaints and how to forgive, Paul assumes that these new cultural norms will be challenging for citizens living abroad. While we are not in the final kingdom yet, we are still very much a part of the true kingdom. The King is calling us to fall in line with our true identity by developing the cultural mindset and behavior of our heavenly kingdom, all while battling our old nature but still maintaining the mindset that we are here for God's glory and the good of the people.

It should come as no surprise, then, that Scripture is full of cultural reminders of our new kingdom ethic. The Beatitudes in Matthew 5 give a wonderful picture of what God's Kingdom is and will be like. Peter gives instructions on how to interact with those around us as citizens of heaven yet still living on earth (1 Pet. 2:11–17). So many of Paul's other letters give us instructions on how to live in light of Christ's life, death, resurrection, and ascension. All of these instructions seem so opposite from our natural, sinful tendencies, as Paul describes in Romans 7. Every day becomes a wrestling match between our old nature and our new nature, similar to balancing two different cultures and all the expectations that come with each culture. The fact that we live in this tension is one of the reasons every Christian is a cross-cultural Christian.

The Sacraments: Gifts of the Kingdom

Remember the young me who wanted to pick a culture and get on with life? Sometimes we as Christians wish we could do the same. Fighting our sinful hearts and dealing with our broken world is no easy task. The anguish should teach us to long for heaven. In the meantime, a soothing comfort comes when we remember that in the midst of our cultural balancing act, our King has not left us alone. Although we are *"sojourners and exiles"* in the world (1 Pet. 2:11), we are also *"fellow citizens with the saints and members of the household of God"* (Eph. 2:19). The thought is astounding! We as the people of God are not only members of the kingdom, but family of the King. God has joined us together as family with the other citizens of the kingdom who also struggle living amidst two cultures.

This family is composed of a multi-everything community (1 Cor. 12:13), consisting of people from all ethnicities, nationalities, vocations, family backgrounds, wage earnings, clothing preferences, sports teams, and more. This eclectic family gathers together regularly, as any family does. We use the language of our home culture, the manners of our home culture, and we even eat the food of our home culture. Far from a fairy-tale experience, this occurs in the church. The church is our refuge. It should be our safe space, our kingdom embassy on earth where we are joined together, diverse, and in unity. The wonder of it all is that as we meet together, our King meets with us, and he gives us gifts from our true home—our home away from home— that remind us of his kingdom and further set us apart from the world. These cultural tokens are the sacraments.

The sacraments of baptism and the Lord's Supper are signs and seals of God's promises to us (Rom. 4:11, 1 Cor. 11:24–25). He promises to be our Savior, to strengthen our faith, to help us be obedient to Him, and cause us to long for home (Matt. 26:26–29; Rom. 6:3–4, 1 Cor. 10:21). He brings us together with other Christians, and their children, and sets us apart from the world (Eph. 2:4–5, 1 Cor.

12:13).[2] The sacraments of baptism and the Lord's Supper are gifts that are foreign to us, for they come from our new King. Through these two cultural gifts, our King reminds us of the greatest gift he has given us: himself. We are baptized in the name of the Father, Son, and Holy Spirit because of our King (Matt. 28:19). We partake of the bread and wine, his body given for us (1 Cor. 11:24). Yet the sacraments are more than a reminder. Our King actively works to strengthen our faith and encourage us as we receive the gifts of the kingdom by faith.

Baptism

It is common and right for Christians to associate baptism with water and cleansing. While there is an element of washing or cleansing, the primary focus of baptism is not on the recipient of baptism (although he does benefit from it), but on the God who is acting through baptism.[3] In baptism, our Triune God signifies and seals our union with Christ and the benefits of this union (Rom. 6:3–4). While the sign and seal by itself does not provide salvation, it does boast of the blessings of receiving Christ by faith and being granted all the gifts signified in baptism (1 Pet. 3:21).

As we think cross-culturally and about the Kingdom of God, when Jesus and all his benefits are received by faith, baptism serves as our rite of passage into the Kingdom of God. It is the means by which God marks a new citizen. God calls us out of one kingdom and brings us into his kingdom with a new cultural initiation rite, a sign and seal of his promises to us.

In my family, an unofficial rite of passage is the food test. When my non-Indian husband first met my parents, a main concern was his ability to eat and enjoy Indian food. Of course, they were also concerned about his religious background, manners, and overall morality, but food was a major component in being welcomed into the family. Gratefully, my husband is able to put down Indian food like no one's business. He loved the variety of dishes my parents prepared.

Since then, they have given him a steady stream of different dishes to try. They are continually improving on that first experience and reaffirming his position in the family regularly by offering him more and more opportunities to eat traditional food.

The analogy is not perfect, but it is helpful. While we do not need to be baptized over and over again, there are ways we can "improve on" our baptisms. The Westminster Larger Catechism describes it this way (in my paraphrase):

> We are to thankfully remember our initiation into the family of God, remember the privileges and benefits sealed to us in this event, be humbled by how we fail to live up to the calling of our baptism, be assured of God's forgiveness, be strengthened by Christ's death and resurrection, avoid sin, live by faith, and walk in brotherly love.[4]

As those initiated into the family, we are called to remember our initiation and make sure our attitudes and actions are reflecting the Kingdom of God. In doing so, we are bound together with others who have been initiated into the family, and we encourage one another. For this reason, baptism is so much more than a one-time personal commitment. It is a gift of our King for the family pursuit of sanctification.

While this kingdom perspective is just one layer of the cross-cultural nature of baptism, there is more to pursue. It is important to note that ideas and examples put forth in

Scripture often meant something different to the original audiences than they do to us. In the American church, however, we often become complacent with our traditional understanding of doctrine and fail to push ourselves to understand the beauty of truth in significant ways. When we neglect a multicultural perspective, we contentedly dwell with an impoverished understanding of intricate truths. What are we missing by neglecting the cross-cultural clues in our understanding of the sacraments? Have we established a standard of understanding that is American instead of biblical? Are we too proud to reach across cultures and centuries to have a well-rounded under-standing of what has perhaps become a little too familiar? There is much to be said on the topic, but for now, let's focus on the cultural background of Jesus when he insti-tuted baptism and the significance given in the original context.

Consider just one aspect of Jewish culture and history as an example. Throughout the Old Testament, the concept of water often coincides with the concept of judg-ment. Noah, who obeyed God's instructions to build an ark, was saved from the waters of judgment on the earth. The writer of Hebrews comments on this, noting that Noah's faith in God's provision for his family, shown by his actions of building an ark, *"condemned the world"* (Heb. 11:7). While the flood of condemnation rained down upon the wicked earth, God provided Noah and his family with a means of salvation from this judgment through the ark. The splash of the rain must have reminded them of the impending doom and God's kindness in making a way of escape. This points us to Christ, the ark of God, by whom we are saved from the same judgment. 1 Peter 3:18–22 explains:

For Christ also suffered once for sins, the righteous for the unrighteous, that he might bring us to God, being put to death in the flesh but made alive in the spirit, in which he went and proclaimed to the spirits in prison, because they formerly did not obey, when God's patience waited in the days of Noah, while the ark was being prepared, in which a few, that is, eight persons, were brought safely through water. Baptism, which corresponds to this, now saves you, not as a removal of dirt from the body but as an appeal to God for a good conscience, through the resurrection of Jesus Christ, who has gone into heaven and is at the right hand of God, with angels, authorities, and powers having been subjected to him.

Unlike Noah who passed through the waters of judgment safely, Jesus was baptized on the cross with the Father's wrath (Luke 12:50). This sacrificial act now carries us through the same waters of judgment and lands us safely in the Kingdom of God. This is why God tells us so beautifully through Isaiah:

Fear not, for I have redeemed you; I have called you by name, you are mine. When you pass through the waters, I will be with you; and through the rivers, they shall not overwhelm you; when you walk through the fire you shall not be burned, and the flame shall not consume you, for I am the Lord your God, the Holy One of Israel, your Savior. (Isa. 43:1–3)

When Jesus instituted the rite of baptism (Matt. 28:16–20), the cultural backdrop of judgment was necessarily involved in the sacrament. Baptism is the means by which God identifies us with the Judgment-bearer and initiates us into his kingdom (Rom. 6:3–4), but it must be obtained by faith. Without faith in Christ, the waters of baptism remain the waters of judgment. It is a chilling warning. Those who are baptized must also have faith, or we will be like the people in Noah's day who saw the ark, scoffed, and remained in their sins to be condemned.

How can these cross-cultural lenses help us understand baptism? First, they help us realize baptism is more than an outward declaration of personal devotion. In many churches in the United States, people view baptism as a cleansing. It is something I must do to demonstrate my devotion to God. There is a feel-good emotion that often prompts both clapping and celebration.

While there are elements of truth to this perspective, baptism is even more beautiful than this. Baptism is a sign and seal from the King who brings us into his kingdom, one that is necessarily cross-cultural because we have a Jewish king. Though the act of baptism happens to an individual, it is not only for the individual. Baptism joins the individual into a diverse community. Further, the community viewing the baptism should be both reminded of their own baptisms as well as how they are to improve upon their baptisms. They also are witnesses to the newly initiated member, remembering the judgment associated with baptism, and are united in prayer for the new recruit. Baptism with water, therefore, should not be viewed as a casual swim in a pool, dunk in the ocean, sprinkling of holy water, or act of simply washing the dirt off our hands. In its fullness, baptism should bring us to our knees in gratitude for our King who underwent the waters of judgment for us, who now calls us to lay hold of the benefits of our baptism by faith as we become members of the Kingdom of God. Understanding baptism in this manner causes us to reach across cultures, back to the Ancient Near East when water maintained this significance.

The Lord's Supper

As baptism initiates us into the Kingdom of God, the Lord's Supper further sustains us until we finally arrive in glory. The Lord's Supper involves giving and receiving bread and wine to remember Christ's death, and in doing so, God nourishes us and grows us in grace (Matt. 26:26–28). In this sacrament, God reminds us of our union with him, prompts us to be thankful, and binds us together as the people of God (1 Cor. 10:14–17).[5]

This meal is more than just a time of remembering, however. Through partaking of the Lord's Supper, the Lord himself gathers his family for a covenant meal. This family is multi-everything. It includes the spectrum of skin tones God beautifully and intentionally designed. It includes those who wear suits and ties and those who wear overalls. It includes those who make minimum wage and those who are CEOs. It includes people who are elderly and those who are younger. It includes ISTJs, ENFPs, and all sixteen Myers-Briggs personality types. It includes every possible diverse combination we can imagine. Our Triune God not only created our intricate diversity, but he also brings us together for a divine meal. This meal nourishes our faith and strengthens our relationships with one another as fellow citizens of the Kingdom of God. It is the cultural food of the kingdom.

Interestingly, a significant part of maintaining any culture while away from home involves gathering together as a family to eat traditional food. There's something about food that brings comfort and peace. My family would gather to enjoy a feast of Indian delicacies. Something about those familiar spices took my family back to the motherland just for one moment. The tastes of the food would elicit scores of memories of their time in India, and of course, the aunties and uncles used it as an opportunity to share all sorts of stories about India with my cousins and me. It was so much more than a meal. We gathered together as a family to celebrate the traditions of our culture and to share joyfully about our common homeland.

Once again, the analogy is not perfect, but it is helpful. As the people of God, we are a family composed of people of all ethnicities, social standings, and wage earnings. While we were always united by blood in Adam, we are newly united by the blood of the second Adam, Jesus, who shed his blood to make us new. Some of us may not share a common country of origin, but we do share a common home as we look forward to our heavenly home. Although we may have different cultural traditions, we share a kingdom ethic in how Jesus taught us to live based on his kingdom culture.

Through Jesus' life, death, resurrection, and ascension, he creates a brand new family from an assorted group of people who may not otherwise have much in common. The sacrament of the Lord's Supper is the most prominent and official covenant meal of the diverse people of God. We gather together to partake of true food and drink. It's the feast of our homeland, not in whole, but in part. It should remind us of our true home and bring us joy.

When my family gathers to remember home and commune with one another, one thing is sure—it is loud. There is an energy and excitement permeating our conversations and attitudes. We are delighted to be together after spending however many days apart, comforted to eat our familiar food with one another, and eager to remember India together, discussing all we have in common. The electricity is what makes our family even tighter.

Can you imagine if our churches had the same electricity when we gathered? Can you imagine if our churches were full of multi-everything people, thrilled to be gathered together to receive this gift from our King? What a testimony of unity amidst diversity that would bring glory to God alone!

Compare this joyful gathering to what often happens in the American churches. The Lord's Supper is often attended by silence as people individually commune with God. Though we sit together in the pew, our hearts are far from one another as we partake, conclude the service, and move on to discussing anything but the covenant meal. The beautiful table set by our Host becomes a private snack eaten hastily over the sink.

Why are we so silent? In my family, when one member is present but intentionally silent, it implies that he or she is mad, hurt, or upset. There is a broken relationship and a level of rudeness in failing to join in the joy of the family. Even the children who throw fits will say, "I'm not talking to you" as they turn away in silence. Due to this cultural cue, when I sit together with the people of God on the Lord's Day to eat the covenant meal with my brothers and sisters, the silence disturbs me to some degree. It seems to highlight our personal relationships with Jesus, but it ignores that Jesus put us in a community, which the sacrament highlights.

I wonder what it would be like for us to converse during part of the sacrament, like a family talking joyfully about home and all we have in common amid our diversity. Silence, however, isn't entirely unwarranted. Scripture reminds us we are to examine our hearts that we may not partake unworthily (1 Cor. 11:28–29). A few moments of silence is appropriate to heed this warning, but complete silence for the entire administration can make the sacrament appear more individualistic and private than it is intended to be. The Lord's Supper is not a private meal, but a communal one, and a vital gift that brings a diverse group of people into unity.

While common food brings the family together, it often excludes those unfamiliar with it. As a child, I once dared to bring Indian food to school for lunch. Some of the girls made fun of me, and I never brought it to school again. Instead of being proud of my heritage and family, I wanted to distance myself from the identity associated with the food. Yet that same cuisine was central in the life of my family, binding us together and reminding us of our home.

In a similar sense, the Lord's Supper is the meal of the family of God. When the outsider observes the traditional meal, he or she is often skeptical and confused. The early church dealt with the consequences of being set apart by the covenant meal. Early letters about Christians reveal that a common perception in that time was that Christians were cannibals, eating and drinking flesh and blood, and mysteriously calling one another "brother and sister," even if they were married.[6] Society at large did not understand how the sacraments brought Christians together as family. Christians are part of a new culture, together in Christ and distinct from the world.

While the Lord's Supper is the covenant meal, there are other cross-cultural and multiethnic layers we must consider. Not only do we join together with others from different cultures and ethnicities, but we also partake of the body and blood of a Jewish man (not European, despite the myriad of pictures suggesting otherwise), who had Jewish traditions informing his actions. The concept of eating and drinking with God is seen several places in the Old Testament, often in reference to cutting a covenant or a covenant renewal ceremony.

In our world today, international treaties are followed by state dinners. In the ancient Near East, however, "the dinner *was* the signing ceremony."[7] For example, Moses describes a meal with God at Mount Sinai where he and several others "beheld God and ate and drank" in the midst of covenant ratification (Ex. 24:11). The covenant meal was more than an act of satiating hunger; it was an act of satiating the soul. On top of breaking bread with his disciples, Jesus also declares the cup to be *"of the new covenant"* (Luke 22:20). This reference should have prompted the Jewish listeners to remember the words of their prophet who foretold of the day God would make a new covenant with his people (Jer. 31:31-36). This language of new versus old is not used because the old covenant failed, but because Jesus is the total and final fulfillment of the old covenant.

This fulfillment also is seen as Jesus intentionally instituted the Supper during the time of Passover (Matt. 26:17–19). Interestingly, Bryan Estelle notes that although the occasion for the gathering was the traditional Passover meal, many of the traditional items that were to be present at the meal were not described or included in the biblical records.[8] He goes on to argue that the focus of this new tradition is not how Jesus fulfills the Passover meal, but rather the inauguration of the coming of the Kingdom of God.[9] The scope of fulfillment is even greater —Jesus fulfills the entire sacrificial system, not just the Passover.

Can you imagine how revolutionary this was? No longer do we need types and shadows, for the Lamb of God, the final sacrifice, our true food and true drink is finally here! Every bleat of the sheep, every blood-stained garment, every ceremonial regulation, every ritual meal anticipated the coming Messiah. Now the Messiah is here, inaugurating a new kingdom and a new feast. Jesus' institution of the Lord's Supper is more than just a remembering.

It is a declaration of the King who has come to redeem his people once for all!

Compare this view to how we tend to view the Lord's Supper in the West. Often we use the Supper as a time to remember what Jesus has done and meditate on his sacrifice for me. Isn't that what Jesus instructed us to do, saying, *"Do this in remembrance of me"* (1 Cor. 11:24–25)? Michael Horton reminds us that in the Jewish Passover liturgy, the idea of remembering meant "participating here and now in certain defining events in the past and also in the future."[10] There is an active connection between the sign and the thing signified, the sacrifice of the past, the covenant meal now, and the future covenant feast of the people of God. It is a remembrance to be sure, but with a celebratory gaze toward the future kingdom and an active strengthening of the soul for today. We eat together with anticipation of the marriage feast of the Lamb (Rev. 19:9).

With the Jewish cultural backdrop, we realize we are not just remembering Jesus as the one who died for me. Instead, we feel the magnitude of our Redeemer who is securing a multi-everything people for himself, fulfilling every anticipation of him since time began. Remember, while we ingest bread and wine, it symbolizes the body and blood of a Jewish man. The Lord's Supper is by nature cross-cultural and multiethnic.

Multiethnic and Catholic

Although I have primarily labored to demonstrate that the sacraments are cross-cultural, we must also remember that they are intrinsically multiethnic and catholic. The signs and seals given to the community of faith, by a king who is both Jewish and God, is for the church made up of a multiethnic people from all tribes, tongues, and nations (Matt.

28:16–20, Rev. 7:9), united because of the judgment Jesus bore on our behalf. God is setting a people aside for himself, a rescued people snatched from judgment, and is joining us together in his kingdom. As Horton writes:

> Every racial barrier (beginning with the Jew/Gentile distinction), every socio-economic wall, every demographic profile and generational niche, and every political-ideological partition that defines this present age disintegrates as the rays of the age to come penetrate.[11]

While we may appreciate aspects of our culture and ethnic identities, all visible identifiers should not separate the family of God. The broadest possible group of people is brought together in Christ and made one. The King shows no partiality in his kingdom (Acts 10:34, Rom. 2:11, Gal. 2:6). All are welcome and made part of the family of God.

Amidst this diverse family of God, there is a unity that can only come from the Triune God. One of the very last things that Jesus prayed for while on earth is for our unity. Acknowledging our sinful nature and the struggle of living in the world as citizens of a diverse kingdom, Jesus prayed for us: *"Holy Father, keep them in your name, which you have given me, that they may be one, even as we are one"* (John 17:11). What an encouraging thought! The one who unites us also intercedes for us, that we may be one body, working together and bringing honor to the Father. As the people of God, we should commit to the same prayer and actively seek to obey in faith.

Jesus' prayer for our unity should also challenge us to consider if we, the church, the family of God, the body of Christ, are truly united. On Sunday mornings, do we display a united diversity that depicts the citizens of heaven? When we witness baptisms, do we focus on celebrating the individual, or do we remember the implications of judgment as we prayerfully stand with our brother or sister, committed to growing in godliness together? When we partake of the Lord's Supper, do we do so privately, as a solemn remembering of Christ's suffering, or do we treat it like the celebratory meal of the family of God? Do we use the opportunity to talk about our homeland and bond with other citizens in the pew, or do we sit silently for the entire administration? What would it look like for the family of God to look more like family and less like acquaintances?

A cross-cultural, multiethnic, and catholic understanding of the sacraments challenges us to broaden our view of the church, of each other, and most of all, of our King who crossed ethnic and cultural barriers to grant us these gifts. If you look at a diamond from one perspective, it is beautiful. If you turn that diamond to see another side, however, you will see other facets catching the light and shining in different ways, making the diamond even more striking than before. The sacraments are more brilliant than a diamond and more precious than a diamond. If we only look at the Supper through a Western lens, can we honestly say that we comprehend with all the saints *"what is the breadth and length and height and depth, and to know the love of Christ that surpasses knowledge"* (Eph. 3:18–19)? The dimensions of Christ's love for us are mysteriously and wonderfully immeasurable, and we need both the historic cultural background of the Scriptures as well as the insights from our multi-everything community to help us grasp them. Let us prayerfully seek to understand the sacraments in a deeper way for the sake of the unity of the people of God, and for the glory of the King.

8

FACE THE MUSIC: WE'RE NOT IN KANSAS ANYMORE

HOWARD BROWN

In 2003, Rev. Giorgio Hiatt and I began the work of planting Christ Central Church (CCC), a multiethnic congregation of the Presbyterian Church in America, in Charlotte, North Carolina. One question we would inevitably get from prospective core group members and various supporters and interested parties was, "What is the worship going to be like?" What is the worship going to be like, at its core, for most people, is a question about music. Music, especially in a multiethnic church, is the great cultural tiebreaker. Whatever a church planter will decide about his music is typically telling of the vision and mission of the church. Music is the soundtrack, vernacular, culture, and sacrificial praise of the church.

The Soundtrack of a Church Movement

Music is cover art to the Gospel. It's an accompaniment to the greatest performance known to humankind—God redeeming us through his Son Jesus Christ. When we look

7

at the Psalms, we see a call to accompany the all-important inspired Word of the God with tempo, proper instrumentation, and vocalization. In the book of Nehemiah, after the wall is constructed, Nehemiah orders God's people to consecrate and celebrate God's work in their lives with a sacred parade on top of the rebuilt wall. It is worship complete with an Old Testament version of a marching band.

As the soundtrack of God's written and celebrated work, music is important. As the accompaniment, cover art, and hype melody for the main act, music in a church, nevertheless, is not most important. We must constantly keep this in mind because it is easy to make music the thing that will transform the message, draw the crowd, keep people's hearts and attention.

But it has been, is, and always will be the *logos*, the living Word of God, alive through the finished work of Jesus Christ, and the continuing ministry of the Holy Spirit that will make the Gospel ministry be what it is.

I love soundtracks on the big screen, especially action and sci-fi movies. When I listen to them, it is as if I get to relive the emotion and message of the movie.

Music in the church must reflect and be subservient to the message and emotion of the Gospel. Our music must go along with and make sense of God's script and action. Music must be true to and follow the biblical cues of its divine director. Music must therefore shape itself to the form of the Word and do its part to amplify the Gospel. God has called his people, the leaders in his church to artistically and technically work with the word and music to accompany God's glorious words and acts among his people.

At Christ Central Church, we decided to take a cue from the Indelible Grace music productions and rewrite the music of traditional hymns. We did this for a number of reasons, which I will discuss later, but we couldn't get away from the richness and theological veracity of the words found in many of those hymns. We wanted the words. The church needed those lyrics, but our church's ministry required a different soundtrack.

Regardless of whether God has called or equipped a church with the gifts and abilities to rewrite music or borrow what has already been put together, the search for the right music must always be a search for the right soundtrack, first for the theological and spiritual truths of the Gospel, and also for the mission and vision of the church.

Do You Hear What I Hear?

In a Christmastime favorite song "Do You Hear What I Hear?," the writer asks if we can hear what she hears, even through the blaring fear and uncertainty surrounding them. The song calls us to hope that somehow we can all hear how and what she hears—good news beyond the sorrow and static of world conflict. The song assumes, like we must, when there is present and historic division among us, we can't and don't always hear what and how others hear.

With humility and intention, when it comes to music in our diverse congregations, we must ask, "Do you hear what I hear?"

Music can make what is being said lost or rejected by how it is stylized or arranged. We see something like this happen in Exodus when Moses and Joshua hear the people worshiping the golden calf.

When Joshua heard the noise of the people as they shouted, he said to Moses, "There is a noise of war in the camp." But he said, "It is not the sound of shouting for victory, or the sound of the cry of defeat, but the sound of singing that I hear." (Ex. 32:17–19)

Joshua and Moses heard the same sound but had different interpretations of what it meant. There is one sound for every song we sing in church on Sunday, but each of those songs with the same words, because of the accompaniment, can mean something different to different people. For one it will sound like war, and to another confusion, and to yet another the most accurate musical interpretation of the truth.

This was the musical challenge we faced in a metro, multiethnic, multigenerational church we were planting. Everyone would come with some kind of musical preference. Some would want an escape from the popular and ordinary. They would want to get away from anything that sounded like the war they lost to past sin. Others would want the familiar feel that most closely matched the "first high" of their worship relationship with God. They would want to feel like they did when faith was brand new or when they felt most deeply changed by God.

We as pastors and ministry leaders needed to not go into the church planting project bull-headed or confident that people would hear what we heard and how we heard it, or that they should. We realized that worship does not start with what comes from and happens on stage, but with who God is reaching and ministering to.

Steal Away: The Uniqueness of Your Mission and People

When a church starts, a new ecclesiastical culture and community is created. Regardless of whether that new community is culturally monolithic or diverse, music in worship attempts to make one community out of many. Ephesians 2:13–16 says:

> But now in Christ Jesus you who once were far off have been brought near by the blood of Christ. For he himself is our peace, who has made us both one and has broken down in his flesh the dividing wall of hostility by abolishing the law of commandments expressed in ordinances, that he might create in himself one new man in place of the two, so making peace, and might reconcile us both to God in one body through the cross, thereby killing the hostility.

Music must be subservient to the Gospel theme demanded in this passage. As a multiethnic church in Charlotte, North Carolina, we worshipped God in the New South, which is the new world coming to the cultural structures and barriers of the Old South. In his book *Down By The Riverside*, Charles Joyner explores the cultural challenges and changes in community that developed out of Lowcountry slave communities. In what was a new world of African slaves and mainly Protestant settlers from Europe, a religious worship community developed for slave and master. Though the term "steal away" has been used to describe the private worship gatherings of slaves from different communities, the term could also apply to Scottish, Irish, French, and English settlers. These settlers, many who were not of the aristocracy, also had to shape a worship that drew on the sounds of the motherland but adapted them to the new world. It is a misconception to assume there was one pure worship group versus another in early American history. All religious worship forms in this country were culturally and religiously syncretistic.[1]

Consider what the Apostle Paul faced in the church of

Ephesus with Jews and Gentiles worshiping in one community. Worship styles were in flux in the mix of such different peoples. That was true then, and it's true now. We are drawing on a history, both pagan and generally gracious, while facing and forming a new world and community with the Gospel.

When slave communities in the Lowcountry would steal away, it was a coming together of different communities and cultures of Africans.[2] Imagine the diversity involved in that steal away worship service. Africans from different parts of Africa, with different religious and social backgrounds, were converted to Christianity and were made disciples from different European denominations. The style and sound of the worship would vary based on their country of origin.

In his controversial documentary on the origins of African American spiritual and Gospel music, Dr. Willie Ruff argues that Black Gospel has, as part of its musical "stew" a main ingredient of Scottish Psalm singing, from Gaelic worship styles brought from Scotland.

The distinctive psalm singing had not been brought to America's Deep South by African slaves but by Scottish migrs who worked as their masters and overseers, according to his painstaking research. Ruff, 71, a renowned jazz musician who played with Duke Ellington and Dizzy Gillespie, is convinced the Florida congregation's method of praise— called "presenting the line," in which the psalms are called out and the congregation sings a response—came from the Hebrides. Ruff explained:

> They had always assumed that this form of worship had come from Africa, and why not? I said to him I had found evidence that it was Scottish people who brought this to the New World, but he just would not believe it.

I asked him what his name was. He said McRae, and I just replied: There you go.[3]

It is not my goal to create a great debate or to lessen the contributions of my people, Blacks, to their own Gospel music, but to emphasize that the history and theology of hymnody is hymnody itself. God made a new community in the spread and embrace of his Gospel. Music is the soundtrack and the production of the Gospel-driven steal away. The music these slaves and their descendants drew on came out of the world God called them to engage and make sense of through the lens of the Gospel.

The church planter, pastor, or ministry leader is entering a new world in the urban diversity of modern cities. A new church's worship and music is a new steal away. So the pastor must ask himself in vision casting, as he looks at the people and community God has called him to build into a new world, "Who are we, where are we, and how are we?" Even with the most adept social engineering and scheming, church cultures can create and embrace something unexpected and beautiful, to the glory of God.

We Bring the Sacrifice of Praise

It makes sense in the safety and intimacy of a new community that the sounds associated with that community soon breed a sense of familiarity and safety for people. But if we aren't careful, we can make that sound a de facto requirement for intimacy or even orthodoxy. To push against this natural tendency, the Apostle Paul admonished the church in Ephesus to let God continue his work of making one man, one body, and one holy community out of many. He encouraged them to go beyond their fear of the unfamiliar and other to move toward worshiping as one.

At Christ Central Church in Charlotte our mantra for worship and music is: You will love it, but not like it. It is worth noting that Pastor Hiatt, now the Senior Pastor at Redeemer PCA in Winston-Salem, and I had different musical loves when we together started CCC. What we ended up agreeing on musically was something neither of us felt completely at home with or comfortable with. We were leaving our musical motherlands and coming into the new world that was Christ Central Church in Charlotte.

We asked people to be willing to do the same.

I believe this is a part of what it means to bring to God a sacrifice of praise. Recognizing that the basis of any sacrifice of praise is the once-and-for-all sacrifice and satisfying work of Jesus Christ, what else automatically gets nailed on the cross and pulled into the "fire"? The Gospel teaches that because of Jesus, our idolatrous musical tastes can burn up. Our idols of what true worship music should sound like can get thrown into the flame and nailed on the cross. Jesus frees us to embrace the new world he is building—and that includes music.

Our ministry team knew when we planted Christ Central Church in a largely segregated city that there would be plenty of fires and crosses, both bad and good. There would be fires of people being angry with how we changed the sound of their and Jesus' favorite-sounding hymns. But we expected and pushed for something else more miraculous in our music—that people would burn piles of Christian music idols.

We did our best to take a bell curve average of those we were hoping to reach. We went to various hangouts in our neighborhoods and visited the most popular churches for the people we were hoping to draw. With the anchor of our theological convictions dropped deep, we sought to create a new, mixed, multiethnic musical sound and style. In

Lowcountry-slave-community-in-the-new-world style (I am from the Lowcountry of South Carolina), we threw all of the backgrounds and musical talent of our core group in the pot. We seasoned toward African American tastes since those would typically be more alienated from Presbyterianism, our denomination. We then trimmed off some of the cultural edges and pulled the "Please God let this work" lever. In the infamous words of Dr. Frankenstein, we can now say, "It's alive!"

Out came a combination of re-tuned, rewritten music, borrowed styles and rifts from popular music, and of course Christian music covers, meticulously picked to match our theological convictions and sounds.

One of the greatest influences in our music development came from Rev. Kevin Twit, a pastor with Reformed University Fellowship at Belmont University in Nashville. When we were working on the music for our church plant, I called Kevin to help me understand how he produced the music in the Indelible Grace hymn series. He gave me a version of Spurgeon's hymnbook that has no notes. It's just a book of verses and refrains.[4] He explained he would sit down with the verses, pray and meditate over their biblical references, and begin worshiping and singing with them.

This experience was a musical journey worth taking. I brought in the help of my brother, Terrence, who majored in music, and our church's musicians. My musical concepts turned into congregationally singable songs matching our vision and theological script. I remember those days spent in the "kitchen," developing new stuff with my brother and band members. Did I mention sacrifice of praise?

In order to create the music around the hymns, we had to be willing to both count and pay the cost. Coming from the heritage of the Black Church, I knew music and musicians were one of the biggest sacrifices of praise there. But if we consider our complicated heritage as a people, it makes sense that our music is complicated. In the new world, the preserved, continued sound created out of Black history is a highly specialized talent, technically unique, and thus not free.

Many church planters might differ with the philosophy of music Christ Central Church used in the beginning. I respect them and have seen the God-will-provide-from-the-congregation approach work too, involving a different set of sacrifices and challenges. There were times, especially when planning the budget, that I would question our decision to hire professional musicians. However, we decided to place a high value on being able to accompany our worship with music that could steal away and call people to a sacrifice of praise. The cost was part of our sacrifice of praise, and we burned larger salaries and more support staff and nicer meeting space to have the music we wanted.

In Nehemiah, it is important to remember the musicians were provided for out of the congregation's offering. In other words, when they were called to be a part of the wall-building band, they were given food and housing help from the community. Based on this example, we felt like we were free to pay for professional musicians and therefore continued to have musicians who could adapt to an ever-changing diverse community.

At Christ Central Church, we have a Hammond organist, an electric guitarist, a bassist, a drum set percussionist, a conga percussionist, and singers. We chose not to have a choir because of the numbers in our congregation and our desire that the congregation be able to sing on every song. Singing together was too much of a unified value for a diverse church like Christ Central Church to lose that opportunity with a traditionally done choir number. In addition, when we first started we met in a popular local music venue and our music was so new and professional that people would just watch and listen. We did our best to make the worship need the voices of the congregation. I admit it did not always work. We continue to move toward more congregational involvement and away from musical performance. It is our hope to be changed providentially and intentionally in our music at Christ Central Church.

Communities are always in flux. In a diverse metro church like ours percentages and neighborhoods change all the time. When we created new music around hymns, in our sacrifice of praise, we committed that no song's music was sacred. This frees us, as things change, to be willing to let the music change or retire or be recreated by the next generation of musicians at our church. Some of my favorites have already bitten the dust! But it is worth it to see God making a new community.

Cultivating the New from the Old

What about established churches who desire to change the accompanying taste of their worship? Maybe the neighborhood has changed, the church has become more diverse, or the church wants to be more welcoming to different cultures. I can't think of a harder and more potentially disastrous thing than trying to make a church's traditional worship more hip and modern in order to reach and be more attractive to new people groups. Jesus said:

> No one puts a piece of unshrunk cloth on an old garment, for the patch tears away from the garment, and a worse tear is made. Neither is new wine put into old wineskins. If it is, the skins burst and the wine is spilled and the skins are destroyed. But new wine is put into fresh wineskins, and so both are preserved. (Matt. 9:16–17)

Jesus' point is a hard one—the religious action, activity, or attempt must follow the heart, which must be made ready by the Lord. The first question a congregation must ask in seeking to update or change its worship is one of the heart: Is this something God has prepared and conditioned through prayer and providence?

This can easily prove the hardest part. Will the hearts of the leadership, called by God to create more diverse worship, melt when members leave and challenge them? Is the leadership prepared for lots of listening and instructing? The practical steps may cause all sorts of issues in the congregation. Singers and musicians who have been faithful for years may be asked to step down or step aside if they are unable to play or lead in the desired style of music. It is important therefore to take a journey toward change with all those who will be most affected. It is of utmost importance that the leadership in the church be patient and pastoral to bring the music leaders and stakeholders of the old style along and then the rest of the congregation. This change should not be quick but gradual as the leadership is attentive to whether the hearts are accepting the new wine the Lord is pouring in from heaven.

Other aspects are relatively easy, as they are practical. A musician who can play both styles of music desired by the church is a rare talent, and most churches have a hard time finding or affording such talent. The most practical way to go about change is by hiring a musician who can work with the present musical staff and worship service. The leadership should slowly introduce new musicians who will be trusted to know how to bring new music to the church. The new musicians should be interviewed as to whether they too are new wineskins for what the Lord is calling them. They should recognize this could be a rewarding but patient process as they work to lead and be led by others. I recommend blended worship for a season or for the life of the church.

I recognize our story will not be exactly like any other churches and understand the way we saw God work will not be the way God works in your music ministry. It is important that you not outpace your resources economically and technically. Not every church is going to be able to commit the money and have all the musician connections to rewrite, retune, or redo the combinations of music that are perfect in the vision and mind of the pastor and church leadership. Some pastors and ministry leaders have no idea how to manage professional musicians and professional church musicians. I have seen more problems with churches hiring a musician and having no knowledge how to manage, set expectations, or hear what they are truly getting. Music should be a sacrifice of praise and help the congregation to enter into worship, but they should not become an all-consuming fire. I say this because your limitations and the limitations of your community is part of the Gospel story of God at work, and the soundtrack should be authentic and true to that.

The unique sound, canned or created, is authentic and true when the limitations of its ministry, and the limitations that Scripture puts on it, becomes a part of the sacrifice of praise. It forces us to not look to our awesome music and creations as the power of the Gospel. That is a good thing. In fact our musical story has changed significantly at Christ Central Church

We no longer produce music at the frequency we did in the early years. Changes in staffing needs, leadership, giftedness, and vision emphasis have taken the time and talent necessary to do what we did. We cannot let musical idolatry and idolatrous nostalgia (often wrongly labeled as theological integrity) trap us into being stiff-necked people.

Otherwise, I believe we will soon be draining spiritual time and energy protecting an idol instead of sharing and ministering the Gospel.

When it comes to worship, and the music we use, we are calling our people to a transformative process. We are hoping and begging that God would be glorified. When he is lifted up we will be drawn to him like a moth to a flame. We hope and pray that music will be the right sound for our being melting, molded and moved by God and his love for us in Jesus Christ.

In the story of the new world of your ministry, I encourage you to find and submit to the soundtrack of its movement. Make sure your music helps them hear what you hear. In the new community of faith that your church will be, steal away to Jesus. In the faithful practice of ministry, let your music be a sacrifice of praise.

CHURCH GROWTH: TIME, PRESENCE, AND CONSISTENCY

ALEXANDER SHIPMAN

Church planting can be described as the best of times, the worst of times, the age of wisdom, the age of foolishness, a season of light, a season of darkness, all rolled into one.[1] Every church planter experiences the joyful and painful marks that come from the church planting roller coaster. There are the scars left from outreach that doesn't produce commitments, battle wounds from fundraising trips that don't lead to any funds, emotional stress from when people leave. There are the sleepless nights of wondering why you wanted to pursue this path, but also the joyous memories and mountain top experiences. There is excitement when you see the Lord move in ways that exceed your expectations and when you witness him add to the number of those being saved through the ministry. There is rejoicing as he raises up leaders and officers in the church and when church members take ownership of the congregation.

Church planting certainly is an up and down journey, with both awesome and awful times, but these times and ministry marks aren't unique to church planting. Established churches experience joys and pains in ministry, too. Both have ministry highs and lows. Both have pleasant and hard realities. Both can be messy and unpredictable. While focusing on church planting, much of what follows can be applied to established churches as well, as they seek to make disciples of all nations.

Theologian and missiologist C. Peter Wagner says, "Planting new churches is the most effective evangelistic methodology known under heaven."[2] For that reason, many pursue church planting. Some reading this book will specifically be curious about the cross-cultural, multiethnic[3] church planting journey, or perhaps making an established church more diverse. They desire to see Revelations 7:9–10 lived out now.[4]

Like all church planters, they search for a model, a system, or a method that will be a rainbow in the sky. They want a rainbow with a pot of gold at the end, and that gold is growth. It's numbers! It's members! It's bodies in seats! Unlike a monocultural, monoethnic setting, there is a nuance when it comes to growth within these types of cross-cultural and multiethnic church plants. These ministry leaders want both numerical growth and growth in diversity. They want people from different cultures and ethnicities to join the church.

They seek answers to the questions that keep them up at night: How will I gather a team? How will the church plant grow? How will we become more diverse? Will it be through evangelism? Will it be through community connections? Will it be through transfer growth? These are sincere questions for all church planting pastors, regardless of the type of church they plant. Pastors of existing churches ask the same questions when they catch a Revelation 7:9 vision for their church. I still ask these questions.

But one critical question faces all cross-cultural, multi-ethnic church planters: What does it take to grow this type of church?

I planted The Village Church in 2008 with fifteen families from various churches and denominations and networks (e.g., Presbyterian, Baptist, Methodist, and non-denominational). We are a cross-cultural, multiethnic church located in Northeast Huntsville, Alabama. The Village Church was a mother/daughter plant that grew out of Lincoln Village Ministry. We currently have 114 members (71 adult and 43 kids/youth) and our average weekly attendance is 76. Eighty percent of our congregation is from the majority demographic and 20 percent of the church is minorities. These numbers reflect the neighborhood in which we are located, and our diversity is more than just ethnic. It mirrors generational, socioeconomic, educational, and political diversity. This makeup then represents a church that seeks to honor God and strives to look like the kingdom of heaven.

In 2011, I attended an event where I had a conversation with a fellow pastor. He wanted to know how I was doing and how things were going. "How many of the community neighbors are visiting church?" he inquired. I told him their presence is slowly increasing but it takes time and consistency to build trust and relationships. In fact, it takes time, presence, and consistency to plant cross-cultural, multiethnic churches.

Time, presence, and consistency are ministry opportunities church planting leaders must accept and embrace. Church planting is not a 100-yard dash, but rather a marathon. This acknowledges that pastors cannot produce members or make the church plant grow. The church grows when the Holy Spirit blesses outreach and evangelistic efforts. Key to this is the "ministry of time."

Ministry of Time

The ministry of time is necessary for anyone desiring to plant a cross-cultural/multiethnic church. It's essential for churches striving to grow in these areas too. This ministry requires new church starts and existing churches to spend time discerning the cost of pursuing diversity. Mark DeYmaz says, "Make no mistake: pursuit of ethnic blends in your congregation is no easy task. It will stretch you and your family in ways you cannot imagine."[5]

DeYmaz makes a point that shouldn't be taken lightly. The path to a Revelation 7:9 church will stretch everyone involved. Don't enter this particular journey simply because it is trendy. Enter it because the Lord has given you a Spirit-filled vision that Revelation 7:9–10 can be tasted on this side of heaven. Enter it because you desire the church be a reflection of its community. Enter it with the mindset that true diversity is sacrifice not assimilation.

Diversity isn't simply assimilating various cultures and ethnicities into a monocultural, monoethnic way of doing church. This approach functionally requires the minority cultures and ethnicities to do all the sacrificing while church continues with business as usual. True diversity requires change. It requires doing things differently. It is wisely integrating the various cultures and ethnicities within a church in such a way to grow a beautiful cross-cultural, multiethnic community.

Revelation 7:9–10 is a wonderful picture of kingdom diversity, but witnessing that picture now isn't easy. Intentionality is required. It will cost something! New and established churches must discern and accept the cost to grow cross-culturally and multiethnically. They must spend time discussing what cultural preferences they are willing to sacrifice in terms of worship, staff, and leadership. These won't be easy changes, but they are necessary for true diversity to grow and be cultivated.

The cost of being cross-cultural and multiethnic should drive pastors to their knees. The task will be overwhelming at times, and the temptation to do what is comfortable and natural will always be present. The leaders will have to trust the Lord to strengthen them and make the vision of diversity happen.

Rev. LeRoy Fountain once told me that God hasn't promised to make provisions for your vision, but he will make provisions for *his* vision.[6] The Lord will provide what is needed for the church to grow cross-culturally and multiethnically. At the end of the day, the church is going to look the way he wants it to look. We must trust him.

Perhaps you are wondering: What does ministry of time have to do with church growth? It has a lot to do with it. Peter Wagner says, "The single most important factor in the success or failure of a church plant is the church planter. As I will reiterate time and again, the leader is the principle key to a successful church plant."[7]

In other words, the planter can be the reason why the church plant does not grow. The reasons can stem from being under-trained, under-coached, under-resourced, or because the planter entered the journey without a true sense of call. For example, if the pastor lacks diversity in his interpersonal friendships and relationships, then he need not move out too quickly to plant a cross-cultural, multiethnic church. A pastor cannot lead others to develop and cultivate what is not developed and cultivated in his own life. We need to be honest with ourselves, which requires self-understanding.

Self-understanding is the second aspect to the ministry of time. Self-understanding is not the same as self-preoccupation. "Self preoccupation shows up in leaders who use others in order to achieve their own ambition. Self-understanding begins and ends with God. This takes time and reflection,"[8] says Reggie McNeal. Planters driven by self-preoccupation will plant churches with themselves at the center. Their focus is self-glory and self-promotion. They will use and abuse others on their way to ministry success and recognition. Self-preoccupation is simply pride, and it attempts to steal Jesus' glory. But the Lord God says, *"I am the Lord; that is my name; my glory I give to no other, nor my praise to carved idols"* (Isa. 42:8). Proverbs 16:18 says, *"Pride goes before destruction, and a haughty spirit before a fall."*

Every planter struggles with self-preoccupation, but he should not live in it with an unrepentant heart, lest he eventually find himself out of ministry. We will struggle with self-preoccupation, but let's be sure to struggle with a repentant heart. Pray that the Spirit will give us self-understanding. Remember McNeal's words: self understanding begins and ends with God.

Proverbs 1:7 says, *"Fear of the Lord is the beginning of wisdom."* Self-understanding is gaining wisdom about who we are. It begins when we cultivate a spiritual walk with the Lord rooted in communion and fellowship. Planters cannot lead people to a fountain from which they themselves do not drink. We must continue to drink from the fountain of Jesus daily. This means we make it a priority to spend time in prayer and in the Word in order to feed our souls.

Second, we must seek self-awareness. All planters must have self-awareness. Some possess the gifts to be a solo church planter, while others have the gifts for a team plant. So do you know yourself? What are your strengths and weaknesses? What is your DISC or Myers-Briggs? Self-awareness in church planting will serve you well. Spending time gaining self-awareness is essential to aligning strengths and gifts with the best planter model.

Next, we must establish healthy self-care practices: exercising, adequate sleep, maintaining a day off, maintaining an accountability group, and taking vacations with family.

Finally, we need to invest in self-development opportunities. Find a church planting coach who has planted a cross-cultural, multiethnic church and talk at least monthly. Consider joining a church planting network that offers monthly or quarterly training opportunities.

Finally, the ministry of time deals with family. This is frequently overlooked in the church planting world because church planting is demanding. It demands so much time from the planter. It's almost like birthing a child! It can rob the planter from having a family presence, and that will eventually hinder the church plant.

Burns, Chapman, and Guthrie stress that "a healthy marriage and family strengthens pastors. At the same time, marriage and family difficulties can derail ministry leaders. Therefore, the health of a pastor's marriage and family is also a priority for the well-being of a congregation."[9] Every planter must make it a priority to build and cultivate a healthy family presence. This can be done by setting proper boundaries to protect family presence and time. For example, the planter and family can keep a family calendar and block off time for family activities and trips. The planter should strive to limit evening meetings when possible. The planter should not sacrifice family for the sake of growing the church plant. He must have balance between ministry and family.

So, ministry of time requires planters to engage the cost of diversity, self-understanding, and family. Once you have done your due diligence here, you can move to the ministry of presence, the second ministry activity you must engage as a planter of a cross-cultural and multiethnic church.

Ministry of Presence

There are two facets to the ministry of presence. The first presence is a launch team presence. This is where the planter gathers and recruits members to join the launch team, the group of people who will help the planter start the church. This team has a start date and end date. Nelson Searcy writes, "Your launch team has one singular purpose: to assist you in launching the church. When the launch service is over the team dissipates."[10] There are two methods you can use to gather a launch team. Use the method that best fits your gifts as a church planter.

The first way to gather a launch team is the team method. This method can be utilized through a mother/daughter church plant relationship. The mother church becomes a resource church for the plant. These resources may include but are not limited to families, finances, and facilities. The families from the mother church will be part of the church planter's launch team. The finances can be used to pay the planter's salary and ministry expenses. The mother church also can provide facilities where the planter and launch team can meet.

However, the team method may follow a completely different process. In my denomination, the Presbyterian Church in America (PCA), a small group Bible study can petition their local presbytery[11] for mission church[12] status. If the presbytery approves, the group, with the help of the presbytery, can move forward in calling a church planter. The team method of gathering a launch team is not new. Peter was accompanied by six men in Acts as he brought the Gospel to Caesarea. Jesus sent out the seventy-two in pairs. The church in Antioch had an ethnically diverse launch team in Acts 11:12–21.

The second method a church planter can use to gather a launch team is what I call the individual/loner method. Church planting experts sometimes call this the parachute method. This is when a planter and family drop into a new community and start a church. This is done without a launch team. Usually, the planter enters the community as a stranger with zero connections and relationships. The planter seeks to build the launch team from scratch, preferably with people from the community.

Not all church planters can utilize the parachute method. Planters who possess self-starter and entrepreneurial gifts fit this method best. The Apostle Paul planted churches using this method. He would parachute into a new community, preach the Gospel, and the Holy Spirit would build a church.

Prayer and wise counsel are necessary before deciding which of these methods to use in planting a cross-cultural/multiethnic church. Both can be effective. However, neither method will naturally lead to an Antioch-type launch team or church. They will not guarantee the reality of Revelation 7:9–10.

Church planting leaders must be intentional in order to grow cross-culturally and multiethnically. Many times the mother/daughter and existing small group teams will be monocultural and monoethnic. Many of them will not have any diversity in their personal relationships. If that is the case, the parachute plant has a much higher possibility to gather a diverse launch team, particularly if the planter already has diverse relationships. The planter can spend intentional time building relationships in the community and inviting different types of people to outreach events. Diversity can still be an issue for a launch team gathered through this method, though, because the diverse launch team might not have any diverse relationships outside the diversity within the initial team. This lack of interpersonal relationship diversity can be seen in established churches as well.

This means church leaders will need to intentionally train the launch team and members in cultural intelligence. This can be done in a weekly gathering time with the team. There are books available to aid in training the team and members in this area.[13] David Livermore says, "Cultural intelligence is reaching across the chasm of cultural difference in ways that are loving and respectful. Love. That's our destination. We're on a journey from the desire to love the Other to a place where we effectively express the love of Jesus to people of difference."[14] This training will equip the team and members with the tools necessary to build cross-cultural connections with others within the community.

The second facet of the ministry of presence is cultivating a healthy relational presence in the community. This requires the planter be mindful of the relationship that is first initiated between the church plant and the community, for the initial relationship will set the stage for what it will be like once the church has its first service. For example, a relationship initiated based totally on one group meeting the needs of another group isn't healthy. A church plant that does this intentionally or unintentionally creates a have-and-haves-not culture. Dr. Anthony Bradley, professor at King's College, said, "Churches serving the poor don't tend to bring the poor into membership. We don't call people we want to invite into our homes 'the poor.'"[15]

A healthy relational presence in a community is about building genuine friendships with one's neighbor. It's neither about a church plant coming into a community as the white knight in shining armor, nor is it about being the next big thing in town. It means a cross-cultural/multi-ethnic church plant will seek to build a family-like community into the life of the church. It's a presence saying all God's people have issues. It's a presence saying all of us are broken before the throne of grace, regardless of race and class. It's a relational presence walking alongside each other in a spirit of mutual brokenness. Rev. Ricky Temple once said people will forget what you preach; people will forget what you say; but people will never forget how you make them feel. Make others feel they are truly welcome to join your church family and community as a friend, not simply someone to whom you serve and minister to. Go over and beyond in your hospitality and greeting in everything you do in the church and community.

Ministry of Consistency

Finally, the ministry of consistency is the third piece the planter must engage. This focuses on the efforts to help the church plant grow organically. Many churches grow fast because of transfer growth, people leaving one church and going to another. Transfer growth isn't bad, but it shouldn't be the only way the church plant grows. We want new people coming to church for the first time, or to re-engage after being away from church.

There are two organic efforts the planter can utilize here. First, there are in-reach efforts, which focus inside the church plant. Second, there are outreach efforts into the community. These two endeavors should not lead the plant off the relationship-building course. Instead, they should create opportunities for building organic relationships.

Cross-cultural, multiethnic church plants grow best when ministry is more relationally driven than program driven.

The planter will have to consistently challenge the church to be intentional in its sphere of influences when it comes to diversity—schools, jobs, kid's activities, and neighborhoods. Let's face it. People go to church with their friends, and our churches are a reflection of our interpersonal relationships. In-reach means the planter will have to train the team in evangelism. I failed to do this in the planting stages of The Village Church, and it's still one of our weaknesses and a personal weak area. But God is giving us grace and fruit. In-reach involves intentionally equipping the team to evangelize and build healthy cross-cultural relationships. Both will lead to church growth. The growth will not be fast. It will be slow and steady, which is fine.

Next, the ministry of consistency focuses on outreach in the community. Outreach is how the church plant practices and lives out an evangelistic and relationship-building lifestyle. This means the planter and launch team must do outreach with the intention of sharing the Gospel and building relationships with their neighbors and community. These activities can be block parties, church picnics, going door-to-door to share the Gospel, inviting people to church, or prayer walks in the community. Outreach also means networking with local business owners and community leaders in order to establish community connections. It's also creating strategic ministry partnerships that will bring the church plant into contact with more people in the community. These partnerships can be with local schools, ministries, nonprofits, and community organizations. The challenge is to be consistent with the outreach activities you do in the community. Your evangelistic and relationship-building activities will take time, presence, and consistency to build trust and see fruit.

It is important not to fall into the trap of thinking God is getting ready to start working in the community because your church plant was recently started. In reality, he has been at work in the community long before he called you. In fact, he is calling you to join in the ministry he's already doing. We need to remember that the ministry belongs to Jesus and will always outlive us.

These ideas will help cross-cultural, multiethnic church plants grow in diversity. They can be applied to existing churches as well. The ministries of time, presence, and consistency will aid these new and existing churches in their journeys toward being Revelation 7:9–10 churches.

They will need to engage the ministry of time—cost of diversity, self-understanding, and family.

They will need to engage the ministry of presence—launch team gathering and launch training.

They will need to engage the ministry of consistency—doing in-reach and outreach.

The journey toward diversity will be challenging, but it is a journey worth taking!

10

ENGLISH AS A SECOND LANGUAGE: AN EFFECTIVE TOOL TO REACH FOREIGN CULTURES

JAHAZIEL CANTU

[Note: ESL (English as a Second Language) is the
common term for what might more accurately be
called either ELL (English Language Learners)
or ESOL (English for Speakers of Other Languages).]

This chapter begins by explaining some of the history of
Mexicans in the United States, but keep in mind that not
all Hispanics in the US are of Mexican descent. However,
many Hispanics and Mexicans do have similar reasons for
coming to the US. According to the US census, we have
55.4 million people making up the Hispanic population,
and Mexicans constitute 63.9 percent of those Hispanics in
the United States.[1]

To understand and eventually meet the spiritual and physical needs of Hispanics (and specifically Mexicans), Christians need to have an awareness of Hispanic perspectives, feelings, culture, and history. Every culture and group of people face distinct and specific challenges, and the Hispanic minority is no different. Understanding Hispanic challenges might help non-Hispanic Christians involved in a Hispanic ministry be more sympathetic with personal interactions and understand why the Hispanic ministry takes on a different ethos.

Discrimination is one of the biggest obstacles Hispanics face as a minority, and it affects their daily lives and culture. This discrimination against Mexican and Hispanic people is not something that began just in the last decade, but it is something that has existed in the United States since at least the 1820s. The American people have often wanted to have separate communities, languages, and customs from the Hispanic people, and specifically from the Mexicans.

When referring to intolerance, it is not the same as the Ku Klux Klan, but rather the inherent intolerance that often guides actions: inappropriate jokes; preconceived notions of people who have a different skin color; laughing at or refusing to understand people's accents; judging members of a race based on previous negative experiences with other members of that race; and treating people differently based on their social status. All of us as Christians should strive to love others and fight these behaviors. Also, Christians should build up and encourage Hispanic brothers and sisters who may bear emotional wounds from intolerant actions against them.

One of the main reasons Hispanics come to the US is to

provide a better financial situation for their families and relatives. Put differently, Mexicans come to the US for The American Dream, since this offers a lot of hope to Mexican people who do not have a high level of education. Those without college degrees were never going to make as much money in Mexico as they could by doing the same work in the United States. In the States, you are able to earn a decent salary without having a college education. In Mexico, on the other hand, it is much more difficult to find any job, let alone one with high enough wages to support a family. Finding reliable work is a primary reason why many Hispanics come to the States. Most migrant workers have not finished college or even high school, and in Mexico or their country of origin it would be difficult for them to sustain their families. The hard-labor jobs that give such pay discrepancies include: construction, maintaining roads, streets, and train tracks, agriculture, yard work, bussing tables, washing dishes, and meat processing.

As Mexican immigrants come to the United States, many employers know they do not have proper immigration documentation. Some choose to take advantage of that and pay them less than they would pay another person with a valid Social Security number. Regardless, the immigrants still see the unfair wages as a better opportunity, and thus Mexican immigration has resulted in the United States having the second largest Hispanic population of any nation in the world, and Hispanics are now the largest ethnic or racial minority in North America.[2]

Current Day Hispanic American Culture

I offer my own personal experience of coming to the US as an adult and working in Hispanic ministry as a glimpse into modern Hispanic American culture and challenges. When

I came to the United States in 2005 to study for a Masters of Divinity, I also began working in a bilingual multicultural church in Dallas, Texas (Cristo Rey PCA). I met many people who had immigrated directly from Mexico several years prior (we refer to them as first-generation immigrants). Having just come from Mexico myself, I actually found it hard to relate to them because their customs were a mixture of American and Mexican. Their culture was no longer Mexican. Instead, the Hispanic American culture is what now belongs to those who were born in a Hispanic country but now live in the US.

After four years living in Dallas, the Hispanic American culture had become my own. I could relate to and understand the spiritual and physical needs which were unique to those who had come from Mexico, such as: cultural identification, maintaining one's heritage, learning the language, facing temptations offered in the US such as debt and materialism, and managing the money they now earned.

The predominant aspect of the first generation of any immigrant population is the reluctance to give up their native language. It is difficult to learn a new language! They do, however, want to integrate into their new home country's culture and embrace new customs. They also want to maintain their heritage and keep old customs within their families. The result is they do not have a clear identity, either from their home country or from the United States. According to the US census predictions, the United States is in the midst of a cultural change. In thirty years, one in three Americans is expected to be Hispanic.[3]

English as a Second Language (ESL) ministry is a key means of reaching out to any foreign culture that does not speak English. It enables churches to meet a practical need of the vast majority of the Asians, Europeans, Hispanics, etc., who want to thrive in the US. My focus here, however, will be on reaching Hispanics through ESL ministry.

By God's grace, since I came to the United States, I have been involved with several churches' ESL ministries in varying roles: director, director's assistant, teacher trainer, student relations, and teacher of Bible studies in Spanish. In some programs, we had 120-plus students; others programs had twenty students.

A common theme among programs of all sizes was the love and kindness the students felt from the teachers. Students inevitably would ask, "Why are these teachers, who have families at home and are not getting paid to teach, taking the time to come help us?" This provided the perfect gateway for discussions about our Father in heaven who sent his only son to save us from the penalty of our sins and death.

ESL Ministry Helps to Reach Out

In the book of Matthew, we read:

> Go therefore and make disciples of all nations, baptizing them in the name of the Father and of the Son and of the Holy Spirit, teaching them to observe all that I have commanded you. And behold, I am with you always, to the end of the age. (Matt. 28:19–20)

This is a key passage to have in mind when starting this type of ministry. Because we live in the United States, the cultures (especially Hispanics) are actually coming to us, not us going to them!

Many immigrant Hispanics are fleeing violence in their countries of residence, while others want to give a better life to their families. Still others come to chase the American Dream. Whatever their reasons, we have a great opportunity as well as burden to share the Gospel with all foreign people who are in the United States short- or long-term.

When Hispanics come to the US, I have found they are more open to hear the Gospel of grace. Those who have left their families behind in Mexico and come to the US alone are living day-by-day with two or three different jobs (perhaps dishwashing, cooking, construction, mowing yards, and cleaning houses). They usually send most of their hard-earned money back to family in Mexico, and therefore they are surviving in the US on the bare minimum. These newcomers frequently are the least fluent in English and suffer the most abuse from bosses or business owners because they do not have proper documentation to work and therefore are seen as having no workers' rights.

This physical and emotional neediness opens these individuals' hearts to the good news of Jesus Christ in a way it might not if they had easier lives. Free ESL classes provide a simple means to meeting these immigrants and developing relationships with them so they feel comfortable listening to teachers and pastors talk about the Gospel.

These "single" immigrants, or those in the US without family members, are more open to leaving their Catholic heritage (especially if it was more devoid of real faith), because they are not feeling as much pressure from loved ones living in Mexico to continue in their grandparents' tradition. They are open to visiting Gospel-preaching churches. On the other hand, because they do not have family accountability close, they are more tempted to do things they would not do with their families (e.g., having an affair, visiting men's clubs, or spending more money on themselves than on their families).

Students in ESL classes face pressures and temptations

all week. When they come to their lessons with loving teachers and other students who face similar daily struggles, they begin to feel comfortable and safe. Their hearts are receptive to a fifteen-minute devotional at the end of classes, and they often are moved to receive Christ as their Savior. They are generally excited to come each week and learn more about both English and the Bible. They learn that the Gospel of our Lord Jesus Christ is the only true solution to their problems and to the situations they are facing.

We have witnessed many families and individuals come to Christ through the ESL ministry. Some families start attending the host church regularly, and some even become members. The church should have a plan for how to integrate new believers into their church family.

How Does ESL Work?

ESL outreach is the most effective program I can recommend to begin a new Hispanic ministry. It is easy to start. The two critical components are volunteer teachers who speak English, and a volunteer who is able and willing to share a devotional in Spanish at the end of the class.

Schedules are flexible when starting an ESL ministry. I have seen programs that offer classes twice per week or just once per week, mornings or evenings. The schedule depends on how many helpers are available to the ministry and what their availability is, as well as the availability of the target population. If there are many stay-at-home mothers of young children, then morning classes would be appropriate. If most have school-aged children and work during the day, then evening classes would get more attendees. It helps to have a director or coordinator to lead the program.

There are several good options for curricula. One is produced by Cambridge University Press: *Ventures*, From Basic to 4th Level. We suggest having the students purchase the books from you so they value and care for them more. You can discount them or offer payments plans if you like. We developed a policy that students could not take the books home until they had paid the book's full price.

Another need, which is almost always present in an ESL ministry, is a nursery or kids program offered at the same time. In our church, we hold the ESL ministry on Wednesday nights because the entire kids program is already in place (nursery and kids classes). We normally follow the local school calendar for vacations and days off.

Marketing for the ESL Ministry

After you have the volunteer teachers and a person to give the devotionals and connect with the students, you need to pass out flyers or use the radio, newspaper, or social media to advertise the classes. I have usually passed out the flyers about two weeks before the first class of the semester, going where high populations of Hispanics are. These locations include Mexican grocery stores, markets, Hispanic restaurants, laundromats, and stores in Hispanic neighborhoods. Schools in Hispanic neighborhoods often allow you to post notices for ESL classes. We even go door-to-door in Hispanic apartment complexes, where these flyers are usually very well received. Handing out flyers has been key for the success of the ministry, since it is personal and tangible.

Churches bless the Hispanic community through ESL, which opens up more opportunities for individuals in their work and daily life. ESL also helps the community better understand and embrace its new culture. Beyond the physical blessing, the true goal of the ESL ministry is to bring the students the Gospel and for them to have saving faith in Christ.

Many of the Hispanic students we have met over the years came from a Roman Catholic background but did not attend church anywhere. Their gods were typically work (some of them worked sixty hours per week) and family.

Most of them:

- Have never heard the Gospel of grace
- Have not read the Bible
- Do not have a church home
- Do not know how to pray
- Do not own a Bible

It is key to have the devotional at the end of the class, and it shouldn't be more than fifteen minutes long. Keeping the lesson short allows for enough Gospel message that the students will want to learn more about saving grace, but will not feel burdened by a long sermon. If it's longer, many will try to leave before the Bible study begins. When they want to know more, they stay after and ask questions about the Bible lesson and the Gospel. They also have the option (and are encouraged to come) to attend a worship service on Sunday.

In my experience, the ESL students who show interest at the Bible study are the ones who start attending the church. Some receive Christ as their Savior and become members. The percentage of students who become members is very small, but usually many will pray to receive Christ as their Savior during the Bible study.

This ministry is a great outreach tool for any foreign culture in the US, and the students are usually open to hear the Gospel of grace. In many cases, the immigrants' homeland had few churches that taught the Gospel of grace.

The primary reason US immigrants do not attend regular Bible studies or ESL classes is because they are more focused on working to provide for their families. Most of them work two or three jobs, and their schedules do not allow them to take advantage of these opportunities to learn about grace and ESL. In addition, persecution sometimes will reach immigrant believers in the US. Some are disowned by their family members in their native country. One of our church's believing families told their relatives in Mexico that they had accepted Christ and were attending a Gospel-preaching (non-Catholic) church. Those relatives discontinued communication because they believed it was a betrayal of the true church. The family was of course sad to be abandoned by their relatives but felt that the church had become their new family.

Students of ESL

Most of the students in ESL classes will be first generation immigrants to the United States. They may have come to the US when they were young or have recently arrived. All of them are in need of learning English, and most importantly, of learning about the saving grace that Jesus Christ gave us through his death and resurrection.

The children and grandchildren of first-generation immigrants tend to embrace the US culture more than their parents or grandparents. While they speak the language of their parents, they prefer to speak English as they progress more through English-speaking schools. The second generation prefers either bilingual or English-only worship services. Second-generation Hispanic Americans carry on the family-centered orientation of their parents, where the children often stay living with parents through college until they get married themselves. As a result, if these families take advantage of the ESL classes and start attending churches that offer an English/Spanish service, it is highly probable the children will want to attend service with their parents and family.

These second-generation children fully identify with most of American culture. The second-generation children of the ESL students typically have no problem integrating into English-only kids programs at church. Catechism classes, youth groups, kids music, and prayer time are great programs that usually already exist in the English-speaking church and can be opened up to the ESL students' children during the English classes. These children experience the love of Christ from Christian adults and other children. As the kids develop friendships with the church's youth, they become excited to return and even want to come on Sundays for worship. The parents (the ESL students) return to church more often when their children are excited to join them.

If the church offers worship in another language, it is good to keep in mind the increasing trend of multicultural families. More and more married couples have different native languages (wife Spanish and husband English, or vice versa). Bilingual services are attractive to such families so that the family can worship together. For example, our current bilingual service is 60 percent Spanish and 40 percent English. The liturgy is written in both languages. The sermon is mostly Spanish, but we summarize periodically in English. With this format, the children are happy in case they don't understand something in Spanish, and also mom and dad can understand what is happening during worship in their native language. The second-generation children love our tradition of "pan dulce" at the end of every service, when we set out sweet bread and coffee and there is a time of fellowship.

The fellowship times we have in our ESL classes prompted one ESL student to eventually start coming to our church. She first came to just the English classes. Then she started to come to our Spanish Bible studies. During that time, she would ask for prayer for her adult son to begin going to church. Several months later, her son called to ask me to marry his fiancé and him, which started a wonderful friendship between our families. They and are now members, and he is training to become a deacon.

The ESL classes and bilingual programs are great tools for beginning and building relationships with multiple generations of immigrant families. In the fellowship we have in our ESL classes and church services, they can see our love for God and one another.

Third Generation

Most third-generation Hispanic Americans only have a Spanish last name. They do not speak Spanish at all and embrace American culture entirely (though they still like to eat Mexican food!). They will feel most comfortable to have everything in a worship service be in English. They sometimes will not attend a bilingual service unless there are strong family relationships within the church. More often, they will migrate to the English-speakers service or nothing at all.

How then can we attract the third-generation Hispanics to our English-speaking churches? Even though they only speak English and are culturally American, they will have inherited the open and friendly behavior and manners of their parents and grandparents. They will rarely seem shy. The English-speaking church should be a warm, welcoming place for all visitors. They will be more comfortable in a warm environment where people socialize and are not shy with strangers.

I have gone to churches as a visitor and been the only one who is greeting and talking with other new visitors! English-speakers can get uncomfortable when talking with strangers, and they will sometimes leave it to the work of the pastors, elders, and deacons. However, it is very important to build a church culture of open hospitality and friendliness if you want to reach out to foreign cultures. The church can have an assigned team to purposefully reach out to visitors and even follow up with them that week and pray for them.

All generations of immigrants desperately need Christ. Our job as a church is to present our Savior and Redeemer to them. And yet, if a church has all programs and elements in place, they will go nowhere without prayer! The church congregation should be regularly praying for the outreach ministries, as well as for individuals' salvation.

Other Outreach Programs for Hispanic Americans

These programs are alternative suggestions to reach out to immigrant communities. Some target the Hispanic Americans more than other cultures, but all can be attractive to foreign cultures if you are seeking to serve the needs of that community. All these programs are tools to build relationships with people to share the Gospel of grace with them.

Outreach Lunch

One Sunday per month, hold an outreach lunch after the worship service. This can be potluck style, but the focus should be on inviting new visitors to church. Encourage the members and regular attenders to pray for a friend, neighbor, or family member they can invite to worship and fellowship. This should be a welcoming and enjoyable opportunity to build new relationships.

Guitar Ministry

If you have someone who knows how to play the guitar, and a church leader who wants to teach the Bible and speaks Spanish, you already have the resources to start this ministry. Set up a sign-up sheet for free guitar lessons for older kids in a Hispanic community. Then while the kids are learning guitar (they are usually bilingual, so the guitar teacher can speak in English), you will need a Spanish-speaking Bible study leader for the parents to hear the Gospel.

VBS in a Park

Many immigrant communities live in apartment complexes or housing subdivisions with a park in a central location. Hosting a free Vacation Bible School in parks near these areas is a great outreach to the community. Such events should be in a safe, central, open place, where the parents can bring their kids and stay nearby to watch. You will have the opportunity to be in contact with kids and parents for an entire week and begin new relationships. If you get their contact information, you can call them again later for other church programs such as ESL classes, bilingual church services, Bible studies, etc.

The VBS curriculum can be all in English, as most of the kids will speak English. It might help to have a Spanish speaker for the very little (pre-K) children. On the final day of the VBS, a good way to bring entire families to the program is to have a fiesta instead of lessons. Include activities such as bouncy houses, piñatas, balloon animals, and (the biggest draw) a simple free meal of hot dogs, chips, juice boxes, or food of your choice.

This type of outreach feels especially welcoming and comfortable for Hispanic families, who frequently have family gatherings that resemble such a party. Before the food, you should have a Spanish-speaker not only bless the food, but also explain the Gospel of grace to the kids and parents. It is also a good opportunity to pass out tracts. I use the booklet "Who Will Be King" or "Two Ways to Live" by Matthias Media. At the end of the fiesta we frequently donate Bibles to anyone who wants one. This type of fellowship should be like an invitation to your church.

Free Garage Sale

Throughout the year, ask your congregation to donate gently used household goods and clothing for a charity outreach. Store the items at the church, and once a year have a free garage sale. Invite your target immigrant community to the event so they can pick up items they need. While providing for physical needs, you also make new contacts to invite to other programs.

Soccer Team for Kids at YMCA

One way to attract Hispanics to the church is by starting a soccer team at your local YMCA. Your church can pay for the t-shirts and any registration fees. This provides good marketing for your church and a way to minister to the children and their parents. This ministry is good at attracting first-generation parents and their second-generation kids.

All programs will need to be promoted and marketed with flyers, text messages, telephone calls, and word of mouth to the target community. Focus on the places immigrants physically visit the most in order to establish a physical presence in their world.

It is important that Christians be ready to preach the Gospel to all immigrant populations that come to the US. Hispanics are the largest population, and we have contact with them every day in our restaurants, grocery stores, yards, factories, and elsewhere. We carry a responsibility to preach the Gospel to them and to love them. The Hispanics are largely open to the Gospel, especially those who have come to the US recently and are feeling displaced. It is a great opportunity to share the love of Christ with them and meet their physical and spiritual needs.

11

MERCY: COMPASSION IN MOTION

C. STANLEY MORTON

It seems like a reasonable conclusion that Christians and acts of mercy would be synonymous, but mercy and the people of God have had an uneasy relationship for years. Recall how Jesus rebuked the Pharisees for inviting certain persons to dinner. The Pharisees invited their friends, brothers, relatives, and rich neighbors, but they excluded the poor, maimed, lame, and blind (Luke 14:12–13). A similar situation occurred in Luke 10:25–37, in the parable of the Good Samaritan.

In the Old Testament, Israel engaged in ardent worship practices such as fasting, but they wondered why God was displeased. Yet his chosen fast included the following:

> To loose the bonds of wickedness, to undo the straps of the yoke, to let the oppressed go free, and to break every yoke... to share your bread with the hungry and bring the homeless poor into your house; when you see the naked,

to cover him, and not to hide yourself from your own flesh. (Isa. 58:6–7)

Why do we struggle with being merciful? Perhaps it is because mercilessness is part of our Adamic nature; that is it is an aspect of original sin. We do not have a natural tendency to be be merciful to our fellow human beings in need. Interestingly, though, mercy is exactly what we need.

We need mercy at the most basic level. Paul wrote, *"But God, being rich in mercy, because of the great love with which he loved us, even when we were dead in our trespasses, made us alive together with Christ—by grace you have been saved"* (Eph. 2:4–5). Our greatest need—reconciliation with God—was met through the mercy of God. Not only are our spiritual needs met in Christ Jesus, but our God knows we have physical needs (Luke 12:30–31). Christianity is a holistic religion that cares for both body and soul.

My aim in this chapter is to encourage churches to extend mercy (i.e., diaconal work or benevolence), specifically toward the urban inner city poor in North America, although there are certainly aspects that could apply to rural areas and places beyond North America. Diaconal work includes both material support and discipleship. I hope this chapter will encourage churches to engage and extend mercy in a fashion that will help the poor rather than aggravate their situation.

The Church and Mercy: The Struggle for Compassion

The modern Evangelical church's struggle with urban mercy can be traced to the rise of urban squalor during the late nineteenth century. The influx of southern European immigrants, the Industrial Revolution, the end of African slavery, and the movement from the rural countryside to urban centers created an explosion of needs that overwhelmed volunteer social welfare networks.

People began to call for justice and mercy as conflicts developed between socioeconomic classes and between labor and management. Exasperated with the sheer magnitude of the crisis of need, crime, and squalor, the Evangelical church began to increase its call for individual spiritual salvation. Other church traditions took a different approach, which later became known as the Social Gospel. This split still reveals itself as many of today's churches struggle to understand where their place is in showing mercy to the urban poor versus sharing the Gospel of Christ that transforms the heart.[1] It is my contention that every church needs to labor to extend the Gospel through our words but also provide deeds of mercy to those in need.

The struggle today to show compassion is fraught with several issues.

- The welfare state

The government provides programs to help the poor. How does the work of mercy within the church correspond to and with the Welfare State? Should the church function as a partner with government or see itself as being displaced by government? Sometimes government programs compete with our discipleship efforts to spur growth in areas of wisdom and discipline.

- What should motivate the church's involvement?

Sometimes the church falls prey to laboring out of guilt

rather than out of obedience to Christ and love for the least of these. Jesus shared that he would judge the nations based on how they addressed the needs of the least of these—the hungry, the naked, the sick, and imprisoned. (Matt. 25:31–45; see also 1 John 3:16–19).

- There are approaches to mercy within the inner city that actually hurt the recipients.

This can occur because we undermine what God may be doing in their lives through their difficulty. Someone may have been making self-sabotaging decisions, and it may take enduring a measure of those consequences to learn that the decisions made were foolish. We also can hurt them when we don't see through their eyes or don't see them through God's eyes. With this skewed view, we can humiliate or even sin against them.

- Compassion at times runs aground on the rocks of the reality of sin among the poor.

The deacons discover that the person they have been trying to help has lied and has extorted funds in excess of what was needed. Clothing provided to help is being sold for drugs. The church then, in an effort to be prudent, can overreact and virtually kill the heart of compassion, especially when the poor are different from the members of the local church in respect to race, class, or culture. All of this can push a church to make mercy a marginal part of its work.

Through the Eyes of the Poor

Let's begin this section by describing life in the inner

city, which I call "The Struggle." It is a combination of factors that together create the drama that inner city folks are all too familiar with.

They are:

Family Structure—ranging from intact families to fractured families

Money—never enough to make ends meet, living hand-to-mouth, and robbing Peter to pay Paul

Employment—temporary agencies or dead-end jobs

Government—a life source of resources and yet with humiliation

Healthcare—often ghetto clinics with a bureaucratic character that still costs

Education—viewed as having little worth, parent-teacher tensions, schools taking on the parental role, parental abandonment, and a myriad of distractions

Housing—behind in rent, having to pay rent when there seems to be better uses for money elsewhere, minimal maintenance, landlord attitudes, and the threat of eviction

There is something peculiarly destructive about poverty, even if we don't subscribe to the idea that an impoverished background will determine a person's future life (Prov. 10:15). Steve Corbett and Brian Fikkert in their book *When Helping Hurts* observe that when poor people talk about poverty they "typically talk in terms of shame, inferiority, powerlessness, humiliation, fear, hopelessness, depression, social isolation and voicelessness."[2] These emotional experiences are part of the sting of poverty. Interestingly, Scripture discusses some of these very experiences.

Shame and Disrespect—James exhorts the church not to make the sinful choice to have the poor man in shabby clothing sit or stand in the obvious place of disrespect while directing the rich person to the place of honor. This passage shows us the poor are so often shuffled to low places. It's no wonder they feel ashamed just because they are poor (see James 2:1–9). This sense of shame makes poor folks want to hide their deficiencies. Don't we all? None of us wants to let people in our lives when we are down. "What will they think once they see us as we really are? Will I be judged? Will I be rejected?" These thoughts also can lead to mistrust, and this mistrust can create relational difficulties for people of means doing ministry with poor people.

Dislike, Even Hatred—The sage states that even the poor person's neighbor despises him (Prov. 14:20). In his book *Merciful,* Randy Nabors cites an example of this dislike by how many political commentators characterize the "powerless and voiceless poor" as "a permanent class...of despicable...human parasites" living off the government.[3]

Powerlessness—The psalmist exhorts leaders to execute justice and maintain the rights of the weak, fatherless, afflicted, and destitute. Without the help of others who have power, these people are powerless to defend themselves (Ps. 82:1–4).

Hopelessness—Sometimes it seems there is no chance of change or improvement in The Struggle. The ladders of progress seem inaccessible to the poor.[4] However, there are ladders that are accessible that hopelessness blinds people from seeing. Part of ministry to the poor is giving hope that opens their eyes.

Inferiority and Marginalization—Ecclesiastes points out that a poor man's wisdom is despised and not heard. He is marginalized (Eccl. 9:16). As stated earlier, James highlights the impulse to have the poor man with tattered clothes stand or sit in the lowest place (James 2:3).

Voicelessness—The sage cries out that those in power should defend the cause of the poor and be a voice for them (Prov. 31:8–9). Job speaks of hearing the cry of the poor and afflicted as an aspect of righteousness (Job 34:28). God will judge the ones who close their ears to the cries of the poor by not allowing them to be heard (Prov. 21:13). One aspect of our modern urban riots is that some urban people feel they will only be heard after such violence takes place.

Fear—What will happen to us? There are fears that authorities will block all possible chances of pursuing their dreams and aspirations. Further, there is fear of being violated or killed by the very people hired to protect the citizenry.

All of these and other emotional experiences often create in poor people what Corbett and Fikkert call "marred identities," identities that embrace poverty and struggle as part of who they are as persons, where "the experience of poverty has sold them the lie that they are the 'needy,' the 'have nots,' the 'valueless,' or even the 'condemned by God.'"[5] Poverty is a condition, not an identity. Only the hope of the Gospel can really set people free from making poverty an identity. I wonder if the Civil Rights Movement would have happened if the protesters' identities had remained marred by poverty and by the image that was created in the twisted mirror of Jim Crow?

Sins Against the Poor

There are ways we can sin against the poor collectively, not just as individuals. That may sound strange. We can easily see individuals sinning against individuals in a myriad of ways, but these sins against any one person who is part of a group or socioeconomic demographic can be rooted in sins against a particular group in general. Consider the following:

Impatience—The disciples told blind Bartimaeus to be silent as he cried out for mercy. They thought Jesus had better people to see than the blind. The more they hushed him, the louder he cried. Jesus intervened by asking for Bartimaeus. At that moment, when Jesus called to him, the able people were pushed to the side to make room for the disabled (Mark 10:46–52). This is the real Cinderella story.

Forget and Ignore—God calls people wicked who don't care about justice for the poor. God warns people who harden their hearts against the needy, and he assures the afflicted that he does not forget them (Ps. 9:12, 18).

Violations and Oppression—There are those who take advantage of the poor. God describes such people as having fangs used to devour the poor and needy of the earth (Think: eugenics in the early part of the twentieth century;

abortion in the latter part of the twentieth century; Prov. 30:14). Scripture identifies oppression through the instrument of government, through unjust business practices or through outright robbery (Deut. 24:12, 14, Ps. 10:2, 37:14, 109:16, Prov. 22:22–23, 28:8, 28:15, James 5:1–6).

Sins of the Poor

What sometimes surprises urban do-gooders is that poor people are sinners too. Working among the poor will mean that both your sin and theirs mix. It is not pretty. The sins of the non-poor can be summed up by a phrase from Corbett and Fikkert—a god-complex. It is the notion that people of means have come to be the saviors of the poor since they are superior to them. The would-be saviors think, "All the poor have to do is become like us." Jesus accused the Pharisees of trying to make proselytes. When they succeeded, the proselytes wound up being twice the children of hell as they were (Matt. 23:15).

Yet there is a moral dimension to modern poverty characteristic of materially poor sinners. R. R. Reno put it this way, "A Christian who hopes to follow the teachings of Jesus needs to reckon with a singular fact about American poverty: Its deepest and most debilitating deficits are moral, not financial; the most serious deprivations are cultural, not economic. Many people living at the bottom of American society have cell phones, flat-screen TVs, and some of the other goodies of consumer culture. But their lives are a mess."[6] Dr. Carl Ellis calls this "dysfunctionality." There is a culture that carries it, "a culture nurtured by structures of oppression and one that wears down initiative and personal responsibility—whose value system elevates and encourages anti-achieverism, fatherlessness, dependency, helplessness, hopelessness, self-sabotaging/self-

179

destructive behavior, fratricide, etc., and in extreme cases, nihilism."[7]

Self-sabotaging attitudes and behaviors are heart-breaking to real urban deacons and practitioners such as: refusing to do high school homework; refusing to restrain job-costing anger when they think they are right; can't get to work on time.

One social commentator identified something he called "touchy pride," where sin gets involved with the quest for respect and a person will erupt into violence for the least perceived slight against them from another person, even if accidental. We see this kind of pride in road rage where a person, cut off in traffic, erupts into a shouting match with the offender or even gun violence. Some people carry the aura of not "to be messed with, or else."[8]

My experience has been that some inculcate from interaction with "the system" a deep sense of normalized entitlement that hinders their motivation and efforts to do what it takes to work and build a life. It is not that people arrogantly assume they are entitled. Rather they come to expect that certain things are supposed to come to them as a matter of course, expectations their forbearers could not have imagined would simply be theirs by some predetermined right.

Scripture lists as other sins that can lead to dysfunctional poverty: excessive pleasure (Prov. 21:17), outright foolishness (Prov. 13:18), addictions (Prov. 23:21), laziness (Prov. 6:10, 10:4, 20:4, 21:25, 26:13, 26:16), and haste (Prov. 21:5). Pray! Pray for your heart when you encounter the sins of the poor lest you become jaded and sink into cynicism. Pray that God would make and keep your heart as soft and harmless as a dove and yet sharp and streetwise as a serpent (Matt. 10:16).

The most fundamental fact about human beings in general and the poor in particular is this—they are made in the image of God (Gen. 1:27, Prov. 22:2). This gives them equal and inherent dignity and worth alongside any and all other humans in the world.

A theme running through the Bible is how God chooses and stands by the poor. Israel, the nation through whom God brought the Savior, was not chosen because it was more numerous than the other nations around them or more righteous than the others, but simply because God set his love on them (Deut. 7:6ff, 9:4ff).

The Father chose to send his Son to earth through a poor couple named Mary and Joseph. They were poor enough that when they brought the sacrifice of purification for dedication of the firstborn male to the Lord, they brought a pair of turtledoves and two young pigeons, the alternative provision for those too poor to bring a lamb (Luke 2:11–24, Lev. 12:8). The heavenly host of angels that announced his birth did so to shepherds, men in an occupation of low social standing.

In fact, Paul wrote that Jesus became poor so we might become rich (2 Cor. 8:9). Jesus, when he declared his mission, made *"preaching the Gospel to the poor"* part of it (Luke 4:16–21). Randy Nabors said that "if we follow Christ, we join him in his commission and in the task he was anointed to complete...*to preach the Gospel to the poor.*"[9]

With all this talk about mercy, what exactly is it?

The Bible defines mercy as pity and compassion toward sinners and toward the miserable and afflicted, but with a desire to relieve them. God begins to show mercy from the day of the Fall to the close of the New Testament. When

Adam and Eve plunged from innocence into a state of sin and misery, God extended mercy. Rather than destroy them immediately, God made them garments of skin and clothed them, which symbolizes a provision for the covering of our sin through the sacrifice and shedding of blood by a substitute. These skins also provided covering for what would soon be life outside the garden. God did not give them what they deserved, immediate death. God would show mercy to human need through his provision for his people Israel, both by how he addressed their physical needs and by the laws he gave them to handle the needy within the covenant community and strangers they encountered outside the community.

In the New Testament we see the mercy of Christ toward the needy in a variety of ways, from healing the sick, to feeding thousands of listeners, to setting free those possessed with evil spirits, to raising up from the dead lost loved ones (see particularly Luke's gospel). The Bible continues to discuss the poor as we look into the epistles where Paul tells of his dialogue with the leaders in Jerusalem when they tell him to remember the poor, to which he replies he is eager to do (Gal. 2:10). Finally, we have in 1 Thessalonians a statement that, to my mind, is God's goal for the poor, wherever they may be: *"But we urge you... to aspire to live quietly, and to mind your own affairs, and to work with your hands, as we instructed you, so that you may live properly before outsiders and be dependent on no one"* (1 Thess. 4:10–12).

This passage says God's plan for the poor is that they be set free from drama and dependency and be able to handle their finances from resources they themselves have earned or developed such that they will be able to live with dignity before a watching world. Mercy ministry should help people realize this reality.

The heart and work of a deacon or deaconess or benevolence servant is captured in the *Book of Church Order of the Presbyterian Church in America* (PCA) sections 9-1, 9-2, and 9-7:

9-1—The office is one of sympathy and service, after the example of the Lord Jesus; it expresses also the communion of saints, especially in their helping one another in time of need.

9-2—It is the duty of the deacons to minister to those who are in need, to the sick, to the friendless, and to any who may be in distress. It is their duty also to develop the grace of liberality in the members of the church, to devise effective methods of collecting the gifts of the people, and to distribute these gifts among the objects to which they are contributed. They shall have the care of the property of the congregation, both real and personal, and shall keep in proper repair the church edifice and other buildings belonging to the congregation.

9-7—It is often expedient that the Session of a church should select and appoint godly men and women of the congregation to assist the deacons in caring for the sick, the widow, the orphans, the prisoners, and others who may be in any distress or need.

So then, as we have opportunity, let us do good to everyone, and especially to those who are of the household of faith. (Gal. 6:10)

The fundamental motivation for doing this work is love, and it is a balancing act between compassion (dignity, respect, generosity, advocacy, and embrace) and prudence (wisdom, empowerment, and instruction).

> By this we know love, that he laid down his life for us, and we ought to lay down our lives for the brothers. But if anyone has the world's goods and sees his brother in need, yet closes his heart against him, how does God's love abide in him? Little children, let us not love in word or talk but in deed and in truth. (1 John 3:16–18)

Diaconal work must be done through relationships. Policies should be developed that support this relational approach. Often churches inadvertently set up programs to distribute mercy that feel cold and impersonal to the recipients, particularly across the racial divide from majority to minorities. I suspect one reason is that upper- and middle-class majority people want to make a difference in as many lives as possible and as efficiently as possible. They want to impact communities of need as a whole and be able to quantitatively measure that impact. Programmatic approaches allow leaders and workers to narrow their focus and "keep track" of how things are going. These kinds of results make for good reports to institutional leaders and donors. This approach often requires rules and structures that will include those who can fit into the program's framework and exclude those who do not.

A relational approach allows you to enter deeply into another's life with dignity and grace. It permits you to work with those who might not qualify for a particular program. This submerges the distribution of assistance into the ups and downs of the recipient's life. This does not lend itself to quantifying. It makes you tell stories. Listen to inner city urban practitioners who have gotten their hands dirty trying to help someone move from poverty and dysfunction (e.g., drugs, sexual immorality, crime, self-sabotaging choices) to stability and Gospel living. They will tell stories because the lives of the people they work with will often elude neat statistics. They can tell you what God has done in individuals, but are at a loss to give you a number that indicates institutional success in a given year. Karen Ellis describes the work of the "urban disciple maker" this way:

> The Christian focus throughout the twentieth century on conversion strategies alone has already been weighed by many and found wanting. Our urban disciple makers understand that discipleship is a much longer and deeper commitment than simply moving an individual from impiety to piety. It involves walking alongside men and women from foolishness to wisdom, and making certain that they know—*tangibly*—that Christ has earned them a valued place and given them a strong, secure and transcendent identity in Him; a place where even sinful choices can be redeemed and kingdom potential realized.... He knows that in pre-conversion discipleship, moving from foolishness to wisdom is a two-steps forward, one-step back proposition, just as it was with Christ and his disciple making. The urban disciple maker also knows that in his context, as young people are drawn into Christ and slowly transformed by the renewing of their minds, a single indulgence in foolishness can result in tragic loss of life and the termination of the entire discipleship process.[10]

Randy Nabors puts it like this:

> Discipleship is not a curriculum. It is a relationship, it is a lifestyle, it is a life experience in community within a local church. That makes it harder, longer and difficult

to quantify. One can't simply say we have trained this many folks in this period of time and as a result, now there is no longer any poverty in this city. Oh that it could be so easy!"

Jesus asked the Samaritan woman for a drink. She must have thought, "What?! Don't you know we don't do this?" There were a lot of ways this woman could not help Jesus. He is God and fully self-sufficient! But Jesus identified the one resource she had that she could use to help him in his humanity: water. He was thirsty.

Samaritans were considered continually ceremonially unclean. So drinking from a vessel of a Samaritan would make one of God's people unclean. The woman knew the significance of his request. It was not a matter solely of thirst. It had social and spiritual ramifications. It opened her up to eventually come clean about her circumstances. Ingenious! In order for us to go deeper than mere relief for poor people, we need to develop a relationship with them that may lead us to a better understanding of their circumstances, a clearer revelation that we truly need them, and the opportunity to tell them about the one who though he was rich became poor for our sake.

Practical Considerations

The overarching goal of our assistance should be to communicate the Gospel of Jesus through building bridges to financial and family stability. We build godly wisdom into the lives of our recipients. There are those who will come to us because of a temporary rough spot, but many others live in chronic poverty. The day-to-day work of a deacon is an art not a science, especially to keep it relational and not descend into cold distribution.

Again, policies and procedures help structure the interactions and relationships so things do not get arbitrary and overwhelming. These give the framework to be able to say yes and no to people in light of the resources of the church. Policies, forms, and procedures help the deacons get information needed to make good assistance decisions, provide means to train others, and foster building those relationships that are vital. Materials on these matters are available from The Chalmers Center and through the New City Fellowship Network.

There is much discussion as to whether the church should assist only those who are attendees or members of the church. Many passages of Scripture seem to limit aid to the covenant community (I John 3:16–18, Deut. 15:7, Acts 4:32–37). However, Jesus also teaches us in his parable of the Good Samaritan that our neighbor goes beyond "just us." As Tim Keller writes, "Jesus expands the concept (of neighbor) by showing that anyone in need is our neighbor."[12] Paul, in Galatians 6:10, suggests that priority should be given to attendees and member of the local body, but that priority should not exclude everyone else.

At one church I served, we set the priorities this way: 1) members and regular attendees, 2) referrals from members or regular attendees and affiliates of the church (irregular attendees), 3) referrals from sister organizations in the city (other churches, rescue missions, shelters); 4) requests from those in the larger inner city community.

You'll need a set of priorities to help guide your decisions and practices.

The needs deacons typically attempt to meet are emergencies (food, transportation, critical medical, financial setback support, and utilities), housing assistance (i.e., security deposits, rent delinquencies), and educational needs (tuition assistance), to name a few. It all depends on the needs of your locale. Diaconal practitioners everywhere will tell you not to assist with cash.

Be careful not to burn out your troops with compassion fatigue. Diaconal work in the inner city is involved and intense. It will drain everyone involved. Take on only the number of people you can, share the ministry among the group, and make sure there is adequate Sabbath rest for them. Burned out deacons are very hard to bring back to life.

I will end with the following suggestions given by Robert Lupton in his book *Toxic Charity*: 1) Discern—Is the need crisis (emergency) or chronic (constant)? 2) Never do for others what they can do for themselves; 3) Sustainability is a litmus test; 4) Consider unintended consequences; 5) Listen to what is not being said. If the work of God is to be done in a life through another, both the giver and the recipient have to come to the table in mutual humility.[13]

12

COME AS YOU ARE, BUT DON'T STAY THAT WAY: NAVIGATING ISSUES OF ASSIMILATION AND INCLUSION

LANCE LEWIS

It was February of 1983. I remember the exact year and month because at the time I was a freshmen at a branch campus of Penn State. A good friend and I participated in an InterVarsity (IV) retreat that included a Sunday morning church service.

The church was not one with which we were familiar. To give just a little background, neither my friend nor I grew up in overtly Christian homes. By God's providence we came to faith through the witness of a close friend and immediately joined his church, which was in our neighborhood. It was a Pentecostal church, and as you might surmise, was quite demonstrative in its expression of worship. That doesn't mean our services were ecstatic free-for-alls with no order. Rather, they were joyful, enthusiastic times of praise and worship. We took great comfort in and drew great strength from the nearness of God's presence along with the strong belief that the God we worshiped on Sunday would be active in our lives throughout the remainder of the week.

Imagine our surprise when the cultural expression of worship at the church we attended for the retreat was so utterly different from what we were used to. It was like night and day. Where we were emotionally jubilant and flexible with the order of worship, they were emotionally restrained and regimented. Where we felt like one big family coming to our Father's house for a celebration, this service had the feel of a formal ceremony whose participants came to hear a lecture. Where we reveled in our freedom to express verbal affirmation within each element of our service of worship and especially the sermon, this church gave the distinct vibe that such outbursts would be extremely disruptive. Whereas we lingered in our Father's presence for two to three hours each Lord's Day, they wrapped up everything nice and neat in an hour and fifteen minutes. As if all that weren't enough, the pièce de résistance was the baptism of a new believer, who wore his three-piece suit!

Upon leaving, my friend and I were thoroughly convinced of at least two things. First, we questioned whether these people truly knew the Lord. To us their worship seemed to be little more than a dead, moribund ritual. Second, we would never set foot in that place again.

What I didn't know then was that I had embraced a particular subculture. For the purpose of this chapter I'll define culture as a particular set of customs, traditions, beliefs, assumptions, history, habits, attitudes, expressions, behaviors, etc. that belong to a specific group of people.

Within the cultural category there are macro and subcultures. A macroculture is one to which a wide scope and variety of people subscribe, such as American culture.

For example, American macroculture was on display when I overheard a new immigrant express her enthusiasm at celebrating her first Thanksgiving. One characteristic of macroculture is that it's transmitted in a number of ways and reaches almost everyone under its influence. For instance, the American Thanksgiving holiday is taught by many elementary schools as well as referenced in a number of media outlets (think of *A Charlie Brown Thanksgiving*).

Within macrocultures there are subcultures. Subcultures are those cultures that are peculiar to specific groups within macrocultures. Christian churches are one example of a subculture. Moreover, there are several smaller subcultures within the larger Christian subculture. Subcultures have a number of things in common with macrocultures, beginning with the reality that each one has the unspoken but real expectation that those who choose to associate with the group will conform to that culture, even if it means laying aside one's existing or previous culture. For example, there is no law mandating immigrants (or for that matter anyone) celebrate Thanksgiving. However, it is the expectation of most Americans that those who choose to come to this country should want to celebrate our national holidays.

In many ways, the characteristics of macro and subcultures are the same. The first and perhaps primary aspect of culture is that it actually exists. There is no human institution, including the church, which is absent of the human imprint of culture. If you truly think your church is a-cultural then you're just not looking at it hard enough. This is why one of the initial steps in cultivating a church culture, which promotes genuine unity across cultural and ethnic lines, is to recognize your church has one (or will have one if you're still in the planning stages).

A second aspect of culture is its importance to us. Our subculture has a certain significance that is tied to our identity. It's what helps us identify with our group (or tribe) and gives us a sense of belonging or place.

The third aspect of culture, and related to its importance, is its function in facilitating our sense of ease, welcome, safety, and rightness. A good example of this occurred several years ago when a group of musicians from Reformed University Ministries began to retune several well-known hymns. They drew a strong and negative reaction from others who completely rejected this practice and wanted it to stop immediately. What was the big deal? The big deal was that this particular part of their subculture was extremely important to them, and they did not want it changed.

A fourth characteristic of subcultures is the presence of traits that are built upon unspoken and perhaps informal foundations. These traits, such as the expressive emotion-filled worship from my Pentecostal experience, as well as the reserved, restrained worship of the church we visited, are obvious to newcomers or outsiders. What's not so obvious are the informal foundations that lay at the basis of these traits.

A fifth characteristic of a particular culture is the belief that it is not only right but normative. During my early years as a Pentecostal, I was fully convinced that the way we worshiped was the normal and most accepted way to worship the living God. Since any given subculture is seen as normative by those who embrace it, there is little wonder why newcomers are expected to assimilate to the norms and expectations of that culture.

For our purposes I'll use the following definition of assimilation. It is to bring into conformity with the customs, attitudes, etc., of a group, nation, or the like; to adapt or adjust. To assimilate is to shed your previous culture (i.e., your customs, traditions, history, habits, attitudes, expressions, behaviors, etc.) in order to wholly adopt another.

Two more aspects of culture are worth mentioning, one more obvious than the other. First, since the foundations of a particular subculture aren't necessarily front and center, the culture itself can seem not only unfamiliar, but foreign and even unwelcoming to outsiders and newcomers. The last (and not so obvious) aspect of church subculture speaks to the issue of why we're so determined to hold to it tightly. Many—if not most—who hold to a specific church subculture are convinced that it's steeped in biblical truth. This conviction is what contributed to our jarring experience in worship during the InterVarsity retreat. Because we mistook our core cultural convictions for core theological convictions, we were absolutely certain that this church could not be biblical, regardless of its confession of faith.

We Are the Borg

"We are the Borg. Lower your shields and surrender your ships. We will add your biological and technological distinctiveness to our own. Your culture will adapt to service us. Resistance is futile."[1]

The Borg Collective, the ultra enemy of the United Federation of Planets, came into popular conscience in the mid-90s in the Star Trek storyline. What made the Borg such a tantalizing enemy (and so different from other zombie motifs) was their collective culture that was so different from and antithetical to the Federation. It's little wonder that war ensued when they showed up on the Federation's doorstep and introduced themselves using their now-infamous greeting.

In some ways churches offer more subtle yet similar demands of those who wish to join them. While we may not force prospective members to "lower their shields and surrender their ships," there is the strong presumption that they should lower any expectation that aspects of their previous subculture will be welcomed. They are expected to surrender their desire to express elements of that culture in their newly chosen church.

Those entering a new church subculture can get the distinct impression they will submit to cultural conversion (i.e,. assimilate) and in time serve the group by bringing others like them to do the same. Granted they may still pine away for aspects of their previous culture and even suggest ways the existing church can adjust for the sake of becoming more welcoming to souls from other cultural backgrounds. In the end though they find resistance really is futile.

This is why intentional multicultural churches can play such a key role in presenting a more accurate biblical witness to our society. Scripture convinces me that the living God has appointed his church as the vehicle through which he will get glory in Jesus Christ (Eph. 3:21). And one of the primary ways God gets glory from his church is by our tangible, expressed display of biblical, Christ-centered unity across ethnic lines in local congregations.

Since the validity of our witness, along with God's settled and determined will, provide a sufficient motivation to begin and cultivate multicultural churches, the challenge is how to navigate the foundations of various church subcultures. Recall that I previously wrote that while the presentation aspects of a particular subculture is quite obvious to even outsiders, the foundations of what's presented are not. By the way, just so we're on the same page, I define a multicultural church as one that attempts to incorporate at least two existing church subcultures with the hope of achieving a new kind of church subculture that is potentially accessible to a wider group of people. That is much easier said than done.

To Assimilate or Not to Assimilate?

Where does one start with such an endeavor? We should acknowledge our need for churches that feature souls from a variety of ethnicities. We must get to the point where it's understood that according to Scripture multicultural churches present a more accurate picture of God's grand promise (Gen. 12:1–3), his great commission (Matt. 28:18–20), and his glorious vision (Rev. 7:9–17).

To sharpen my point, we must adjust our mindset and embrace the reality that the time has passed for believing we can have a full, relevant, and accurate witness by replicating mainly monoethnic, single-culture churches. The first step toward normalizing authentic multicultural churches is the conviction that the strength, faithfulness, and relevance of our witness is tied to pursuing genuine redemptive unity within the local church.

If you think starting intentional multicultural churches is a weak cave-in to political correctness or just the latest fad sweeping the church, you're mistaken. Moreover, you may have allowed your present cultural and political ideology to blind you to what Scripture actually teaches on this issue.

Yet subcultures by their very nature develop blind spots. To deny that a culture has blind spots is an indication of both arrogance and a sense of superiority. It is arrogant because culture itself is a necessary though sinfully flawed part of our humanity. For example, speech is an integral, indispensable, and God-given part of our humanity. Yet because of Adam's rebellion against God in the Garden of Eden, human speech, like all other aspects of our humanity, is infected by sin. Added to our natural human tendency of sinful speech, however, is the fact that for some of us there are times we use speech in unwise, unkind, hurtful, and sinful ways toward others and don't realize it. My wife brought this to my attention once when I used a common slang term to refer to a Philadelphia police van. Once she explained it to me, I acknowledged she was right and that I needed to stop using that term immediately. Now, in my view it would have been arrogant of me to ignore this correction and adopt the attitude that what I said couldn't be offensive since I didn't mean it to be or that those who might be offended just needed to have thicker skin. The fact is, I was blind to the reality that this was a pejorative term and needed my wife to bring it to my attention so I could stop using it.

A denial of cultural blind spots is also a sign of cultural superiority in that we believe that something so innately human is beyond correction. Few if any of us would affirm that our walk with the Lord is perfect to the point that no area of our lives needs correction. The same holds true for the church of which we're a member, no matter how biblical, faithful, and holy the church. Since that's true, how is it we act as if the cultural expression of that church is beyond correction? To say, whether outright or implicitly, that our church's cultural expression is so complete that change is unnecessary is to declare that it is perfect, and thus those outside of it must not only assimilate to it but be grateful for the privilege of doing so.

Related to our need for souls from a variety of ethnic groups for a biblical witness is the desire to love them. For some this may seem like a given to the extent that it need not even be mentioned. But my experience within the Evangelical church (in the Presbyterian Church in America) during the past twenty-five years and the general experience of the Black community, including the Black Church, has proved that that's not always true. Frankly, it seems that in large part the conservative Evangelical church went from an active hostility and malice toward the Black community during our first few centuries in this country to a resigned indifference and apathy the last few decades. To wit, a few years after America outlawed segregation, more and more evangelical churches began to open their doors to Black people, with many leaving the traditional Black Church and assimilating into mainly white Evangelical congregations.

My observations reveal that a fairly significant majority of Evangelicals still believe that multiethnic churches are unnecessary. That doesn't mean they're against them, just that a multiethnic church is a nice thing to have, much like having wifi in your car. It's a nice thing to have, and though it has its advantages it's certainly not vital to the operation of the car itself.

One consequence of this thinking is the perpetuation of monocultural churches that cater to one specific group of people. This happens even though in the mind of these churches "everyone is welcome." The challenge is that while everyone may be invited, a good number may not actually feel welcome unless they're willing to assimilate. Having embraced this attitude toward multicultural churches, what follows is a limited opportunity to demonstrate love toward those who are different.

"But Lance, isn't that the case with Black people too?"

Not necessarily. My observations and experiences over the past twenty-five years reveal that a greater percentage of Christians not only attend mainly white Evangelical churches but desire to be part of multiethnic churches. What many of them do not want to do is assimilate completely.

But you don't have to take my word for it. Right now do a mental checklist of your churchgoing friends and acquaintances. My guess is you'll discover a larger percentage of your Black friends attend mainly white, monocultural Evangelical churches than your White friends who attend mainly Black monocultural churches.

Does this mean that those Blacks in mainly White churches aren't loved by their fellow congregants? Of course not. My overall point is that the mainly white Evangelical churches have largely failed to love black people, including black Christians. How can I say this? The answer would take at minimum another chapter or more realistically another book. Suffice it to say that during the four hundred years African Americans have lived in this land we've seldom been the objects of love by the wider Evangelical church. Far too many times it's been Evangelicals who've sided against us and with those who oppressed and mistreated us. Seldom have Evangelicals stood up to defend our basic human rights, Constitutionally given American rights, or even our lives. I realize that for some this is hard to believe and might well be dismissed out of hand. For those who are hesitant to take my word on this, I'd ask that you take some time to study Evangelical reaction to and positions on the latter part of the Civil Rights Movement. Black people, in many respects, were not loved.

What's Love Got to Do with It?

Biblical love is the virtue that moves us to stretch beyond ourselves for the good of someone else. Love isn't stuck on making sure everything is fair. It is motivated to go beyond stark fairness and demonstrate lavish grace. Love causes us to refuse wholesale assimilation because we recognize that some aspects of our brother's and sister's subculture are important to them, and we'd be blessed to encourage it within our church.

Love determines to not just look out for our own interest, concerns, and issues, but catapults us into considering the interest, issues, and concerns of others (Phil. 2:1–11). Love realizes that everything doesn't have to be my way all of the time and that it is in fact good when others express aspects of a subculture different from mine. Romans 14 (especially verse 15) is a good passage to reflect upon. The Apostle Paul wrote of cultural differences that were causing division between some within the church. One of the important factors to note about these differences is that each group viewed them as a critical part of their relationship with the Lord (see verses 6–8).

Like many of us today, they had mistaken some of their core cultural preferences for core biblical convictions. Paul's admonition to them was to accept each other, differences and all, and to prize and pursue relating to each other in love instead of always insisting on having their own way (see verses 13–15). It also appears that Paul's admonition concerning the supremacy of love in 1 Corinthians 13:4–7 can also be applied to the way we work through the issue of cultural expression within our churches.

Biblical love doesn't get hyped by winning arguments and being right. It replaces the drive to be right at all cost with the desire to listen, learn, engage, care, be considerate, and sacrifice my rights not just for the sake of my brothers and sisters in Christ, but for the the supreme pursuit of Christ's kingdom, of which his multicultural worshiping community—called the church—is an integral part. Love doesn't adopt an attitude that communicates "Why do we have to do this?" Rather it embraces the mindset that says "Hey, why aren't we doing this?"

Further, healthy multicultural churches begin with the

building blocks of a strong sense of mutual need and love. For those who desire to plant a multicultural church, this must be true of every single individual on the launch team or core group. It is not enough just for the pastor and his wife to have a compelling sense of need and love. It must be evident across the breadth of the team or the church will not work as hoped. At best, people from the sub-dominant group will be expected to assimilate. At worst, they'll be ignored.

I'd strongly encourage you to refuse to cater to anyone who views a multicultural church as their opportunity to convert people from a different cultural group to their way of thinking regarding various aspects of culture and politics. My experience reveals that when this is done, people from the minority group (i.e., the group that is sought after) are seen as projects to be corrected and not people to be loved. Additionally, my experience has shown that those who lead with an agenda to change others in these areas come off as both condescending and paternalistic. This is especially so when those who engage in such behavior have little or no contact with the minority group and no genuine relationships with persons within that group with whom they disagree on issues of race and culture. Consequently, those within the minority quickly get the sense that the church's agenda isn't so much unity and fellowship as much as it is wholesale assimilation. Whatever you do, please refuse anyone who sees contact with the target group as an opportunity to impose their own ideological or cultural views. This shouldn't be done since your passion is for genuine redemptive unity and not superficial and unloving uniformity.

For existing churches that wish to follow God's call in this area, a time of intense, focused prayer and Scripture study is in order. Keep in mind this would represent a significant change in an existing church's subculture akin to a Presbyterian church considering joining a Baptist denomination. It's the kind of change that must be prayed through, thought through, examined by those inside the congregation and outside counsel, explained, worked through with Scripture, and then waited upon. Be advised that not everyone will go for something like this (remember our subcultures are extremely important to us).

In my opinion, such a decision should be church-wide since it will affect all who regularly participate in the life of the congregation. If after a time of prayer and examination, a church isn't ready to make this change, I'd recommend they consider helping to sponsor and participate in a multicultural church plant. In fact, I'd highly recommend suburban churches consider this option for two reasons. First, America's suburbs are becoming increasingly diverse. Secondly, there are probably members of existing suburban churches who are quite passionate about multicultural churches and would be best served if encouraged to pursue that passion with others like them.

Ground Rules

Upon answering the call to start or transition to a multicultural church you'll have a few initial decisions to make with respect to assimilation and integration. You may recall our definition of assimilation is to bring into conformity with the customs, attitudes, etc., of a group, nation, or the like; to adapt or adjust.

Now let's work with a standard definition of the term integration. In short, to integrate is to bring together or incorporate parts into a whole. Embedded in the idea of integration is the reality that everyone will, in some way, participate in some degree of assimilation. An initial question then for those planting or transitioning to a multicultural church is how much assimilation do you expect of the group?

In general, there are two schools of thought concerning this. The first is that the group that wishes to initiate the multicultural church should bear the lion's share of the assimilation. The goal of this approach is to make the sought after group's experience as seamless as possible and to demonstrate that they, their history, present circumstances, and subculture are valued, cherished, and taken seriously. The second approach looks to combine elements of the two church subcultures with the hope that no one group bears the brunt of assimilating.

Once you and your group have settled on an initial approach, it's time to do some research. You can begin by checking out a few examples of the church subculture you'd like to incorporate. Observe what they do and how it differs from yours. Take note of what you believe might work well with your group and what you may need to leave out. Be sure you and your group discuss what parts of the service not only differ from yours, but how you could grow to love and appreciate them. Finally, put yourselves in the shoes of someone who decided to leave that church for yours. What would they have to give up? What do you think they'd miss?

We can too often believe that when a person leaves one church subculture for another, he or she is gladly leaving behind everything with no remorse or regrets. However, that's not always the case. Many times they're willing to make significant sacrifices to assimilate into your church but would gladly welcome the integration of a couple of aspects of the culture they left behind.

Pointed conversations with those with whom you'd like to connect is another avenue of research. You can start with those members of the church or core group. Ask them what, if anything, would make the church even more inviting to people from their background. Ask them, "What made you feel at home in your previous church?" If possible, have them ask a friend or family member who currently attends a church within your friend's previous subculture to visit and give their impressions and suggestions regarding how you could be more welcoming to people from that subculture.

Attempt to incorporate at least one element from the other church subculture into your worship service. For example, a Pentecostal church, of which I was member, devoted part of the Sunday morning congregational prayer for a time of private prayer. The pastor would stand at the front of the church, and those who wished would come up to pray with him. During this time, the congregation would sing along with the choir or remain in quiet prayer themselves. While this extended the time spent in worship (not that we minded), it was a precious time of prayer and met the need of those who had an urgent need for prayer that Sunday. I introduced this element of worship to a church I served. Although we did it just once per month (the first Sunday to coincide with Holy Communion), it became one of the most anticipated and appreciated parts of our worship.

Finally (and most importantly), be sure to draw from and point to Scripture, as it both prescribes and describes various expressions of worship. One of the best ways to do this is by explaining why you do what you do in a church newsletter or website. I'd especially encourage you to examine the Psalms, which were used as calls to worship. Psalm 33:1–2 says:

Shout for joy in the LORD, O you righteous! Praise befits

the upright. Give thanks to the LORD with the lyre; make melody to him with the harp of ten strings! Sing to him a new song; play skillfully on the strings, with loud shouts.

It's important to recognize that the weekly worship service is just one area where a particular church features its subculture. There are several other areas of church life in which it's also evident. For example, a significant yet informal characteristic of church subculture is the topic of conversations among members before and after the weekly worship service, as well as other church gatherings. This is where having been an active member of churches that featured distinct subcultures comes in handy. I noticed the conversations in Pentecostal churches ranged from what was going on in our lives, our walk with the Lord, issues of race, and stuff happening in our church. The conversation in Evangelical churches also consisted of regular life happenings and church life. Added to this was a steady diet of politics. One subject that was rarely if ever discussed was that of race.

Are these aspects of church subculture wrong? No, not necessarily, but they could be potential blind spots that might convey an unintentional expectation of assimilation for those who are a part of the church. How can this be avoided? One possible way is to be aware and accepting of the type of subculture different people bring to the church. Once they give evidence of that subculture (for instance someone begins to discuss politics in a church that's not used to such conversation or another person brings up the topic of race where the subject is viewed as off-limits), existing members of the church can engage them in the subject, show genuine interest, and even inquire as to why it's important to them.

Why is this necessary? One reason is it communicates that no one has to check important parts of who they are at the church door. It also affirms that those who come to the church will be loved and not just tolerated. Finally (for the purposes of this chapter), it conveys that everyone is truly welcome as opposed to only being welcome if they become just like us.

Exceedingly and Abundantly

You may be familiar with these words as they appear in the KJV translation of Ephesians 3. Millions of believers have read these words with great comfort, believing that our great God can and will work in extraordinary ways in our lives. I for one believe this is true! It's the placement and context of these words, however, that should give us even more cause for awe and marvel at the greatness of our glorious Lord. For the context has to do with what the living God is doing to get glory from his church.

What does it mean for God to get glory from us? In short, it means that we display, demonstrate, reflect, highlight, and emphasize his person, nature, character, sovereignty, providence, and holistic salvation as they culminate in the person and work of the Lord Jesus Christ. How did God choose to do this? As I wrote elsewhere in this chapter, he's done so by saving a people for himself from souls of every ethnic group throughout the world and by his wisdom and power that brought them into one unified, multicultural worshiping community called the church.

Who else but the living God can bring people together who would normally remain stuck in their hostility, indifference, and bitterness? Who else could cause people to want to remain together not by erasing their God-given ethnicity but by willingly submitting to each other out of genuine love and for the advance of Christ's Kingdom? Driven by the Spirit, the Apostle Paul, who was raised among a people who prized their ethnicity, culture, and heritage, wrote of the miraculously wondrous thing God had done with his church, using phrases that would thunder home the truth that only God could have done this.

This is why an authentic multicultural church can be such a beautiful display of God's wisdom, power, and love. It starts with a passion to see God's glory through his church. It's a passion that moves a group of people to subsume their own rights for the privilege of consistently demonstrating Christ's loving-kindness and the biblical virtues we so prize. It's what causes a group of people to willingly give up some of the important aspects of their own subculture so they can begin the journey of knitting their lives to a group of souls whom they could just as easily view with distant indifference. Pursuing biblically commanded unity through multicultural churches isn't a deviation into the sphere of liberal theology, nor is it replacing a focus on the Gospel with one on social issues. Instead, it's simple obedience to our Lord and Savior Jesus Christ who by his cross has intentionally brought together people from different ethnic groups, backgrounds, and countries and formed us into one beautiful multiethnic worshiping community called his church.

Let me conclude by finishing my "We're not in Kansas anymore" moment. It turns out that the church we visited in February of 1983, that we vowed never to return, was the congregation of which we became members in May of 1990. It was truly a surreal moment when we, along with our wives, became members of Tenth Presbyterian Church in Philadelphia under the pastorate of the late Dr. James Montgomery Boice. It was even more poignant and meaningful to me when nineteen years later to the month, I became an ordained minister of the Presbyterian Church in America in the very same church in which I had vowed to never visit again. What a God, what a Savior, and what a church!

Now unto him that is able to do exceeding abundantly above all
that we ask or think, according to the power that worketh
in us, unto him be glory in the church by Christ Jesus
throughout all ages, world without end. Amen.
—Eph. 3:20–21, KJV

13

WORD AND WITNESS: CHURCH LEADERSHIP FOR TWENTY-FIRST CENTURY GOSPEL MISSIONS

DARRYL WILLIAMSON

In Lewis Carroll's classic 1872 novel *Through the Looking-Glass*, Humpty Dumpty plays fast and loose with semantics. He slyly attempts to repurpose the word "glory" in a way that seems completely at odds with Alice's understanding of its meaning:

> "When *I* use a word," Humpty Dumpty said in rather a scornful tone, "it means just what I choose it to mean—neither more nor less." "The question is," said Alice, "whether you *can* make words mean so many different things." "The question is," said Humpty Dumpty, "which is to be master—that's all."[1]

Brazilian educator Paulo Freire understood Humpty Dumpty's insight about words and their relationship to the dynamics of power when he said, "There is no true word that is not at the same time a praxis. Thus, to speak a true word is to transform the world."[2] Freire believed words drive thoughtful movement, framing the scenery of our actions, and words interpret the world for us, giving meaning and purpose to all we do. So then, the actions that flow from words are very much determined by who's speaking and what they mean by their words.

What is meant by the words "the Gospel"? What kind of actions flow from those words, what does the church look like when guided by those words, what kind of mission does she pursue, and how does one's understanding of the Gospel relate the church to the broader culture? Let's take a look at how this plays out, depending on who's speaking.

According to R. C. Sproul, the definition of the Gospel has a very targeted, personal, and redemptive scope:

> The Gospel is called the "good news" because it addresses the most serious problem that you and I have as human beings, and that problem is simply this: God is holy and He is just, and I'm not. And at the end of my life, I'm going to stand before a just and holy God, and I'll be judged.[3]

From here, Sproul explains that Jesus has atoned for the sins of those who have placed their faith in him, and he has imputed his own perfect righteousness to those same believers, so they can stand before a holy God wrapped in Christ's righteousness. That is very good news indeed!

Pastor Tim Keller on the other hand, says:

> The Gospel is the good news that through Christ the power of God's kingdom has entered history to renew the whole world. When we believe and rely on Jesus' work and record (rather than ours) for our relationship

to God, that kingdom power comes upon us and begins to work through us.[4]

Both of these definitions of the Gospel are profoundly biblical. Yet it is easy to see how each of them will forge different actions and mission boundaries, particular ministerial language, and even different kinds of Christians. Those centering on R. C. Sproul's meaning will pursue extensive efforts of personal evangelism, seeing the world as primarily a fishing pond for heaven. Conversely, Tim Keller and those who listen to him labor to interpret the cultural landscape of the city as a Gospel-mission strategy and to engage urgent cultural matters as a redemptive witness to the kingdom of Christ, through both speech and church life.

Both approaches are valid. And within a given local church, Gospel messages like these will be connected to a vision crafted and promoted by its leadership, anchored in their perceptions, experiences, convictions, and felt priorities, as they pursue their understanding of Gospel missions.

With this in mind, what are the words that best communicate the good news of Jesus Christ to twenty-first century America, and who are those best-suited to speak those words? Or we can ask it this way, given the ethnocultural revolution that the twenty-first century is bringing America: What Gospel speech and speakers are needed to connect with and proclaim the Gospel to that changing cultural landscape?

The face of American society and culture is browning and yellowing rapidly, along with the face of American Christianity. If the church is going to speak to a potentially balkanized nation about the oneness of the body of Christ and the power of the Gospel, it will no longer be allowed to stand up islands of monoethnic Christianity across the

American landscape, separated by deep prejudices, conflicting worldviews, and a profound lack of "phil-adelphia," brotherly love. If the twenty-first century American church continues the cultural and racial division of the eighteenth through twentieth centuries, we will all need to seriously question whether the Spirit of God truly dwells among us.

The aim of this essay is to consider what kind of leadership is needed in local American churches to effectively reach the richly variegated cultural landscape unfolding before us. To pursue this, we must take on three vital questions:

1. What are the priorities for Gospel missions in the twenty-first century American church? To tackle these, we will need to briefly look at one of the biggest failures of the twentieth-century church and how the ethnic diversity of the American twenty-first century will topple the church's witness if she cannot incorporate cultural diversity in her organizational DNA.

2. Who are the right kinds of leaders, and what are the right kinds of leadership teams for American churches in the twenty-first century? Here we will need to outline a profile for church leaders and leadership teams (i.e., how they should see the world and experience American culture so they can reach it effectively.

3. What is the right strategy for developing and deploying this kind of leadership? This really is the vital question, is it not? We will need a new vision for what ministry and theo-

logical education is, and how leadership is further trained and mentored in local church communities.

Priorities for Gospel Missions

Pastor John Piper has influenced at least two generations of pastors and seminarians through his preaching and writing emphasis on the sovereignty of God, reformed theology, holy affections, and a radical missions-mindedness, so there is no mistake in meaningfully considering his insights. Heading into the year 2016, he was asked what he thought were the biggest challenges facing the Evangelical church. He answered with questions of his own, two of which stand out to me: "Is true knowledge being disseminated about God [in our churches]? Is the whole counsel of God really being taught in the church?"[5]

Though I wholeheartedly agree with him that these are great concerns for the twenty-first century American church, I would like to refine his answer to speak to the massive cultural sea change underway among us. The biggest challenge facing the twenty-first century American church is, how does it regain moral and spiritual credibility after its spectacular failure around racial and ethnic injustices in the nineteenth and twentieth centuries, at home and abroad? Indeed, nearly every ethnicity emerging on the twenty-first century American stage has its own plaintive tale recounting its cultural encounter with American Evangelicalism, and every one of those ethnicities and nationalities are searching for the redemptive language to explain and redeem those histories. Let's begin by looking back at the American story of racial prejudice and Jim Crow.

In the preface to his 1903 classic *The Souls of Black Folk*, W. E. B. DuBois boldly stated, "The problem of the Twentieth Century is the problem of the color line."[6] This is prophetic language as it relates to the American church because the color line was not only its twentieth-century problem but its manifest spiritual problem, as race-segregated churches, icons on the American cultural scene, are the most basic and obvious counter-argument to the church's claim to possess divine presence and truth. When we see American Christianity littered with an abundance of distinctly white and black churches, we are observing a legacy of spiritual failure and historical proof of a profound lack of love among white, Evangelical Christian leadership. Allow me to explain with a brief reference to the history of America's church and pivotal moments in its racial-congregational history.

Jonathan Edwards Jr. and other leaders of the early nineteenth century Reformed tradition, while advocating for the abolition of American slavery, openly expressed fear and disgust of having a free black presence in the United States, especially the "mongrel breed" it would create as races intermarried.[7] Instead of using the prospect of freed slaves to showcase an emergent new humanity in the Ephesians 2:15 sense, along with connecting the liberation of bondsmen to proclaim the far-reaching values of the new American republic, these leaders resorted to carnal race-class self-preservation, guarding Whiteness at the expense of Christian factionalism.

Another case is the late eighteenth century St. George's Methodist Episcopal Church of Philadelphia, which found it necessary to segregate worship and prayer service attendees by race, causing resentment and confusion among black attendees. The leaders of the Negro congregants, Richard Allen and Absalom Jones, chose to escort their followers out of these affronts to their God-given equal humanity and form the AME Church.[8] These kinds of actions and policies continued in the American Evangelical church as denominational organizations sought to maintain segregation as official policy well into the mid-twentieth century, resisting advances of civil rights initiatives.[9]

My point is to remind that the source of the American church's segregation came about through abject spiritual failure by her leadership on issues of race, racial justice, and cross-racial fellowship by professing followers of Christ. Immense theological questions surface as we weigh this failure and what it portends for the credibility of the American Christian witness. It was Jesus that said that the world would know we are his disciples by the love we show one another; so America's Christian history concerning racial injustice is truly nearly damning.

What about today? Can the church simply go back and get it right? Not quite. Life rarely offers do-overs. The agenda for the twenty-first century church cannot be to simply make amends for the failures of the twentieth century. It is imperative that the principles of racialization that marked American Christianity not be repeated. However, it is equally vital that we accept that the largely black-white binary for considering American cultural-racial priorities is a relic of the past. American cultural identity is now spiked with the flavors and sounds of the Global South —Latin American, African/Caribbean, and Asian cultures. These are creatively mixing in with the urban vibe of African Americans and Latinos, while not losing the contributions of American Whites. This transition is profound and glorious. This is the cultural canvas upon which the American church must live out the truth and force of the Gospel in the twenty-first century.

The Pew Research Center published the results of a recent study on American immigrant population growth, and among its notables is that by 2065, 18 percent of the US population will be foreign-born, up from 15 percent in

2015. Another 18 percent will be second-generation immigrants with at least one foreign-born parent, up from 12 percent in 2015.[10] Other key forecasts of the American demographic landscape include:

- No single racial or ethnic group will be a majority.
- Asian, Hispanic, and Black population percentages will increase respectively from 6 to 14 percent, 18 to 24 percent, and 12 to 14 percent, with the growth of each largely driven by immigration and prolific birth rates of immigrant families.
- Within each ethnic group, the percentage of foreign-born vs. native-born will actually decrease from 2015 to 2065, except for Blacks, whose immigrant percentage population will increase from 8.9 to 16.5 percent due to immigration from Africa and the West Indies; and Whites from 4.1 to 8.1 percent, immigrating primarily from Europe.

What does all this mean? Since there will be no single racial or ethnic majority, there will likely be no dominant ethnic culture. Whatever will serve as the basis of cultural dominance, perhaps based on class or region or education, for example, it is likely not to be visibly identifiable by ethnicity, and certainly not White ethnicity.[11]

The stage is then set for the demise of what scholar Soong-Chan Rah has called the "western, white cultural captivity" of the church, which basically explains that what the Evangelical church considers objective biblical thinking is really ethnocultural preferences.[12] These preferences in the minds of white Evangelical Christians pose as Christian thinking or a biblical worldview.

Thus, it cannot be overstated how welcome such change would be to non-White Christians who are commonly trying to persuade others to place their concerns at the heart of the church's agenda. Some possible contemporary implications of this change could include the end of having to explain to White ecclesiastical leaders why justice matters or no longer having to accept the referencing of non-European theological resources missiological edge cases. In other words, it may be no longer necessary to convince those who hold ecclesiastical power the importance of issues deriving from cultural and ethnic marginalization, such as explaining why racial and social injustices are kingdom priorities for the church and not meddling in the world's affairs.

Another notable change in the aforementioned trend, as alluded to earlier, is the decline of the binary black-white ethno-racial landscape that has dominated American conversations about racial reconciliation over the past fifty years. Ethnic social hermeneutics will necessarily take on new tones in the twenty-first century as large portions of American society will have no generational connection to the lived experiences of America's dark Jim Crow past.

So the vision and scope for racial reconciliation must be broader than black-white, and conversations in this regard will need to be inclusive of a wider set of experiences. The reasons for pursuing racial-cultural unity in the church must be theologically deeper than just loving across divides and healing old wounds. It is important that new immigrants do not discount the legacy of injustices experienced by American Blacks, and correspondingly African Americans must understand that these new arrivals have their own histories of injustice and marginalization, and coming to this country was their hope-filled response.

So what does this mean for the priorities for Gospel missions in the twenty-first century American church? Well, white conservative Evangelicalism will not likely be the reference for Christian identity in America given that African Americans, Latinos, West Indians, and Asians bring their own set of experiences and traditions to bear on how the church should interact with the culture—e.g., priority of social justice, less emphasis on classic American patriotism, identities connected to national homelands, etc.

Yet it is no better to simply replace white conservative Evangelicalism with ethnic Christian identities. Men and women of conviction and vision will need to chart a course of a new emergent identity in Christ that incorporates, redeems, and yet transcends ethnicity. This requires clear biblical, theological, and cultural reasoning to offset the convenience and comfort of settling into ethnocentric Christian identities.

As America becomes home to an even greater mix of cultures, showcasing a transcendent unity will be vital to being a compelling witness in this new, excessively diverse society. Community and unity across cultures and ethnicities proclaims the power of the Gospel and elevates the values of kingdom culture above all competing ethnic identities and cultures. Grace will surely trump race in such a setting.

The Right Leaders and Leadership Teams

I recently took part in a denominational survey about diversity and was taken aback by questions that approximated versions of, "How do you feel about persons of color coming into your congregation?" This language represents what many people perceive and people of color fear about the development of multicultural churches: that they are typically led by White pastors and are focused on diversifying White churches and institutions.

I have had no conversations with National Baptists, Full Gospel Association members, or Church of God in Christ pastors about a desire for increasing diversity in their organizations. Indeed, it was almost twenty years ago when Henry Lyons, the now-disgraced former president of the National Baptist Convention, USA, urged the men of his convention to reject participation in the racial reconciliation-focused Promise Keepers men's movement. The NBC instead formed a hollow response called Trusted Partners, born out of the group's participation in Louis Farrakhan's Million Man March.[13]

What is more, it is commonly believed that multiethnic churches will under serve Blacks and Browns, working to disempower individuals from those backgrounds by moving them out of leadership and into support roles and focusing them on "cultural initiatives" within predominantly White churches or denominations. Consultants who advise churches on transitioning from White monocultural to multicultural churches point out that congregations do not typically experience conflict when people of different races arrive, but resentments surface when those new groups ask for a stronger voice in how the church is run.[14]

So, Black Church leaders are not commonly motivated to diversify their institutions, and White church congregants are eager to diversify but not as apparently eager to concede power and leadership. No doubt, the risk in the minds of all is losing their identity and power in their own church organizations.

Becoming a church that reflects the emerging multiethnic and multicultural landscape in America will not be easy. Showcasing the power of the Gospel in a diverse community requires boldness, conviction, and the power of the Holy Spirit, along with the understanding that retreat into ethnic enclaves is not a Christ-glorifying option. The early church put this principle to the test in Acts 6:1–6 in what we could label the Grecian Widow Controversy. This bit of early church history is well-known, but allow me to note a few contextual elements:

1. The Grecian widows were being neglected by a community led by Hebrews.
2. By all indicators, this was an issue of negligence and not intentional discrimination. Therefore, the community was spiritually healthy, if somewhat culturally dysfunctional.
3. Church leadership did not explain away the oversight, but owned it. They recognized the pain caused to their siblings in Christ was a Gospel priority, requiring attention and focus, even though the neglectful behavior was unintended.

We are right to be struck by the decisiveness of the church to not only solve this problem, but to address it on four different dimensions: spiritual, practical, cultural, and structural. Let's flesh these out and then connect them to the twenty-first century American church.

First and most importantly, these men were "full of the Spirit," and the twelve recognized that God-centered, Spirit-empowered leadership would be required to navigate these difficult cultural waters. These would be men of the Word and also men of prayer. They would be humble men who would act in the best interest of those they were serving and not out of the narrowness of their own backgrounds. Men who fit this profile don't need to be taught to feel the pain of the disenfranchised, because from the depths of their Christlike love they see all fellow saints as their dearest brother or sister.

Second, these men were good, practical choices because of their stellar reputations and wisdom. We should not imagine that general relationships between the Hellenists and the Hebrews were tension-free. Most scholars believe the former were Greek-speaking Jewish Christians and the latter were Aramaic-speaking Jewish Christians who really were the enfranchised, empowered group in the early Jerusalem church. The men chosen would need to be aware of and sensitive to those social dynamics while showing no hints of bigotry in the views of both sides.

What is notable in this text is the apparent agreement of the entire church (verse 5) that the right way to guard against the neglect of Grecian widows was to empower Grecian leaders with this new, church-wide responsibility. Greek men like Stephen, Philip, Prochorus, Nicanor, Timon, Parmenas, and Nicolaus were not merely commissioned to look out after their own, but they were empowered to implement this new program across the entire believing community. There would be no schism resulting in two different churches. Unity across cultures was considered an issue of integrity and of Gospel importance. Preserving Hebrew hegemony was of little concern. One can only imagine how the American church, and indeed American society, would have fared if St. George's Methodist Episcopal Church had responded to Richard Allen and Absalom Jones with empowerment and sympathy instead of derision and exclusion.

Last, and perhaps most notably, was the decision to solve the problem by making institutional and structural change. The answer would be to fashion a new class of leadership within which the Grecian men would serve. If it is true that these seven were the first deacons, then the Lord is showing us how theology and ecclesiology is forged in the hot ovens of social necessity. American social dynamics in the twenty-first century will no doubt create opportunities to sharpen our theological pencils and to refine our understanding of the basic elements of Christian identity and practice. Thus, there is need for a culturally diverse leadership that is ready-made to engage the multi-ethnic landscape that is the American culture in the twenty-first century, without the burden of trying to defend or retain ethnic Christian and church identities such as Black churches, White churches, Latino churches, Asian churches, etc.

Strategy for Developing and Deploying Leaders

In my senior year at Boston University in 1987, I had the privilege of serving on a student-faculty committee to fashion the core curriculum for the College of Liberal Arts, now called the College of Arts and Sciences. I was not given to silent submission in those days, so I quickly spoke up when the core reading requirement of "great books" included only readings from white, Western thinkers.

What had begun for me as attempts at calm reason, descended over a few meetings into emotional outbursts of exasperation. How could an elite national university, just over ten years from the dawn of the twenty-first century, think it could prepare its students for future business leadership, social policy formation, and cultural expression if its big ideas were only developed in the incubator of a single intellectual and social tradition, even one as rich in variety as the Euro-American tradition? What about Asian thinkers, African intellectuals, and Latin American philosophers, and their vast responses to the conditions of their societies and respective histories? Do they have nothing to add to civilization and our collective understanding of humanity?

This memory surfaces as I think about the development of Christian leaders for the twenty-first century. What resources will they use to formulate their core theology and missional understanding? Can the awesome legacy of the European Protestant Reformation serve as the only biblical and theological framework for twenty-first century American theological education and seminary curricula? Do we really believe we can equip church leaders of the twenty-first century armed only with rigorous reflections on the Synod of Dort, the Westminster Confession of Faith, or the 1689 Baptist London Confession? As sound and helpful as they are, they are not adequate to interpret the twenty-first century missional landscape with the full force of biblical revelation.

American Evangelicalism has largely ignored many of the biggest socioeconomic issues of our time, or it has not found sufficient biblical or theological impetus to prioritize these concerns in either preaching or discipleship. Some of these issues include:

- The nineteenth century evangelical church's inability to find a biblical basis for opposing the enslavement of Blacks, whether they be Christians or not.[15]
- Recent tensions in the Church surrounding the shooting of unarmed black men, teenagers, and children by police officers and security guards.
- How American Christians should respond to injustices at home and economic injustices

abroad, including the many forms of modern slavery.

- How Christians should biblically respond to immigration, as it continues to rise.
- Does Christian advocacy for human dignity and life imply support for some form of healthcare for all citizens?
- As stewards of God's creation, should we not advocate for a biblically informed balance between economic productivity and environmental sustainability?

Can the Gospel be effectively preached in the twenty-first century while ignoring these issues? It is important to have church leaders who understand the critical nature of these items, informed not just by exegesis, but because these are pressing in on the church, requiring interpretation and Spirit-guided action.

Thus, church leadership teams need to be diverse, ethnically and culturally, if the church is going to be poised to reach diverse cities. Just as the Lord made it clear to Peter that he would need to set aside his dearly held understanding of what it meant to be sanctified before God if he would be a missionary,[16] the church today needs to make substantial adjustments in how its mission is pursued.

To that end, these are some of my convictions for critical action items in light of the above:

1. Churches should place a premium on diverse leadership teams with non-White American lead pastors who will pursue multiethnic and multicultural community life. This is the core issue. Diverse leadership teams, led by blacks, browns, and yellows, will showcase that the American

church is emerging out of its past racial biases, overcoming the White hegemony that often plagues multicultural churches.[17]

2. Church plants should intentionally consist of ethnically and culturally diverse core teams (church members) who understand the importance of #1 above. A diverse congregation more easily attracts diversity, while not in any way discounting the Spirit's work in building churches. The premium on diversity is best lived out early in the life of a church, and a diverse core group of church members assures that.

3. Don't plant multiethnic churches out of White suburban churches. This is really an extended play on the themes outlined above. Large, successful suburban churches will *Ouch* bring models and practices that worked in their context. Yes, they may honestly labor to contextualize within a broader cultural mix what has worked for them. But multiethnic church plants will culturally mature faster when working within its own diverse team and not having to contend with the oversight of the mother church and its culturally biased worship models and ministry priorities.

4. Run toward social issues, not away from them. Social issues and public policy affect the lives of Christians materially and substantively, so they cannot be avoided. What we think and feel about these concerns impact relationships in the church, and many of them are thoroughly addressed in Scripture. So it is incumbent upon pastors to teach and preach on these matters. It is necessary for Chris-

tians to live in awareness of God's expectations about them, so they are relevant to biblical discipleship, resulting in a deeper unity.

5. Incorporate diverse theological resources into the ministerial education of pastors and church leaders. Theology is not formed in a social vacuum, but includes profound references to cultural priorities and urgent matters. This is seen in the European Reformation (examine Luther's 95 Theses sent to the Archbishop of Mainz). Accordingly, a theological agenda that guides pastors in the twenty-first century American church must include insight from African, Asian, and Latin American voices (e.g., Simon Chan, Amos Yong, Soong-Chan Rah, Anthony Bradley, Jarvis Williams, Juan Martinez, Christina Cleveland, and Vincent Bacote) alongside those of the Euro-American tradition (e.g., John Frame, Thomas Schreiner, Richard Pratt, Tom Nettles, Bruce Waltke, Sandra Richter, Don Carson, etc.).

Ethnically and culturally diverse leadership teams often led by blacks, browns or yellows are best suited to guide the American church into the eclectic cultural waters that is the twenty-first century. Teams like this are well positioned to proclaim the Gospel to a new nation of cultures and identities. They also are best equipped to help the American church finally overcome its historical failures around race. And we all pray for and feverishly long for that day.

14

BE STRONG AND COURAGEOUS: PRINCIPLES AND PITFALLS OF TALKING ABOUT RACE IN THE CHURCH

JEMAR TISBY

How many human beings have to become hashtags before the church initiates a sustained dialogue about race in America? As an African American, the issue of racism is constantly on my mind because it can be a matter of life and death. As a Christian, I look to God, his word, and his people for guidance and support. Yet many churches avoid the topic of race. Some argue that such issues are too divisive. People hold strong opinions about this sensitive subject and could get into arguments and cause rifts in the congregation. Others say that race is a topic beyond the scope of the church's mission. It is a social issue but not a Gospel issue.

In my experience working on issues of racial reconciliation and racial justice, I have come to understand that fear is the underlying reason the church fails to delve into the topic of race. Pastors and church leaders worry about how church members will respond if they talk about such a controversial subject. They worry how the tithes and offerings might be affected. They fear the reaction of members who have been at the church for decades and may have even lived through the Civil Rights Movement. They harbor anxiety about speaking on a subject they don't understand themselves.

While wisdom must be exercised about any sensitive topic, the topic must still be addressed. Christians can and must talk about race. Believers cannot cede one of the most pressing topics in American culture to people who have not recognized Jesus as Lord. Instead of following the culture, followers of Christ should lead the way in conversations about racial reconciliation.

In this chapter I will offer basic principles for creating a safe place for discourse when talking about race. For the sake of precision, clarity, and brevity I will confine my examples and applications to issues between Blacks and Whites in the United States. The principles of empathetic communication, however, are universal. Anyone in any context can follow these guidelines to assist in talking about race or other topics like gender, class, and politics.

In addressing black and white race relations, I will often take the white Evangelical church as my frame of reference. According to the Pew Research Center, in 2014, 76 percent of evangelical Christians were White.[1] According to estimates by Lifeway Research, about eight in ten Evangelical churches are racially homogenous.[2] White evangelical churches have a difficult time discussing race due to the lack of racial diversity present in their congregations and the concomitant lack of multiple perspectives. Conversely, Black people and other minorities typically don't have a problem talking race. The problem is their predominantly White churches don't talk about it enough. What they want is the opportunity to discuss race openly and be heard with empathy.

Hearing with Empathy

Hearing with empathy is the first step for creating a safe place for racial discourse. Listening is difficult. Often people aren't really hearing one another. They are waiting for their chance to speak.

Racism has silenced African Americans for centuries. They have been denied literacy education, excluded from higher education, and had their concerns pushed aside by both the culture and the church. Minorities have lifetimes of experiences to share, and they need the opportunity to do so. But many people are just entering into these discussions. The process of listening with empathy won't be easy, especially for White people. It means having to listening to the stories of African American acquaintances and friends firsthand. It also will entail listening to voices from the past by reading books on US history and African American literature. Listening with empathy will mean finding contemporary voices, even from non-Christians, who are doing excellent work in discerning the times and offering insights.

Christians, particularly those in the racial majority, will have to listen so that it feels uncomfortable. We all want to talk. We all want to share our perspectives. But this is speaking too soon. Assuming you know more than you do about our historical and present racial reality can demolish dialogue. The last response hurting people need is one that denies their pain or explains it away. Many people in the majority fear racial dialogue because they are afraid they'll say the wrong thing. This is a legitimate fear. This may be hard to accept, but because of America's racialized culture,

White people are initially going to have to listen far more than they speak. This will be particularly hard for people in leadership positions who are supposed to "know the answers" and teach others. Just recognize that when it comes to racial dialogue, leading often means listening. You will know it's time to talk when minorities start asking you to talk.

To Black people and other racial and ethnic minorities, the world isn't the way it's supposed to be. That means we'll have to be more patient than we'd like, more patient sometimes than we can bear. We'll have to forgive the stumbling and bumbling of people who love Jesus and should know better, but don't. We'll have to endure their ignorant comments and patronizing attitudes. We'll have to listen when they really just can't help but speak even though they still have much to learn. But the reward comes when you see your brothers and sisters in Christ start to get "woke." We can rejoice when all that patience pays off in them becoming advocates and allies in the struggle for racial reconciliation and justice. Our long-suffering will yield dividends when we see the cultural scales fall off the eyes of a fellow believer and we all can more truly resemble the household of God.

Starting the Conversation

The remainder of this chapter focuses on actionable items that pastors, leaders, and churches can take to help their constituents express themselves in racial dialogue. The recommendations, of course, are not exhaustive. They are intended to provide a beginning. These are not "steps" as if following one after the other will automatically lead to healthy conversations about race. No single practice is sufficient. A combination of habits must be cultivated to craft a context for racial conversation. But all the practices I'm about to explain have been tested in real life and have proved helpful when implemented wisely.

First, talk about race. Take the plunge. Don't avoid the topic. Learn by doing. Some reading this may still be hesitant to broach the topic of race, especially in a church setting. Talking about race can be daunting. It might paralyze you to think about preaching on race when you haven't done it much. That's all right. You'll get there. But there are less intimidating steps you can take in the meantime. I know you have apprehensions but do it.

An easy way to bring it up is in prayers from the pulpit. The pastoral prayer is an opportunity for lifting up the needs of the body as well as the nation and the world. But don't stop there. Use your small group ministry to "field test" ideas. Talking about race in front of an entire congregation can be intimidating. One person with a crazy comment could derail the entire discussion. Smaller groups minimize this risk.

Pastors and church leaders also should think about conducting listening sessions. Gathering with small groups of African Americans and other minorities just to ask them, "What's it been like for you?" can yield transformative information. Ask them what it's been like at the church or the ministry. Ask if they've experienced any microaggressions.[3] Let them offer their insights and suggestions about how to make the ministry more racially inclusive. As you venture into these conversations, don't worry about espousing a racist viewpoint or making an accidentally racist statement. You will. But if you set up the conservation correctly, people will understand your intentions and give you grace.[4]

If you have set your face like flint to talk about race in your context, then next comes the question of content. This one should be straightforward. Start with the Bible. As Christians we should always begin with the Bible because this is our normative truth. It is our agreed upon standard for interpreting reality. We will only perpetuate the problems of racism and segregation if we approach these issues from any other ground than God's Word. We should start with the Bible for another more practical reason, too. People who are skeptical about racial conversations and the racists in your congregation (yes, you have them; every congregation does) will be more receptive if you talk about Scripture than if you start with so-called "social" issues.

When I talk about race from a biblical perspective I talk about "one race and two races." Biologically speaking, the Bible makes clear that we are one human race. Acts 17:26 concisely demonstrates this concept. It says, *"And he made from one man every nation of mankind."* Briefly, this means that people of different races and ethnicities are the same species. There was actually a time in the United States when people in power had to debate whether Indians, Africans, and mixed-race people were fully human, or whether they even had souls. While this view is outdated even for the most racially obtuse people, church leaders must still acknowledge how the Bible understands humanity. From there guide the conversation to the image of God and the dignity of all human beings (cf. Gen. 1:26–28).

In another sense, though, the Bible talks about two races. First Peter 2:9 says, *"But you are a chosen race, a royal priesthood, a holy nation, a people for his own possession, that you may proclaim the excellencies of him who called you out of darkness into his marvelous light."* In God's kingly power, he has determined before the beginning of time who will receive the promise of eternal life by faith and who will remain in their rebellion for eternity. The verse from 1 Peter explains how the former group is the chosen "race," those who are redeemed by grace through faith in Jesus Christ. The other race is the unredeemed. From a salvific standpoint, then, there are two races—the saved and the lost. This can be couched in God's sublime plan of salvation that always included an ethnically diverse group of believers from Genesis to Revelation. Diversity is not an accident in God's plan, it is intentional and it is beautiful.

Deciding to talk about race is one thing, starting the conversation with Scripture is another, but actually sitting in front of people and initiating dialogue represents a different challenge. I start every conversation about race among Christians the same way. I say, "If we have confessed with our mouths and believed in our hearts that Jesus Christ is Lord, then we are now all the adopted children of God. The Father has united us by the Holy Spirit through the sacrifice of the Son. Therefore we are connected by a bond stronger than biology. We may not have a natural connection in the world, but we have a supernatural connection through the Holy Spirit who unites us to himself and to each other. Therefore no earthly divisions can separate us. We should be able to talk about such controversial topics as race and leave knowing that we are still brothers and sisters in Christ."

Christians can discuss race like no other group of people because we have a unity like no other group of people. This means we can speak the truth. We can point out blind spots, racist statements, and racist ideas. But speak the truth in love. We don't seek to belittle anyone. We extend grace where there is contrition and patiently endure one another.

Never neglect this. Open with prayer and say some version of the words above. It's like setting the Lord's Table. Every time a congregation partakes of the bread and the wine, the pastor explains what it means and what it doesn't. Even if a member has partaken in the sacrament a thousand times, he or she still needs to hear the words of institution. The same is true for starting a dialogue about race.

Addressing Common Misperceptions

Even though the topic of race in the United States offers volumes of potential conversation topics, a few issues perennially surface. I will mention and briefly explain the blind spots inherent in each subject and how to avoid the pitfalls.

Color Blind/I Don't See Color

The assumption behind the color-blind theory of race relations is that if we intend to treat all people equally then we must avert our eyes from a person's skin color and evaluate by individual merits alone. The problem with color-blindness, though, is that it flattens out relevant differences between individuals and people groups. As an African American, I want you to see the color of my skin. My pigmentation speaks to an experience of America that you must understand. It also speaks to the strength of a people whose past and present you must appreciate. I also come with a culture that has been birthed from generations of Black people learning to survive in a hostile nation. I don't want the centuries of struggle my ancestors endured to be bleached away. Instead, I want people to see me and glory in the stunning diversity of God's creation.

The other issue with color-blindness is that it assumes we will treat people impartially. The reality is that when we say we don't see color, we really mean we see white. Even in an effort to act in a color-blind fashion, the culture will still default to the dominant White culture. Black people and other minorities will still be expected to adapt and assimilate into the majority while their own cultural distinctiveness gets submerged.

Racism is a Skin Issue Not a Sin Issue
People who say, "Racism isn't a skin issue. It's a sin issue," intend to get at the ultimate reason the world is not the way it should be. That reason is sin. Ever since Genesis 3, human beings have inherited a sinful nature and have been turning away from God. Romans 3 states *"All have sinned and fallen short of the glory of God"* and *"there is no one who does good. No, not one."* The problem with the sin/skin distinction is that it spiritualizes an issue that has tangible effects. God created humans as embodied, spiritual beings. The physical world matters. Redemption that does not take temporal, material, physical issues into account, along with the spiritual, is a disembodied, ephemeral version of the robust Gospel found in Scripture.
Christians who jump to the sin/skin dichotomy usually think that racism will end if we just preach the Gospel. I've got bad news. Christians are racists, too. Believing in Jesus Christ as God's only begotten son and putting your faith in him for salvation will not magically rid you of racism. It takes intentionality and direct intervention to unlearn sin. Of course, we do this in the power of the Spirit, but that is not treating racism as simply a sin issue. Pointing to sin as the root of racism, as correct as this may be, is only a partial truth. The logical and tragic end of racism is violence against black and brown bodies. Ta-Nehisi Coates says it this way in his book *Between the World and Me*: "[A]ll our phrasing—race relations, racial chasm, racial justice, racial profiling, White privilege, even White supremacy—serves to obscure that racism is a visceral experience, that it dislodges brains, blocks airways, rips muscle,

extracts organs, cracks bones, breaks teeth. You must never look away from this."[5] Never make racism such a spiritual issue that you don't deal with the violence affecting the bodies that hold the souls.

Race Is a Social Issue Not a Gospel Issue

Churches can split over race. Indeed, entire denominations have separated over issues of slavery, racism, and the place of minorities in majority White churches. It happened to Methodists in 1844. It happened to Baptists in 1845. It happened to Presbyterians in 1861. Even today, bringing up race can result in deep and bitter divisions. Wouldn't it be easier if the church could avoid the topic altogether? For much of the history of the church in America, the solution to racism in the church was to say that it was not an appropriate issue for the church to decide. In one example, Baptist leaders decided to invoke the separation of church and state to sidestep the question of whether believers could own slaves. "Slavery was consequently redefined as a political issue outside the province of churches. While Baptists continued to insist on their broad authority over their members, a claim that included master-slave relations, they ceded the issue of the morality of slavery to the civil state when it proved too divisive."[6]

Instead of attending to the moral implications of slavery and racism, church leaders surrendered resolution of the issue to the state. The mentality that race doesn't concern the church has persisted. People still try to shut down racial dialogue by saying the Gospel doesn't address it, and it should be left to the civil authorities. But, as others in this book have ably shown, the Gospel speaks directly to issues of hatred, diversity, and favoritism. Like any other topic, church leaders should exercise wisdom and give biblical counsel about the topic of race, but no one should say it's not a subject for the church to discuss.

Talking About Race Only Perpetuates the Problem
Some Christians contend that talking about race only perpetuates the very issue it's trying to solve. They think, "If people would just quit talking about race, we wouldn't have all these issues." At one point my thirteen-year-old car started rattling. Something in the engine was amiss. But I figured I'd wait to see if the problem corrected itself. It didn't. A few weeks later the car wouldn't start. Ignoring the problem, acting as if it didn't exist, didn't make it go away. It only made it worse. The same will happen with racism if Christians try to wish it away by not talking about it.

Talking About Race Makes You a Leftist/Liberal/Marxist
Most evangelical Christians identify as politically and socially conservative. They are on the right-hand side of the spectrum in our culture. The opposite side resides on the left. People on the right have correctly pointed out some terrible problems with a more socially liberal stance, not the least of which is advocating for at-will abortion under the banner of "women's reproductive rights." But because the other side of the ideological spectrum has serious issues in one area, doesn't mean they can't be extremely helpful in other areas.
For one, the left has done well to recognize the diversity present in this nation and bring the concerns of minorities to the fore. Honestly, theological progressives and secular scholars have outpaced the US church in offering insightful critiques and thoughtful suggestions about race and justice. It would be wise for Christians to learn from them. Race, however, gets lumped in with the "liberal agenda" so this

237

shuts down conversation about the topic. Believers must recognize that talking about race doesn't mean one has adopted an entire political disposition. Christians should also be wary about labeling and libeling entire groups of people simply because they hold different views.

Excursus: Christian Engagement with Black Lives Matter
On February 26, 2012, George Zimmerman shot and killed Trayvon Martin, a seventeen-year-old African American who was walking back to his house from a trip to the convenience store. Over a year later, on July 13, 2013, a jury acquitted Zimmerman. That night a woman named Alicia Garza, wrote on her Facebook page, "Black people. I love you. I love us. Our lives matter." Her friend, and fellow community organizer, Patrice Cullors, then shared the post with the hashtag #blacklivesmatter.

Since that day in 2013, Black Lives Matter has become an international movement for justice. The hashtag has become a rallying cry for the numerous incidents of police-involved shootings that have left many unarmed African Americans dead. These bloody encounters have been caught on cell phone video and shared hundreds of thousands of times. Marches in the name of Black Lives Matter have taken place all over the country and even as far as places like Britain and Australia.

While Black Lives Matter has mobilized a new generation of civil rights activists, many Christians view the movement with skepticism. Some decry BLM's methods. They think they condone violence (they don't), are anti-police (they aren't) or are too militant. Other Christians take issue with their vocal advocacy of homosexuality and transgenderism. Still other Christians support the movement. They see it as a way to get involved with racial justice and promote the movement in word and deed. Americans also exhibit a large partisan divide, which also roughly corresponds with the racial divide, when it comes to the BLM movement. According to a study by Pew Research, 64 percent of Democrats support or somewhat support BLM, while this is true for only 20 percent of Republicans. On the other end of the spectrum, just 8 percent of Democrats oppose or strongly oppose BLM, while 52 percent of Republicans express some opposition.[7] Any modern conversation about race in America will undoubtedly include the topic of Black Lives Matter, and it likely will be divisive. How, then, should Christians talk about BLM?

In a conversation about Black Lives Matter, it is important to distinguish the principle from the organization. As a principle, Black Lives Matter is both an affirmation of the image of God in people of African descent and a lament over the brutalization of black bodies. It is a historical and existential reality that in the United States Black people have not been valued as image-bearers because of their skin color. Black Lives Matter reasserts the dignity of Black people as human beings, and Christians can wholeheartedly affirm this.

The statement, black lives matter, is also a lament. In his book *Prophetic Lament: A Call for Justice in Troubled Times*, Dr. Soong-Chan Rah writes, "Lament in the Bible is a liturgical response to the reality of suffering and engages God in the context of pain and suffering."[8] He goes on to say, "Lament is an act of protest as the lamenter is allowed to express indignation and even outrage about the experience of suffering." Lament is a way to denounce tragic outcomes and the unjust systems that produce them. As Christians, the Black Lives Matter movement presents us with an opportunity to mourn with those who mourn and to bear one another's burdens.

Black Lives Matter as an organization is a decentralized,

multi-city, multifaceted entity. Activists have formed chapters of Black Lives Matter across the country, but there is no single leader or group of leaders. Even the founders deny they lead the movement. BLM features a thirteen-point platform that includes items as varied as "diversity" and "restorative justice" to "queer affirming" and "transgender affirming." Christians must unreservedly affirm Black Lives Matter as a principle, but we must critically engage Black Lives Matter as an organization.

The goal in discussions concerning Black Lives Matter as an organization should not be to persuade people to get involved or not. That is a matter of conscience. Involvement also depends greatly on the particular circumstances and composition of a local chapter. People who are curious about the organization should visit the website and meet with local activists if there are any in the area. Many Christians will simply not get involved in BLM, which is fine. But inaction is not a solution. A multitude of other organizations, some with an explicitly Christian background, do similar justice and reform work. The goal in a discussion of Black Lives Matter, both as an organization and a principle, is understanding.

Be Strong and Courageous

I believe we are in the next wave of the Civil Rights Movement. Conversations about race will not go away. They will become increasingly relevant in the near future. Pastors, church leaders, and other Christians cannot remove themselves from internal dialogue or the national conversation. But as I stated at the outset, fear often prevails over faith. But to this I say, *"Only be strong and courageous"* (Josh. 1:6). At some point there comes a time when you must stop researching and internalizing data only and start talking. Be assured. You will mess up. You will stir up strong emotions. You will have difficult conversations after the conversation. Be assured. It's worth it.

Your brothers and sisters of color, especially African Americans, are hurting. We come limping to church on Sunday morning or Wednesday night or during a meeting with a pastor longing to hear words of empathy and encouragement. But when other church members or church leaders respond with opposition, silence, or indifference, it cuts. The church, the one place we are supposed to find refuge, becomes just another place of marginalization and pain. For the sake of your neighbors, then, talk about race. Most importantly, for the sake of the reconciliation Christ has already accomplished on the cross, talk about race.

15

INDIVIDUALISM VERSUS COLLECTIVISM: THE POLARIZING EFFECT OF TAKING SIDES

CHRISTINA EDMONDSON

I feel a strong desire to tell you—and I expect you feel a strong desire to tell me—which of these two errors [individualism or collectivism] is the worse. That is the devil getting at us. He always sends errors into the world in pairs—pairs of opposites. And he always encourages us to spend a lot of time thinking which is the worse. You see why, of course? He relies on your extra dislike of the one error to draw you gradually into the opposite one. But do not let us be fooled. We have to keep our eyes on the goal and go straight through between both errors. We have no other concern than that with either of them.[1]

This chapter will look broadly at the concept of culture and specifically explore the role of the cultural orientations of individualism and collectivism within the contemporary multicultural or multiracial American church. Applying the strength of community, while seeing and respecting the individual narratives of all those who are a part of the royal priesthood of believers, brings us closer to the biblical narrative of the multicultural catholic and local church. So it is essential that in this global and multicultural reality we take culture seriously. Yet cultural chauvinism has long plagued even the most well-intentioned evangelistically minded believers and denominations. The consequences related to normalizing and at worse deifying one's worldview and ethnic identity show up throughout the pages of Scripture and throughout the passages of history.

However, seeing into and appreciating cultural difference takes tools of exploration like self-awareness, humility, vocabulary, and often a guide. Culture only questions itself when in contrast to culture. Like a fish, it is not until it is pulled by the fisherman's hook and launched into the crisp air that it knows more deeply and truly its water bias. Unlike the fish, our entrance into another culture will not necessarily end in our demise; however, our shock, resistance, and denial can be just as jolting. Certainly, the interplay of cultural difference is visible in multiracial and multicultural churches despite the fierce pull to concede to dominant group homogeneity.

We can think of dominant group homogeneity as the lived experience of all members of a group filtering their own identity through the norms and standards of the group with both political capital and/or numerical advantage. In other words, in the American culture, this can be an expected over-accommodation to White male identity. We will attempt to push back on the assumption that dominant group identity is right or more aligned with the design of the biblical church as we discuss this topic.

Cultural Orientation

Simply speaking, cultural orientation is defined as the degree to which individuals are influenced by and actively engage in the customs, values, norms, and practices of a specific culture. Two of the primary cultural orientations that impact our lived experience of the contemporary multicultural church are individualism and collectivism. In today's politically charged atmosphere, these terms have deep associations that require disentanglement for the purpose of this discussion. For example, when teaching undergraduate students about these differences, I often start with a simple free association activity. "Students, what does the term individualism bring to mind?" Typical responses include "America, the West, capitalism, and business." Likewise, I offer students the opportunity to consider the term collectivism which usually evokes responses like "Asia, Africa, socialism, and the family." It is at this point that I offer students the opportunity to consider where they might place the New Testament church within the individualism/collectivism continuum. I invite you to do the same as we continue to explore how culture shapes our local church environment. However, first let us briefly consider why cultural orientations garner such controversy and trepidation.

Individualism and Collectivism

To begin, cultural orientations elicit great controversy because of our inclination to moralize seemingly opposing or different worldviews. The C. S. Lewis quote at the beginning of this chapter, in part, reminds us of this temptation. However, let's first practice the skill of suspending judgment and explore some terms and application. Here is a question to start our journey: What if individualism and collectivism both sought to pursue positive outcomes? Individualism pursues the good of the single being a benefit to society, versus collectivism, which pursues the good of the society for the sake of the individual. We define individualism as a moral, political, or social outlook that stresses human independence and the importance of individual self-reliance and liberty. To exist, it opposes most external interference with an individual's choices, whether by society, the state, or any other group or institution (collectivism or statism), and at its base it opposes the view that tradition, religion, or any other form of external moral standard should be used to limit an individual's choice of actions.

In order to further unpack this concept, we can look to politics. There is no doubt that the American dominant two-party political system is rooted in individualistic values, which can be seen when exploring the surprisingly similar core arguments for both gun and reproductive rights. I, the individual, bear the right to govern, protect, and preserve my body by the standards I deem moral and owed to me. Of course, politically, we all then interject our ethical codes that we personally deem valid and self-preserving. The history of the United States, for example, shows we often disagree about these limits based on our sense of personal autonomy and system of moral codification. As can be seen, collectivism often has a different locus of validation and moral endorsement.

Collectivism as a system favors the group, its preservation, cohesion, and values, over the individual. Identity is tied to and informed by the community in this orientation. Recently, I chatted with a former student who shared she had likely disappointed her traditional African grandmother and was given the cultural insult that she was "not a very good Somali girl." This woman had broken from culturally prescribed gender norms by pursuing a vocational identity largely focused on academics and career attainment versus homemaking and the passing of familial traditions and customs. An American example of this might include a son's decline of taking over the family business or a daughter's decision to leave her family's beloved African American church tradition.

With Western and/or individualistic ears these narratives might seem to be necessary steps in the normal process of coming of age and launching from one's family shadow, but consider the potential implication of each of these examples. It is possible that the story and struggle of a people erodes as its youth redefines itself and minimizes the history of its elders. Just look to the American church and consider what happens when liturgical practices and doctrinal "staples" are considered shadows and antiques of the past and personal preference, comfort, and ambition alone prevail? While some might proclaim, "God is doing a new thing" or "See, the church is always reforming," I would imagine there would be many who might argue the erosion of the community's core beliefs will lead to the erosions of that very community.

The truth is that many Americans live along the continuum between individualism and collectivism. It is often not quite as binary and clear as the definitions above. However, within our faith communities, unchecked individualism can lead to self-centered living that resists alignment with the community of God's admonitions and correction. Collectivism, separate from the Word of God, can lead to ignoring the least of these who may live in the minority or with limited political sway. In other words, our socially constructed political orientations must submit to the direction of Scripture. And as we can see from Lewis' quote in the opening, it can be helpful to embrace binary terms. Yet, when considering the forming of diverse church communities these cultural orientations have very real ramifications.

Culture in the Local Church

For starters, what does it mean for Black, Asian, Indigenous/tribal natives, and Latino/a Americans who, within a group, affirm more collectivist orientations to engage with and alongside Anglo American, typically more individualistic, brothers and sisters in Christ? How might these orientations impact the preaching, hearing, and sharing of the Gospel? How does cultural orientation inform church discipline or church governance? How about issues of social engagement, justice, and benevolence? These, along with many others, serve as guiding questions for those seeking to cultivate racially, ethnically, and economically diverse worship communities.

Let's explore briefly how cultural orientation generally and individualism and collectivism specifically, might shape soteriology, the theology of the local church, and the local church's role in doing justice.

Who and What Is the Church?

Nothing beats how enlightening watercooler work conversations can be. While chatting with a male colleague about our respective weekends, he quipped that he missed church that weekend in the midst of all his adventures, but that it was no big deal since he-himself is the church. Huh?! I laughed assuming that his comments were meant to be a joke, but I realized he was serious along with many folks who take church attendance and membership to be an expression of a personal preference versus a biblical command, a command that is both for our individual and collective good. A dominant individualistic view of church might ask: Does this church meet my needs? Are my gifts being used? Does this sermon apply to my personal situation at this very moment?

The local church through the lens of individualism requires attentiveness to here and now. The immediacy of relevance, the value of personal benefit, and consumeristic accommodation rub up against the calling to worship God in assembly for individual and communal good. This is a good that may or may not manifest in the here and now. Additionally, as my colleague's words highlight, the view that an individual believer is sufficient in representing the church demonstrates a divorce from the catholic, multigenerational, and multicultural church that represents Christ's bride. While a personal Savior died for our very personal salvation, Christ through the Holy Spirit is bringing forth a diverse kingdom of believers. A purely me-centered soteriology breeds messiah complexes and squelches evangelistic zeal.

"How?" you might ask. If salvation is only about me and mine, my church community may only reflect a commitment to reaching those who remind me of my own identity. Over time, a country club of shared values posing as a church emerges, that consciously or unconsciously requires shared political interests and ways of understanding for admission.

Salvation

I have often wondered how individualistic mantras like "pull yourself by your proverbial bootstraps," "the importance of being one's own man," or "the quest for ownership" has perverted the only-the needy-ought-to-apply

Gospel of Jesus Christ. The God of the oppressed—those oppressed by their sins and the sins of this world—seeks and saves sinners. Christ's perfect life, sacrificial death, and triumphant resurrection are extended to a broken people, called out to live together as they, in community, reflect Christ's love to the world. Yet at the same time, our own personal and particular repentance is required. The prophet Isaiah, before the cherubim crying, "Holy, Holy, Holy" (Isa. 6:3), represents both a wicked people and a wicked man desperately in need of personal rescue and redemption. Isaiah's guilt is palpable as he is experiences the piercing holiness of God. He is also a man in a collectivist culture feeling the weight of communal shame.

If we are indeed our brother's and sister's keeper, we communally bear responsibility for their burdens and brokenness. Shame and guilt, taboo emotions in many cultures, are a part of the necessary discomfort in the journey to repentance, repair and reconciliation. When people break the rules of the community or institution, they feel guilty in individualistic societies. Guilt is individualistic in nature whereas shame is often felt in more collectivist-oriented cultures. Shame is about a collective obligation to the other. Isaiah holds the tension of both shame and guilt in this vivid text.

How we see the purpose of the local church is impacted by our individualistic and collectivist lens. With a purely individualistic orientation, where we place ourselves at the center of its purpose, the local church is like an addendum to our lives or simply an optional fixture. Conversely, when church is only about the community's cohesion and our allegiance to it, we can find ourselves overlooking the moral failures of leaders and minimizing the suffering of those individuals abused and hurt by the church. Keeping Christ at the center of our theology of the local church, not just as a means to satiate our own desires or maintain the community's perceived unity, requires a dogged loyalty to sound biblical teaching, desperate and consistent prayer, and authentic fellowship among the royal priesthood of believers. Ultimately, both hyper-individualism and hyper-collectivism distract us from our desperate need for a Christocentric orientation that places Christ as the center of our lives, and from loving Jesus, his church, and image bearers as our chief calling.

A Christocentric orientation takes its marching orders from the Word of God. It demonstrates its love of God by obedience to his Word, and sacrificial love for his church and image-bearers. It is a love that reflects a commitment not simply to self-interest or the group's interests but to God's interests. Certainly, God's interest includes his people doing justice and good.

Multicultural Church and Justice

We ought to approach Scripture with humility, openness, and awe. However, the truth is we are likely to approach God's Word with our biases that we read into the text with our own narratives, longings, and cultural orientations. Take for instance, this scenario. You are a member of a historically oppressed minority and gender group. You gravitate to passages about overcoming obstacles and being affirmed as an image bearer in a world that sees you as inferior.

It's not surprising that through the pages of American slave narratives we see comparisons to the Hebrew slaves of Exodus and their cry unto God for emancipation from the ruling Egyptians of the day. We only need to look to the work of Harriet Tubman and her association as the black Moses as an example of this phenomena. Conversely, if you are the "Egyptian of the day," positioned in a place of morally unquestioned social power and privilege, you might miss the themes of social justice in Scripture in the same way that someone else might overstate or misinterpret them.

The Bible reminds us: *"He has shown you, O mortal, what is good. And what does the LORD require of you? To act justly and to love mercy and to walk humbly with your God"* (Micah 6:8, NIV). Here in the book of Micah, like in many passages, we find both beautiful and controversial words. The controversy lives in its exposition and application. If these words, like many from the prophets and into the development of the church in the New Testament, are a calling to see, serve, and correct the broken systems by acting justly, then cultural orientation really matters. Consider how the multicultural local church might offer a most dynamic lens through which to interpret and forum to act the call of these texts.

More on the Multicultural Church

The United States has historically encouraged individualism, while cultures in South Korea or Ghana lean more toward collectivism. However the United States is far from monolithic and includes various minority cultures. For example, African Americans and members of the Navajo or Cherokee tribes demonstrate a stronger leaning toward collectivism. Group identity is salient, and cultural conflict styles vary and impact intercultural interactions for these groups. However, can you imagine an African American elder, with a collectivist orientation and an engagement conflict style that is direct and emotively expressive, discussing benevolence with an Anglo-American elder, with an individualistic and discussion conflict style that is direct and emotively restricted? Both are earnest in their desire to serve the local church and honor God, but are possibly speaking past each other and serving no one to the local church's potential. Such a scenario can cause annoyance and even despair, especially when we unwittingly use cultural instincts to reach a resolution.

However, we are not left to figure these matters out without powerful resources. The church must have an unwavering commitment to the Word of God and its faithful exposition, especially is multicultural communities. One could argue, that it is in these communities that we are able to best expose our worldview bias and resist misusing Scripture to justify our cultural mores or acquiescing to the culture's elite. While it is true that so much of our engagement with Scripture is informed by our cultural lens, we require community and Spirit-informed reading and interpretation of Scripture. The budding church shown in the New Testament was diverse in gender, social status, and ethnic background. This diverse community would sit at the feet of Jesus and learn from his Word about the revealed Messiah and his blood-bought church. If we are willing to look, we find a dynamic, diverse church in the pages of the New Testament.

The Bible gives us examples of both individualistic and collectivist orientations at work within the Old and New Testament. This helps us resist the urge to pit one orientation against the other. As noted earlier, individualism puts the focus on doing whatever's best for "me" and collectivism puts the focus on doing whatever's best for the community. Jesus' earthly life narrative is marked by self-sacrifice while maintaining in-group identity and allegiance. Yet, Jesus' journey on our behalf is ultimately connected with the will and desire of God the Father. We must not ultimately seek out what we want (individualism) or take our cues from the community without questions (collectivism) but rather ask what does God require of us and how must we express gratitude for his unmerited favor. God created humans for himself (Isa. 43:7), not for their own or any other person's sake. A godly cultural orientation would be to do what is best according to God, his Word, and his Kingdom (Matt. 6:33a).

So while, for example, we can see collectivism or individualism in play within the Scriptures, we must be cautious of projecting our cultural orientation without questioning it. There are verses in the Bible that illustrate collectivism and individualism to a certain extent.

Collectivism Themes
Better that one man dies than the whole nation perish (John 11:50)
Pooling resources, so no one lacks (Acts 2:44–45; 4:32–35)
Give so there can be equality (2 Cor. 8:12–14)
Everyone benefits from the return of the lost one (Luke 15:6–9)

Individualism Themes
Individual accountability (Luke 19:15)
Seeking the one lost lamb (Luke 15:3–10)

The go-to illustration of the design and make-up of the church is found in 1 Corinthians in the body of Christ analogy. In 1 Corinthians 12 Apostle Paul presents individual believers as parts of a body. The body represents the church. Each part is distinct, yet connected and interdependent. The parts function as they should only when they are a part of the body as a whole. A foot is distinct and important but only fully useful when connected to a leg (1 Cor. 12:18–20). Finally, the body as a whole is an amazing organism, but only when all the parts warrant honor and care (1 Cor. 12:25–26).

This chapter has discussed cultural orientation specifically related to the concepts of individualism and collectivism. Now we will shift to how, broadly speaking, understanding cultural orientation has relevance for the local church and not just the mission fields. We will conclude with several recommendations designed to serve local churches as they determine, navigate, and appreciate their own cultural makeup and orientations.

Recommendation #1: Leaders Must Lead the Way

Local ministry leaders must see themselves as cultural beings. They model cultural intelligence by communicating that the church need not look past race, gender, and vocation, for example, but rather serve church and community members that are culturally embodied by learning about diverse cultures and their relationship to each other. This posture resists the game of color-blindness and instead embraces each individual's narrative and its corresponding people group.

Such practices help leaders to minister to the whole person and present the God of the Bible who has something to say about the skin we are in and our cultural journeys. To assess a church community's sense of its own cultural identity, try this activity. Give a group of members an image of a gingerbread man on a sheet of paper. Distribute crayons or colored pencils. Ask each person without delay and much instruction to drawn on the gingerbread man the typical member at the church. Or you can modify the exercise and ask them to draw who thrives at ABC Church. Conclude with a small group discussion about the pictures, and identify the groups that might feel excluded based on the images. Consider whether this image reflects the members in your immediate neighborhood.

Recommendation #2: Know Your Lane

Pastors and clergy leaders often come from diverse academic, professional, and personal experiences. However, it is not likely that most clergy leaders are sociologists, anthropologists, or intercultural trainers. We can use the diverse vocational identities of the believers to help diverse people to grow together in unity. Be open to bringing specialists and hearing from different voices. Our autopilot will produce homogenous communities that fall strictly in the comfort zone of the leadership or most influential members. Use the knowledge and experiences of brothers and sisters in the faith from academia, industry, and other denominations. For example, conducting a diversity accessibility audit of your church will help you to potentially see blind spots that are causing avoidance or lack of persistence of potentially diverse members. A church's dominant culturally informed style of handling conflict will send messages about who and what emotions are valued.

Recommendation #3: Have You Made the Case?

The United States history and reality of racial and cultural disparity, dysfunction, and segregation is well documented and felt throughout our country. Despite the common biblical interpretation that Scripture calls us to resist racialized sin, we find our churches, neighborhoods, and peer groups mostly homogenous. America's high concentration of Christians has not manifested into enough spaces that look like the church in glory, despite the nation's ethnic diversity. Leadership must be equipped to make the case for the sacrifices, resources, and education needed to create church communities that by the grace of God are accessible, welcoming, and edifying to diverse and even contentious groups. Members of local churches passionate about fulfilling this mission need each member equipped with their "why is pursuing diversity in the church biblical, important, and worth it" elevator speech.

I am often asked why I would engage in this kind of work. In other words: Is dealing with the messy side of culture and the implications of harmful biases worth it? Isn't it exhausting? Aren't people resistant and bigoted? It would be easier to directly answer those questions while focusing on the weakness of people, but let's think about their Creator. The greatest creation shaped by the hands of the Divine is the human being. Despite sin, the image of God is retained, and cultures all over the world and throughout time still show forth something unique and beautiful about our Maker. Jesus declared us worth it, and he makes us worth it through justification, sanctification, and glorification. He has shown unfathomable grace to the nations who will make up the church in glory. Let us too show grace to the nations and pursue what God pursues.

ENDNOTES

Introduction: Do We Need Another Book On the Church?

1. Michael Emerson and Christian Smith, *Divided By Faith: Evangelical Religion and the Problem of Race in America* (New York: Oxford University Press, 2000), 16ff.

Chapter One: The Most Segregated Hour

1. Martin Luther King Jr, "Proud to be Maladjusted," speech presented at Western Michigan University, Kalamazoo, MI, Dec. 18, 1963, http://wmich.edu/sites/default/files/attachments/MLK.pdf, p. 22.

2. Dan Harris and Blair Soden, "Segregated Sundays: Taking on Race and Religion," ABC News. January 21, 2008, http://www.abcnews.go.com/print?id=4165468.

3. Bob Smietana, "Sunday Morning Segregation: Most Worshipers Feel Their Church Has Enough Diversity," *Christianity Today*, January 15, 2015, http://www.christianitytoday.com/gleanings/2015/januar

y/sunday-morning-segregation-most-worshipers-church-diversity.html.

4. By cross-cultural, I refer to churches that intentionally attempt to be accessible to a broad range of persons in racial, ethnic, gender, class, and ability terms. In addition, these churches inculcate an environment of understanding, empathy, and celebration of cultural variety.

5. Gerald F. De Jong, *The Dutch Reformed Church in the American Colonies* (Grand Rapids, MI: Eerdmans, 1978), 154, 163; Edgar J. McManus, *A History of Negro Slavery in New York* (Syracuse, NY: Syracuse University Press, 1966), 4.

6. Lorenzo J. Greene, *The Negro in Colonial New England* (New York: Atheneum, 1969), 61, 64.

7. Carter G. Woodson, *History of the Negro Church, Second Edition* (Washington, DC: The Associated Publishers, 1945), 7.

8. Woodson, *History of the Negro Church*, 7.

9. Luther P. Jackson, "Negro Religious Development in Virginia," *Journal of Negro History* 16, no. 2 (April 1931): 168–239, 174.

10. Henry H. Mitchell, *Black Church Beginnings: The Long-Hidden Realities of the First Years* (Grand Rapids, MI: Eerdmans, 2004), 27.

11. Albert J. Raboteau, *Slave Religion: The "Invisible Institution" in the Antebellum South* (New York: Oxford University Press, 1978), 128.

12. Mechal Sobel, *Trabelin' On: The Slave Journey to an Afro-Baptist Faith* (Princeton, NJ: Princeton University Press, 1988), 190.

13. Raboteau, *Slave Religion: The "Invisible Institution" in the Antebellum South* (New York, Oxford University Press, 1978), Chapter 3.

14. Carol V. G. George, *Segregated Sabbaths: Richard Allen*

and the Rise of Independent Black Churches (New York: Oxford University Press, 1973), Chapter 2; Richard S. Newman, *Freedom's Prophet: Bishop Richard Allen, the AME Church, and the Black Founding Fathers* (New York: NYU Press, 2008), 58–68.

15. Bishop William J. Walls, *The African Methodist Episcopal Zion Church: Reality of the Black Church* (Charlotte, NC: AME Zion Publishing House, 1974), 45.

16. Woodson, *History of the Negro Church*, 74–75.

17. Ira Berlin, *Slaves Without Masters: The Free Negro in the Antebellum South* (New York: Oxford University Press, 1974), 284ff.

18. Andrew Murray, *Presbyterians and the Negro—A History* (Philadelphia, PA: Presbyterian Historical Society), 53.

19. Woodson, *History of the Negro Church*, 58–59; Murray, Presbyterians and the Negro, 53; John Hope Franklin, *The Free Negro in North Carolina 1790–1860* (New York: W. W. Norton, 1971), 170, 177.

20. Murray, *Presbyterians and the Negro*, 54.

21. Ibid., 30–39.

22. William E. Montgomery, *Under Their Own Vine and Fig Tree: The African American Church in the South 1865–1900* (Baton Rouge, LA: Louisiana State University Press, 1993), 142.

23. General Assembly (1993) of the Presbyterian Church (U.S.A.), "All-Black Governing Bodies: The History and Contribution of All-Black Governing Bodies" (Louisville, KY: Office of the General Assembly, 1996), 39ff.

24. "Resolution On Racial Reconciliation On The 150th Anniversary Of The Southern Baptist Convention," Southern Baptist Convention, Atlanta, GA, (1995): http://www.sbc.net/resolutions/899/resolution-on-racial-

reconciliation-on-the-150th-anniversary-of-the-southern-baptist-convention.

25. "Facts and Myths for the PCA on Racial Reconciliation," Reformed Musings, June 16, 2016, https://reformed-musings.wordpress.com/2016/06/16/facts-and-myths-for-the-pca-on-racial-reconciliation/.

26. Sarah Eeekhoff Zylstra, "Should Denominations Apologize for Racial Acts They Didn't Commit?," Christianitytoday.com, Sept. 18, 2015, http://www.christianitytoday.com/ct/2015/september/presbyterian-church-america-pca-race-apology.html.

Chapter Two: Regaining What We've Lost

1. Afua Hirsch, "Our Identity," TEDx Tottenham, January 6, 2015, http://www.youtube.com/watch?v=TzhCpv9ynrM.

2. Duane Elmer, *Cross Cultural Connections: Stepping out and Fitting in around the World* (Downers Grove, IL: InterVarsity Press, 2002), 64.

3. Ibid.

4. Minna Shkul, ed., *New Identity and Cultural Baggage: Identity and Otherness in Colossians*, ed. J. Brian Tucker and Coleman A. Baker, Kindle Edition, T&T Clark Handbook to Social Identity in the New Testament (London, UK; New York, NY: Bloomsbury Publishing, 2014), Location 9215.

5. Herman Bavinck, John Bolt, and John Vriend, *Reformed Dogmatics, Volume 4: Holy Spirit, Church, and New Creation, Logos Edition*, 4 vols. (Grand Rapids, MI: Baker Academic, 2008).

6. John M. Frame, *Systematic Theology : An Introduction to Christian Belief, Logos Edition* (Phillipsburg, New Jersey: P&R Publishing, 2013), 1021.

7. Ibid., 102.

8. *For he himself is our peace, who has made us both one and has broken down in his flesh the dividing wall of hostility by abolishing the law of commandments expressed in ordinances, that he might create in himself one new man in place of the two, so making peace, and might reconcile us both to God in one body through the cross, thereby killing the hostility.* (Eph. 2:14–16)

9. Steven R. Guthrie, *Creator Spirit: The Holy Spirit and the Art of Becoming Human* (Grand Rapids, MI: Baker Academic, 2011, Kindle Edition), 75.

10. Korie L. Edwards, *The Elusive Dream: The Power of Race in Interracial Churches* (Oxford, New York: Oxford University Press, 2008, Kindle Edition).

11. Soong-Chan Rah, *Many Colors: Cultural Intelligence for a Changing Church* (Chicago: Moody Publishers, 2010, Kindle Edition), 87.

12. J. Daniel Hays, *From Every People and Nation : A Biblical Theology of Race, New Studies in Biblical Theology* (Leicester, Eng.; Downers Grove, IL.: Apollos; InterVarsity Press, 2003), 142.

13. Of course, I realize a relatively easy counter argument to this point is that Paul seems to do just that! For example, in Ephesians 2:11–16, he clearly categorizes the Christians in the Ephesian churches as either having been Gentiles/ "the uncircumcision" or Jews/ "the circumcision" as the primary identity before faith in Christ. But Christ has killed the hostility and made both one. However, to be a Gentile means to belong to a people-group that does not profess faith in the God of Israel. It does not mean that all Gentiles were a common people-group, nationality, or culture.

14. Hays, 141.

15. Eph. 4:5–6

16. Alexander Jun, "Unintentional Racism," Doug Serven,

ed., *Heal Us, Emmanuel: A Call for Racial Reconciliation, Representation, and Unity in the Church* (Oklahoma City, OK: White Blackbird Books, 2016), 25.

17. Derek Thomas, *Acts, Reformed Expository Commentary* (Phillipsburg, NJ: P&R Pub., 2011), 323.

18. Aaron Kuecker, ed. *Ethnicity and Social Identity*, ed. J. Brian Tucker and Coleman A. Baker, Kindle Edition ed. T&T Clark Handbook to Social Identity in the New Testament (London, UK; New York, NY: Bloomsbury Publishing Plc, 2014), Location 1725.

19. Brad Christerson, Korie L. Edwards, and Michael O. Emerson, *Against All Odds: The Struggle for Racial Integration in Religious Organizations* (New York: New York University Press, 2005), 33–34.

20. Miroslav Volf, *Exclusion and Embrace: A Theological Exploration of Identity, Otherness, and Reconciliation* (Nashville: Abingdon Press, 1996), 37.

21. Dennis E. Johnson, *The Message of Acts in the History of Redemption* (Phillipsburg, N.J.: P&R Pub., 1997), 102.

Chapter Three: The Gospel

1. By racial reconciliation, I simply mean the need for diverse human beings from different ethnic and racial groups to be reconciled first to God and secondly to one another and to intentionally pursue each other in love in Spirit-empowered, reconciled community with each other.

2. To see this point developed, see Williams, *One New Man*.

3. See Williams, *One New Man*.

4. For a recent book discussing the Gospel, race, and racism and that offers practical examples as to how to pursue reconciliation and Christian unity in Christian spaces, see the diverse essays in Jarvis J. Williams and Kevin M. Jones (eds.), *Removing the Stain of Racism from The Southern*

Baptist Convention: Diverse African American and White Perspectives (Nashville: B&H, 2017).

5. For a book uncovering things that keep us apart, see Christena Cleveland, *Disunity in Christ: Uncovering the Hidden Forces that Keep Us Apart* (Downers Grove, IL: InterVarsity Press, 2013).

6. For an important work on Evangelicals and race, see Michael O. Emerson and Christian Smith, *Divided by Faith: Evangelical Religion and the Problem of Race in America* (Oxford: Oxford University Press, 2001).

7. For a work about race and racism in antiquity, see Benjamin Isaac, *The Invention of Racism in Classical Antiquity* (Princeton, NJ: Princeton University Press, 2004).

8. For an important work about race and Scripture in the Protestant Atlantic World, see Colin Kidd, *The Forging of Races: Race and Scripture in the Protestant Atlantic World, 1600–2000* (Cambridge: Cambridge University Press, 2006). For brief comments about the construction of race in the Bible, see Jarvis J. Williams, "Biblical Steps Toward Removing the Stain of Racism from the Southern Baptist Convention," in *Removing the Stain of Racism from The Southern Baptist Convention: Diverse African American and White Perspectives,* eds. Jarvis J. Williams and Kevin M. Jones (Nashville: B&H, 2017), 26–27.

9. For a discussion of some ways the category of race has functioned in the American experience, see Brian Bantum, *The Death of Race: Building a New Christianity in a Racial World* (Minneapolis: Fortress, 2016).

10. For a brief discussion of race as a social construct, see Williams, "Biblical Steps," 20–24.

11. For a bibliography on race, see Williams and Jones (eds.), *Removing the Stain,* 149–58, 165–66.

12. For a recent work on race amongst Southern Evangeli-

cals, see Carolyn Dupont, *Mississippi Praying: Southern White Evangelicals and the Civil Rights Movement, 1945–1975* (New York: NYU Press, 2015).

13. See discussions in Williams and Jones, *Removing the Stain*.

14. The phrase race as a "social fact" is from Teresa J. Guess, "The Social Construction of Whiteness: Racism by Intent, Racism by Consequence," *Critical Sociology*, Volume 32, Issue 4 (Brill: NV, 2006): 649–73, esp. 654.

15. For a brief discussion of this, see Williams, "Biblical Steps," 2–24.

16. For this point, see Matthew J. Hall, "Historical Causes of the Stain of Racism in the Southern Baptist Convention," in *Removing the Stain of Racism from the Southern Baptist Convention: Diverse African American and White Perspectives*, eds. Jarvis J. Williams and Kevin M. Jones (Nashville: B&H, 2017), 7–14.

17. For a discussion of this, see sources cited in Williams, "Biblical Steps," 22–23.

18. For example, see the sociological work of Emerson and Smith, *Divided by Faith*.

19. For this point, see Emerson and Smith, *Divided by Faith*.

20. For a discussion about racial reconciliation as a Gospel demand, see Williams, "Biblical Steps," 31–43.

21. For a recent work on justification, see Thomas R. Schreiner, *Faith Alone: The Doctrine of Justification—What the Reformers Taught. . . and Why It Still Matters* (Grand Rapids: Zondervan, 2015).

22. For a discussion of Jesus' death and justification in connection with the extent of the atonement, see Jarvis J. Williams, *For Whom Did Christ Die: The Extent of the Atonement in Paul's Theology*, Paternoster Biblical Monographs (Milton Keynes, UK: Paternoster, 2012). For a

discussion of Jesus' death and justification in the context of racial reconciliation, see Williams, *One New Man*. For a discussion of Jesus' death and justification in the context of representation and substitution, see Jarvis J. Williams, *Christ Died for Our Sins: Representation and Substitution in Romans and Their Jewish Martyrological Background* (Eugene, OR: Wipf and Stock, 2015).

23. For a helpful work discussing the king and for a bibliography, see Thomas R. Schreiner, *The King in His Beauty: A Biblical Theology of the Old and New Testaments* (Grand Rapids: Baker, 2013).

Chapter Four: Multivocality in the Church

1. Thomas, R. Roosevelt and Marjorie I. Woodruff, *Building a House for Diversity: How a Fable About a Giraffe & Elephant Offers New Strategies for Today's Workforce* (New York: AMACOM, 1999).

2. Steven Monsma, "Honoring Religion as a Source of Diversity and Unity," *Journal of Education* (2005): https://eric.ed.gov/?id=EJ764584

3. Thomas F. Pettigrew and Joanne Martin, "Shaping the Organizational Context for Black American Inclusion," *Journal of Social Issues* 43.1 (1987): http://onlinelibrary.wiley.com/doi/10.1111/j.1540-4560.1987.tb02330.x/abstract.

4. Mark Chavez, "National Congregations Study" (Tucson, AZ: Department of Sociology, University of Arizona, 1999).

5. Michael Emerson and Christian Smith, *Divided by Faith: Evangelical Religion and the Problem of Race in America* (New York, NY: Oxford University Press, 2000).

6. Keith Lawrence, Stacey Sutton, Anne Kubisch, Gretchen Susi and Karen Fulbright-Anderson, *Structural*

Racism and Community Building (Washington, DC: Aspen Institute Roundtable on Community, 2004).

7. Ibid.

8. Kathryn Ecklund, *Implicit Bias and Micro-Aggressions*, from SCORR Conference (2006): http://open.biola.edu/resources/implicit-bias-and-micro-aggressions.

9. Rebecca Kim, *God's Whiz Kids: Korean American Evangelicals on Campus* (New York: New York University Press, 2006).

10. Soong-Chan Rah, *The Next Evangelicalism: Releasing the Church from Western Cultural Captivity* (Downers Grove, IL: IVP, 2009).

11. Michael O. Emerson and George A. Yancey, *Transcending Racial Barriers: Toward a Mutual Obligations Approach* (New York: Oxford UP, 2011).

12. Amanda E. Lewis, "'What Group?' Studying Whites and Whiteness in the Era of 'Color-Blindness,'" *Sociological Theory* 22.4 (2004): 623–46, http://journals.sagepub.com/doi/abs/10.1111/j.0735-2751.2004.00237.x.

13. Michael O. Emerson and George A. Yancey *Transcending Racial Barriers: Toward a Mutual Obligations Approach* (New York: Oxford UP, 2011).

14. Jacob Jenkins, "A 'Community' of Discipline: The Paradox of Diversity Within an Intercultural Church," *Western Journal of Communication* 78.2 (2013): 134–54, http://www.tandfonline.com/doi/abs/10.1080/10570314.2013.845793.

15. Lydia Veliko, "Criteria for Unity and the Limits of Diversity: Towards an Ecclesiology of United Churches," *Ecumenical Review* 62.1 (2010): 30–40, http://onlinelibrary.wiley.com/doi/10.1111/j.1758-6623.2009.00044.x/full.

16. Korie L. Edwards, *The Elusive Dream: The Power of Race in Interracial Churches* (Oxford: Oxford UP, 2008).

17. Steven Monsma, "Honoring Religion as a Source of Diversity and Unity," *Journal of Education* (2005): https://eric.ed.gov/?q=source%3a%22Journal+of+Education%22%2bISSN-0022-0574&ff1=dtySince_1998&ff2=locUnited+States&id=EJ764584

18. Gordon W. Allport, *The Nature of Prejudice* (Cambridge, MA: Addison-Wesley), 1954.

19. Mitchell J. Chang, "Racial diversity in higher education: Does a racially mixed student population affect educational outcomes?" (Dissertation, University of California, Los Angeles, 1996).

20. Mitchell J. Chang and Alexander W. Astin, "Who Benefits from Racial Diversity in Higher Education?" http://www.diversityweb.org/digest/w97/research.html

21. Alexander W. Astin, "Diversity and Multiculturalism on the Campus," *Change: The Magazine of Higher Learning* 25.2 (1993): 44–49, http://www.tandfonline.com/doi/abs/10.1080/00091383.1993.9940617.

22. Patricia Gurin, Eric L. Dey, Sylvia Hurtado, and Gerald Gurin, "Diversity and Higher Education: Theory and Impact on Educational Outcomes," *Harvard Educational Review* 72 (2002): 330–65.

23. Jonathan R. Alger, "A Supreme Challenge: Achieving the Educational and Societal Benefits of Diversity after the Supreme Court's Fisher Decision," *Journal of Diversity in Higher Education* 6.3 (2013): 147–54, https://www2.apa.org/pubs/journals/features/dhe-a0034355.pdf.

24. Daniel Espinoza-Gonzalez, Kristen French, Stephanie

Gallardo, Ethan Glemaker, Saraswati Noel, Michelle Marsura, Elaine Mehariya, Nadia Saldaña-Spiegle, Brendan Schimpf, and Chelsea Thaw, "Decolonizing the Classroom Through Critical Consciousness: Navigating Solidarity en la Lucha for Mexican American Studies," *The Educational Forum* 78.1 (2014): 54–7.

25. R. Ghosh, M. Galczynski, *Redefining Multicultural Education: Inclusion and the Right to be Different* (Canadian Scholars' Press, 2014).

26. Michael O. Emerson, David Hartman, "The Rise of Religious Fundamentalism," *Annual Review of Sociology* 32 (2006): 127–144.

27. George Yancey, Ye Jung Kim, "Racial Diversity, Gender Equality, and SES Diversity in Christian Congregations: Exploring the Connections of Racism, Sexism, and Classism in Multiracial and Non Multiracial Churches," *J Scientific Study of Religion Journal for the Scientific Study of Religion,* 47.1 (2008): 103–11, http://onlinelibrary.wiley.com/doi/10.1111/j.1468-5906.2008.00394.x/abstract.

28. Siduri Haslerig, Laura M. Bernhard, Marcia V. Fuentes, A. T. Panter, Charles E. Daye, and Walter R. Allen, "A Compelling Interest: Activating the Benefits of Classroom-level Diversity," *Journal of Diversity in Higher Education* 6.3 (2013): 158–73, https://uncch.pure.elsevier.com/en/publications/a-compelling-interest-activating-the-benefits-of-classroom-level-.

29. Joel Perez, "Living Into Multicultural Inclusive Ministry," *Anglican Theological Review,* 93.4 (2011): 659–667, http://ezproxy.tangaza.org/cgi-bin/koha/opac-search.pl?q=se,phr:%22Anglican%20Theological%20Review%22.

30. Kathleen E. Jenkins, "Intimate Diversity: The Presen-

tation of Multiculturalism and Multiracialism in a High-Boundary Religious Movement," *Journal for the Scientific Study of Religion,* 42.3 (2003): 393–409, http://onlinelibrary.wiley.com/doi/10.1111/1468-5906.00190/abstract.

31. Lalonde Roxanne, *Unity in Diversity: Acceptance and Integration in an Era of Intolerance and Fragmentation* (Diss. Carleton University, 1994. Ottawa: Ontario, 1994).

32. Loes Meeussen, Sabine Otten, Karen Phale,\ "Managing Diversity: How Leaders' Multiculturalism and color blindness Affect Work Group Functioning," *Group Processes & Intergroup Relations,* 17.5 (2014): 629–644.

33. Nancy T. Ammerman, *Congregation and Community* (New Brunswick, NJ: Rutgers University Press, 1997).

34. Kevin D. Dougherty, "How Monochromatic Is Church Membership? Racial-Ethnic Diversity in Religious Community," *Sociology of Religion,* 64.2 (2003): 65–85.

Chapter Five: Liturgy

1. Matthew Anderson, *Presbyterianism: Its Relation to the Negro* (Philadelphia, PA: John McGill White & Co.), 81.

2. Ibid., 7–8.

3. "William Still: An African American Abolitionist," Berean Institute, http://stillfamily.library.temple.edu/stillfamily/exhibits/show/william-still/people-and-places/berean-institute.

4. James K. A. Smith, *Desiring the Kingdom: Worship, Worldview, and Cultural Formation* (Grand Rapids, MI: Baker Academic), 155–214.

5. Robert E. Webber, *Ancient-Future Worship: Proclaiming and Enacting God's Narrative* (Grand Rapids, MI: Baker Books), 29–56.

6. Carl Ellis, *Free At Last? The Gospel in the African*

American Experience (Downers Grove, IL: InterVarsity Press, 1996), 52–53.

7. NAACP, "Criminal Justice Fact Sheet," naacp.com, http://www.naacp.org/pages/criminal-justice-fact-sheet.

8. American Civil Liberties Union, "Written Submission of the American Civil Liberties Union on Racial Disparities in Sentencing," aclu.org.

9. Michael Emerson, *Divided By Faith: Evangelical Religion and the Problem of Race in America* (New York: Oxford University Press, 2000), 1. Quotation taken from Democracy in America, by De Tocqueville, public domain.

Chapter Six: Preaching

1. John Owen, *The Works of John Owen*, edited by William H. Goold; reprint edition (Edinburgh: Banner of Truth, 1965), vol. 9, 455.

2. To call the Gospel "cross-cultural" is to acknowledge the fact that, in his person and work, Jesus Christ crossed over into our dis-integrated world in order to destroy the vertical and horizontal polarization caused by the fall. The creational wholeness, peace, and flourishing that once existed has been definitively recovered through the death, burial, resurrection, and ascension of Jesus Christ. The express intent of the work of Christ was the reconciliation of heaven and earth (Col. 1:19–20) and the re-creation of a new humanity, a new citizenry, and a new family (Eph. 2:14ff). According to our distinctly Christian hope, that shalom which initially began in seed form (Gen. 1–2) will grow to fully blossom in glory (Rev. 7:9ff; Rev. 21–22). This is the good news of the Gospel which has been under-appreciated, under-explored, and under-realized in most American Christianity.

3. Frank Houghton, *Thou Who Wast Rich Beyond Splendor*, (OMF International, 1938),

https://www.gettymusic.com/thou- who-wast-rich-beyond-all-splendor/.

4. Eleanor Smith, "The Good-Luck Charm That Solved a Public-Health Problem," *The Atlantic,* January 2014.

Chapter Seven: The Sacraments

1. For our purposes, I am referring to "culture" as the beliefs and behaviors associated with one's identity, and "ethic" as the code of conduct, or moral standard of living that shapes relationships.

2. "A sacrament is a holy ordinance instituted by Christ in his church, to signify, seal, and exhibit unto those that are within the covenant of grace, the benefits of his mediation; to strengthen and increase their faith, and all other graces, to oblige them to obedience; to testify and cherish their love and communion one with another; and to distinguish them from those that are without" (Westminster Larger Catechism, 162).

3. "Baptism is a sacrament, wherein the washing with water in the name of the Father, and of the Son, and of the Holy Ghost, doth signify and seal our ingrafting into Christ, and partaking of the benefits of the covenant of grace, and our engagement to be the Lord's" (Westminster Shorter Catechism, 94).

4. "The needful but much neglected duty of improving our baptism, is to be performed by us all our life long, especially in the time of temptation, and when we are present at the administration of it to others; by serious and thankful consideration of the nature of it, and of the ends for which Christ instituted it, the privileges and benefits conferred and sealed thereby, and our solemn vow made therein; by being humbled for our sinful defilement, our falling short of, and walking contrary to, the grace of baptism, and our engagements; by growing up to assurance of pardon of sin,

and of all other blessings sealed to us in that sacrament; by drawing strength from the death and resurrection of Christ, into whom we are baptized, for the mortifying of sin, and quickening of grace; and by endeavoring to live by faith, to have our conversation in holiness and righteousness, as those that have therein given up their names to Christ; and to walk in brotherly love, as being baptized by the same Spirit into one body" (Westminster Larger Catechism, 167).

5. "The Lord's Supper is a sacrament of the New Testament, wherein, by giving and receiving bread and wine according to the appointment of Jesus Christ, his death is showed forth; and they that worthily communicate feed upon his body and blood, to their spiritual nourishment and growth in grace; have their union and communion with him confirmed; testify and renew their thankfulness, and engagement to God, and their mutual love and fellowship each with the other, as members of the same mystical body" (Westminster Larger Catechism, 168).

6. Pliny, "Pliny to the Emperor Trajan," "Triny to Pliny," Letters: Georgetown.edu, http://faculty.georgetown.edu/jod/texts/pliny.html.

7. Michael Horton, *The Christian Faith: A Systematic Theology for Pilgrims On the Way* (Grand Rapids: Zondervan, 2011), 799.

8. Guy Waters and Ligon Duncan, eds., *Children and the Lord's Supper* (Christian Focus, 2011), 42.

9. Ibid., 42.

10. Michael Horton, *The Christian Faith: A Systematic Theology for Pilgrims On the Way* (Grand Rapids: Zondervan, 2011), 799.

11. Ibid., 846–47.

Chapter Eight: Face the Music

1. Charles Joyner, *Down By The Riverside: A South Carolina Slave Community* (Chicago: UPress, 1984) 142–43.

2. Joyner, 143.

3. "Black Music from Scotland? It Could Be the Gospel Truth," Scotsman.com, August 31, 2003, http://www.scotsman.com/lifestyle/culture/music/black-music-from-scotland-it-could-be-the-Gospel-truth-1-1293195#ixzz44UWayBb1.

4. Charles Spurgeon, *Our Own Hymnbook* (London, England: Pilgrim Publications 1975).

Chapter Nine: Church Growth

1. Charles, Dickens, *A Tale of Two Cities* (Dove Publications, 1999), 1.

2. C. Peter Wagner, *Strategies for Growth* (Glendale: Regal, 1987), 168.

3. Cross-cultural deals with people from different cultures (like generational, socioeconomic, nationality, educational and race). Multiethnic deals people from different ethnicities (like African American, Caucasian, Asian, or Hispanic). A church can be multiethnic but still be monocultural, especially if all the members are from one socioeconomic class.

4. *After this I looked, and behold, a great multitude that no one could number, from every nation, from all tribes and peoples and languages, standing before the throne and before the Lamb, clothed in white robes, with palm branches in their hands, and crying out with a loud voice, "Salvation belongs to our God who sits on the throne, and to the Lamb!"* (Rev. 7:9)

5. Mark DeYmaz, *Leading a Healthy Multi-Ethnic Church* (Grand Rapids: Zondervan 2010), 56.

6. Rev. Fountain is ordained in the Southern Baptist

Convention. He currently serves at the New Orleans
Baptist Association as a church health strategist.

7. C. Peter Wagner, *Church Planting for a Greater Harvest*
(Ventura, CA: Regal Books, 1990), 11.

8. Reggie McNeal, *A Work of Heart: Understanding How
God Shapes Spiritual Leaders* (Jossey-Bass: San Francisco,
2000), 17.

9. Bob Burns, Tasha D. Chapman, and Donald C. Guthrie,
Resilient Ministry (Downers Grove, IL: Intervarsity Press,
2013), 170.

10. Nelson Searcy and Kerrick Thomas, *Launch: Starting a
New Church from Scratch* (Baker Books: Grand Rapids,
2006), 142.

11. The Presbyterian Church in America's Book of Church
Order (BCO) 13-1 states that a Presbytery consists of all
the teaching elders and churches within its bounds that
been accepted by the Presbytery. When the Presbytery
meets as a court it shall comprise all teaching elders and
ruling elders as elected by their Session.

12. BCO 5-1 states a mission church may be properly
described in the same manner as the particular church is
described in BCO 4-1.It is distinguished from a particular
church in that it has not permanent governing body, and
thus must be governed or supervised by others.

13. Mark DeYmaz, *Building a Healthy Multi-Ethnic
Church*; Livermore, David, *Cultural Intelligence*; Emerson,
Michael, *Divided by Faith*

14. David A. Livermore, *Cultural Intelligence (Youth,
Family, and Culture): Improving Your CQ to Engage Our
Multicultural World* (Grand Rapids: Baker Publishing
Group, 2009, Kindle Edition), 17.

15. Anthony Bradley, Twitter Post. June 17, 2014, 12:06
pm. http://twitter.com/drantbradley.

Chapter Ten: ESL

1. "Hispanic Roots, United States Census Bureau," census.gov, http://www.census.gov/content/dam/Census/newsroom/facts-for-features/2015/cb15-ff18_graphic.jpg.

2. "FFF: Hispanic Heritage Month 2015," United States Census Bureau, census.gov, September 14, 2015, http://www.census.gov/newsroom/facts-for-features/2015/cb15-ff18.html.

3. Sandra L. Colby and Jennifer M. Ortmon, "Projection of the Size and Composition of the U.S. Population: 2014 to 2016," United States Census Bureau, census.gov, March 2015, http://www.census.gov/content/dam/Census/library/publications/2015/demo/p25–1143.pdf.

Chapter Eleven: Mercy

1. Harvey Conn, *The American City and the Evangelical Church: A Historical Overview* (Grand Rapids, MI: 1994), 49–74.

2. Steve Corbett and Brian Fikkert, *When Helping Hurts: How to Alleviate Poverty Without Hurting the Poor ...And Yourself* (Chicago:Moody Publishers, 2009), 53.

3. Randy Nabors, *Merciful: The Opportunity and Challenge of Discipling the Poor Out of Poverty* (North Charleston, SC: CreateSpace Independent Publishing Platform, 2015), 16.

4. Randy Nabors discusses how a relationship with the living God can "overwhelm" the hopelessness those trapped in poverty experience, 16–17. Also Corbett and Fikkert, 53 and Psalms 9:18.

5. Mark J. Bowers, "Faith & Finances Toolkit: Planning for a Financial Education Ministry," ed. Jerilyn Sanders, Amy

Kuenzel, (Lookout Mountain, GA: Chalmers Center for Economic Development), 19.

6. R. R. Reno, "The Preferential Option for the Poor," *First Things* (June 2011): https://www.firstthings.com/article/2011/06/the-preferential-option-for-the-poor.

7. Dr. Carl F. Ellis Jr., "Racism Alone? — Reflections on the Current National Divide," http://drcarlellisjr.blogspot.com/search?updated-min=2014-01-01T00:00:00-05:00&updated-max=2015-01-01T00:00:00-05:00&max-results=2.

8. Thomas Sowell, *Black Rednecks and White Liberals* (San Francisco: Encounter Books 2005), 6–13.

9. Nabors, 113, author's italics.

10. Karen Angela Ellis, "Step Out The Boat: Following the Urban Disciple Maker," https://karenangelaellis.com/2014/12/12/step-out-the-boat-following-the-urban-disciple-maker.

11. Nabors, 86.

12. Tim Keller, *Ministries of Mercy: The Call of the Jericho Road,* 2nd ed. (Phillipsburg, NJ: P&R Publishing, 1997), 15.

13. Robert D. Lupton, *Toxic Charity: How Churches and Charities Hurt Those They Help (And How to Reverse It)* (New York: HarperCollins, 2011), 128–132.

Chapter Twelve: Come As You Are, But Don't Stay That Way

1. From *Star Trek, First Contact,* 1996.

Chapter Thirteen: Word and Witness

1. Lewis Carroll, *Through the Looking Glass* (London: Macmillan Publishers, 1872), 205.

2. Paulo Freire, *Pedagogy of the Oppressed* (London: Bloomsbury Academic, 1968), 75.

3. R.C. Sproul, *"What is the Gospel?"* Ligonier Ministries, October 26, 2015, http://www.ligonier.org/blog/what-is-the-Gospel.

4. Tim Keller quoted by Trevin Wax, *Gospel Definitions: Tim Keller*, The Gospel Coalition, March 7, 2008, https://blogs.theGospelcoalition.org/trevinwax/2008/03/07/Gospel-definitions-tim-keller.

5. "What Are the Biggest Challenges Facing the Evangelical Church?" Desiringgod.com, December 30, 2015, http://www.desiringgod.org/interviews/what-are-the-biggest-challenges-facing-the-evangelical-church-in-2016.

6. W. E. B. DuBois, *The Souls of Black Folk* (New York: Dover Publications, 1903), 2.

7. John Saillant, *Black Puritan, Black Republican* (Oxford: Oxford University Press, 2003) 100–101.

8. Milton Sernett, ed., *African American Religious History, Life Experience and Gospel Labors of Richard Allen* (Durham, NC: Duke University Press, 199), 145–46.

9. "Southern White Fundamentalism and the Civil Rights Movement," Phylon, vol. 40 no. 4 (1979): 334–341; *Mississippi Praying: Southern White Evangelicals and the Civil Rights Movement*, 1945–1975, Carolyn Renee Dupont, (New York University Press, 2013).

10. "Modern Immigration Wave Brings 59 Million to U.S., Driving Population Growth and Change Through 2065," Pew Research Center—Hispanic Trends, http://www.pewhispanic.org/2015/09/28/modern-immigration-wave-brings-59-million-to-u-s-driving-population-growth-and-change-through-2065.

11. I recognize that the vestiges of racial dominance and sub-dominance can continue into an era of no racial-minority if gains are not made in the area of sociocultural and economic empowerment, i.e., if meaningful enfranchisement continues to escape large numbers of African

Americans, even if White cultural dominance is absent, they could still find themselves significantly marginalized.

12. Soong-Chan Rah, *The Next Evangelicalism* (Downers Grove: IVP Books, 2009), 22.

13. Bill Broadway, "Promise Keepers—And Doubters," *Washington Post*, Sept. 13, 1997, https://www.washingtonpost.com/archive/local/1997/09/13/promise-keepers-and-doubters/f6519a6a-d94b-4f63-b8db-b409d42199cd/?utm_term=.0f36b7b3d894.

14. Laura Meckler, "How Churches Are Slowly Becoming Less Segregated," The Wall Street Journal, wsj.com (October 13, 2014): https://www.wsj.com/articles/a-church-of-many-colors-the-most-segregated-hour-in-america-gets-less-so-1413253801.

15. Mark Noll, *The Civil War as a Theological Crisis* (Chapel Hill: The University of North Carolina Press, 2006), 31–50.

16. Acts 10:13–15.

17. Even with non-White Senior Pastors, multicultural churches whose leadership teams are not diverse but are largely White tend to reinforce White hegemonic practices. Korie L. Edwards, *The Elusive Dream: The Power of Race in Interracial Churches* (Oxford: Oxford University Press, 2008), 117–138.

Chapter Fourteen: Be Strong and Courageous

1. "Chapter 3: Demographic Profiles of Religious Groups," Americas's Changing Religious Landscape, Pew Research, March 12, 2015, http://www.pewforum.org/2015/05/12/chapter-3-demographic-profiles-of-religious-groups/?utm_content=bufferea5e2&utm_medium=social&utm_source=twitter.com&utm_campaign=buffer.

2. Bob Smietana, "Sunday Mornings in America Still

Segregated—and That's Okay with Worshipers," LifeWay Research, http://lifewayresearch.com/2015/01/15/sunday-morning-in-america-still-segregated-and-thats-ok-with-worshipers.

3. Defined by Columbia professor, Derald Sue, as "brief and commonplace daily verbal, behavioral, or environmental indignities, whether intentional or unintentional, that communicate hostile, derogatory, or negative racial slights and insults toward people of color." "Racial microaggressions in everyday life: Implications for clinical practice." Sue, Derald Wing; Capodilupo, Christina M.; Torino, Gina C.; Bucceri, Jennifer M.; Holder, Aisha M. B.; Nadal, Kevin L.; Esquilin, Marta, *American Psychologist*, Vol 62(4), May-June 2007, 271–286.

4. Don't expect grace if you talk about race over social media. The audience is too ideologically scattered and it's too easy for people to hide vicious comments behind the anonymity and distance of a screen. If you're new to this conversation on race, stick to listening to others and reposting content you think is worthwhile. It may take a long time before you can enter the conversation with constructive statements. That's just fine.

5. Ta-Nehisi Coates, *Between the World and Me* (New York: Spiegel and Grau 2015), 10.

6. Monica Najar, *Meddling with Emancipation: Baptists, Authority, and the Rift over Slavery in the Upper South*, Jones J, *The Best American History Essays* 2007 (Palgrave Macmillan, New York).

7. Juliana Menasce Horowitz, and Gretchen Livingston, "How Americans View the Black Lives Matter Movement," Pew Research Center, http://www.pewresearch.org/fact-tank/2016/07/08/how-americans-view-the-black-lives-matter-movement.

8. Soong-Chan Rah, *Prophetic Lament: A Call for Justice in*

a Troubled Time (Downers Grove, IL: IVP Press, 2015), 21.

Chapter
Fifteen: Individualism Verses Collectivism

1. C. S. Lewis, *Mere Christianity* (New York: MacMillan, 1952), 185–186.
2. John D. Kelly, "Seeing Red: Mao Fetishism, Pax Americana, and the Moral Economy of War," in *Anthropology and Global Counterinsurgency*, ed. John D. Kelly et al. (Chicago: University of Chicago Press, 2010), 77.
3. Ibid. 81–82.

Made in the USA
Columbia, SC
22 April 2020